DON BRADMAN
CHALLENGING THE MYTH

This fascinating book takes a very different look at Australia's most popular sporting hero, Sir Donald Bradman. Unlike the mostly reverent literature on 'The Don', this book explains how his iconic status was created and sustained, and what his popularity and heroism say about the meaning of Australian nationhood. Brett Hutchins' unique analysis reveals the mythical character of so many representations of The Don, and connects them to broader social phenomena and the cultural contexts in which they were created. Hutchins considers the many ways in which Bradman has been represented – as a symbol of Australian masculinity, as the quintessential Australian boy from the bush, as the 'battler', and as the hero at a distance from the political. Drawing out the ideological content of these representations, Hutchins is able to show that many of the truisms we take for granted about Bradman and his role in Australian culture are open to challenge.

Brett Hutchins' achievement is to change the way we think about Donald Bradman.

Brett Hutchins has published on various social and cultural issues in Australian sport, as well as commenting on the Bradman phenomenon in the media. He teaches sociology at the University of Tasmania.

DON BRADMAN

CHALLENGING THE MYTH

BRETT HUTCHINS

PUBLISHED BY THE PRESS SYNDICATE OF THE UNIVERSITY OF CAMBRIDGE
The Pitt Building, Trumpington Street, Cambridge, United Kingdom

CAMBRIDGE UNIVERSITY PRESS
The Edinburgh Building, Cambridge CB2 2RU, UK
40 West 20th Street, New York, NY 10011–4211, USA
477 Williamstown Road, Port Melbourne, VIC 3207, Australia
Ruiz de Alarcón 13, 28014 Madrid, Spain
Dock House, The Waterfront, Cape Town 8001, South Africa

http://www.cambridge.org

First published 2002

Printed in Australia by Ligare

Typeface Life Roman (*Adobe*) 11/16 pt.   *System* QuarkXPress® [BC]

A catalogue record for this book is available from the British Library

National Library of Australia Cataloguing in Publication data
Hutchins, Brett.
Don Bradman: Challenging the myth.
Bibliography.
Includes index.
ISBN 0 521 82384 6 (hbk).
1. Bradman, Donald, Sir, 1908–2001. 2. Cricket players –
Australia – Biography. 3. Cricket – Australia – History.
I. Title.
796.358092

ISBN 0 521 82384 6 hardback

Waiver

CONTENTS

ACKNOWLEDGEMENTS

This book is dedicated to the memory of my grandparents. They are sadly missed and I wish they were here to enjoy its publication.

I would also like to thank the following people who helped in various ways in the preparation of the manuscript: John Bale, Helen Bowskill and Peter Vallance, Keitha Brown, Mike Brown, Angi Buettner, Leigh Dale, Kathryn Dwan, Lena Edgerton and Sam Altinger, Liz Ferrier, Martin Gregg, Gideon Haigh, Chris Hallinan, John Harms, Lisa Hunter, Ian Jobling, Geoff Lawrence, Malcolm McLean, Abby McLeod, Jim McKay, Maryann Martin, Toby Miller, Kristin Natalier, Brian and Gill Pauli, Murray Phillips, David Rowe, Phil Smith, David Studham and Graeme Turner. Both individually and collectively your help has been greatly appreciated and your involvement has made this a far better book than it would have otherwise been.

A special thank you is extended to Janine Mikosza who has been the most important part of my life and work for many years. Your love, tolerance and insights are without peer.

Many of the above people influenced the writing of this book through comments and criticism. Ultimately responsibility for the arguments and opinions expressed, however, rests with me.

On a personal note, thank you to Dad, Mum and Tania for their support and help over the years. A similar gratitude is due to the Mikosza clan for their support and encouragement.

Two of the chapters in this book have previously been published as a journal article and an essay in an edited collection. Both have been significantly rewritten and expanded for this book in an effort to bring their contents and arguments up to date and in response to critique of them. An earlier version of Chapters 3 appeared in L. Dale and M. Henderson (eds), *Terra Re-cognition: New Essays in Australian Studies* (St Lucia: University of Queensland Press, 2002). Also, an earlier version of Chapter 6 appeared in the *Journal of Australian Studies*, no. 67 (2001), pp. 56–66.

CHAPTER 1

OUR ONE NATIONAL HERO?

There has been one national hero ... The Don ... a title in itself rich with associations of chivalry, but also informal, intimate; the Don came even more to embody the Australian character ideal.[1]

John Carroll, The 2001 Alfred Deakin Lectures

Sport to many Australians is life and the rest is a shadow. Sport has been the one national institution that has had no 'knockers'. ...To play sport, or watch others play, and to read and talk about it is to uphold the nation and build its character.[2]

Donald Horne, *The Lucky Country*

In the course of his 2001 Alfred Deakin Lecture, 'The Blessed Country: Australian Dreaming, 1901–2001', John Carroll made the bold claim that the world's most esteemed cricketer, Sir Donald Bradman (1908–2001), has been Australia's one national hero. Bradman's nomination for the post of *the* Australian hero is perhaps to be expected. As cultural commentator Donald Horne wrote during the 1960s in *The Lucky Country*, sport is often viewed as this country's 'one national institution'.[3] Cricket in particular has long had a dominant presence in Australian popular culture, and we are without question a nation that worships sporting achievement.

While I do not go as far as Carroll does in declaring Bradman the only national hero, he is without doubt an enduring figure in the cultural landscape. Yet few have considered his unique place within the national imagination. The question of why a cricketer – a man who retired from the game over half a century ago – became the embodiment of Australian nationhood is regularly asked, but never has it been thoroughly investigated. This book is just such an investigation, looking in detail at the various ways in which he has been figured on and off the field, in the media and politics and through film and literature. It seems appropriate to begin, however, by briefly recalling a little of his life and the reactions to his death, his extraordinary achievements and his status as hero.

Death of a legend

Sir Donald George Bradman died on 25 February 2001, aged 92 years. Four days later, around 5,000 fans lined the streets of Adelaide to pay their respects as the Don's hearse and its entourage made the one-hour journey to the private funeral.

News of the demise of the nation's greatest cricketer created a 'flashpoint' in contemporary Australian culture, completely dominating television, radio and newspaper reports.[4] Bradman stories spilled well outside the boundaries of routine media coverage, and tributes, dedications and specials poured forth. Flags were flown at half-mast and newspaper headlines announced, 'A Nation's Farewell', 'Death of a Legend', 'The Nation Loses its Hero', 'A Loving Son and Nation Mourn Australia's Greatest Sports Hero', 'The Don: The Greatest Innings Ever' and 'Nation Mourns the Great Don'.

Maudlin 'Bradmania' consumed the pages of newspapers and magazines, hours of radio, half of television news bulletins and current affairs programs, and entire television specials. In a mixture of obituary, nationalism, politics, myth, nostalgia and history, the life and times of Bradman was reviewed. Public veneration flowed in letters to newspaper editors, on talkback radio, via on-line forums, and messages left in condolence books at 4,500 post offices. Former Australian rugby captain, John Eales, said the Don's death was similar to that of American President John F. Kennedy, saying, 'You will always remember where you were the day Don Bradman died.' Political commentator Paul Kelly wrote that Bradman's unrivalled Test batting average of 99.94 runs 'equates with the prime ministership and the great Australian novel' in the antipodean cultural imagination.[5] The *Sydney Morning Herald* editorialised that Bradman's life 'fuse [d] nationalism and sport in an heroic and pure way that has now been lost forever to the trivialities of commercialism and celebrity.'[6] Cricket writer Ken Piesse declared that Bradman was, 'Australia's quintessential sporting hero, a true superstar who had an incredible impact on the game and the Australian psyche'. The Don was compared to Shakespeare, which had followed from earlier comparisons to Einstein and Mozart.[7] Prime Minister John Howard stated: 'In many ways he was the most remarkable figure that Australia has produced in the last 100 years. He had an impact on our country that is difficult to properly calculate'.[8]

We were assured that Bradman's death would not diminish his legend and that his stature as a national hero had moved from unquestioned in life to untouchable in death.[9] These occasionally overstated responses represent an emotional celebration of a man who has been entered into the register of sacred Australian history and who has been framed as a universal symbol of an idealised nationhood.[10] In line with this, most of the journalists, politicians, sportspeople and public figures that honoured Bradman appeared to believe that they were speaking on behalf of *all* Australians, irrespective of people's interest in the Don or cricket, and that the entire nation was in agreement over Bradman's status as *the* Australian hero.

On 25 March, a public memorial service was held in his honour at St Peter's Anglican Cathedral in Adelaide. Over 700 invited guests attended the memorial and a few thousand more watched the service live on screens at the Adelaide Oval and the Sydney Cricket Ground. Those who attended the memorial service included former male Test cricketers Neil Harvey, Bill Brown, Sam Loxton, Doug Ring, Bill Johnston, Ron Hammence, Greg Chappell, Rod Marsh, Bill Lawry, Sir Vivian Richards, Sir Everton Weekes, India's Nawab of Pataudi, as well as the wife of Ray Lindwall, Peggy. Amongst the politicians in the audience were Prime Minister Howard, then Opposition leader Kim Beazley, former South Australian Premier John Olsen and former Prime Minister Bob Hawke. Speakers included members of the Bradman family, former Australian captain and Channel Nine cricket commentator, Richie Benaud, and the then Governor-General, Sir William Deane. The memorial was the culmination of a special 'Bradman week' and was broadcast live on ABC television (to an estimated viewing audience of 1.45 million) and radio, and replayed later on Channel Nine (estimated viewing audience 333,000).

Given Bradman's extraordinary public prominence, the reaction to his death was bound to be exceptional. In the lead-up to the Sydney 2000 Olympic Games, public polls selected Sir Donald as the preferred person to light the Olympic cauldron, even though he was not an Olympian. As of 1998, there were 22 major thoroughfares in Australia bearing the Bradman name, and the PO Box number (9994) in all capital cities for the national broadcaster, the Australian Broadcasting Corporation, is a respectful reproduction of Bradman's 'totemic' Test batting average: 99.94 runs per

innings.[11] An industry built around Bradman's name and image
sells books, videos, songs, souvenirs, prints, autographed limited
edition bats, statuettes, caps, ties, scarfs, jigsaw puzzles, calendars,
biscuits, tea spoons, golf balls, fridge magnets and sunglasses cases.
Spectators can sit in Bradman stands at major venues including the
Sydney Cricket Ground, the Adelaide Oval and Manuka Oval in
Canberra. Visitors to the State Library of South Australia and the
National Library can pore over a full 52 specially bound and
inscribed volumes of Bradman scrapbooks. Just as 'Ruthian' (after
baseball legend Babe Ruth) became an adjective to describe individual success and heroism in America,[12] Australian vernacular has
a term that connotes excellence and endurance: 'Bradmanesque'.

Bradman excelled at cricket, regarded as the 'cornerstone sport
in Australian culture'.[13] Many Australian people are said to relate
more to cricketers than they do to their politicians, and in the
cricketing context, Bradman's achievements are unprecedented.[14]
He is the key reference point with which to consider the merits
of every successful batsman in world cricket. Neville Cardus
marvels that:

> Bradman's achievements stagger the imagination. No writer of boys'
> fiction would dare to invent a 'hero' who performed with Bradman's
> continual consistency. Nobody would even suspend disbelief as he
> read such fiction.[15]

Rather than once again merely reiterating awe or restating
truisms and popularised myths, this book challenges those very
modes of thinking and talking about Don Bradman. Having become idealised as the human character of Australian nationhood,
Bradman is a fascinating subject, and the complexities of that fascination are those that this book attempts to unravel.

Records and achievements

To the uninitiated, cricket statistics can appear both esoteric and boring, yet they are the currency of player evaluation in the game. Bradman's record is the bedrock upon which his heroism is built (see Table 1, Appendix).

The Don's Test career ran from 1928 to 1948, with his first-class career spanning from 1927 to 1949. After scoring a century on debut for New South Wales against South Australia in Adelaide, he was selected for the national team the following season, making an inauspicious start (18 and 1) to his Test career against England in Brisbane. By the Third Test of the same series, however, he had made his maiden Test hundred, a prelude to his record 974 runs in the 1930 Ashes series in England. In his career, Bradman experienced victory in 8 Test series and defeat in only 2. His first loss was in 1928–29 when he was an unestablished 20-year-old youngster and Australia faced a strong England side, and the second was in the controversial 1932–33 bodyline series (see Chapter 4). Also, of the 28 Test matches in which Bradman made a century, Australia won 22, drew 4 and lost just 2, while his 29 Test centuries included 10 double centuries and 2 triple centuries. Upon being appointed captain of the national side in 1936 his startling success continued. The Don never captained a Test team to a losing series, although this has not prevented criticism of the manner and style of his captaincy (see Chapter 7).

Bradman's overall batting record is exceptional: he has the highest average of any Test cricketer (99.94 per innings; South African Graeme Pollock is second, with 60.97); he scored 6,966 runs in 80 innings in 52 Test matches, with 29 centuries and 13 half-centuries (see Table 2, Appendix). This outstanding record saw him selected as *Wisden Cricketers' Almanack*'s greatest cricketer of the twentieth century, by unanimous vote of 100 judges, and also nominated as captain of the Australian Cricket Team of the Century.

Bradman also received numerous awards and honours throughout his lifetime, joining esteemed company both inside and outside sport (see Table 3, Appendix). He received a Companion of the Order of Australia (1979), was voted the greatest male athlete of the past 200 years by the Australian Confederation of Sport, and was nominated by *International Who's Who* as one of only two Australians among the top 100 people who have done the most to shape the 20th century.[16] Yet, while his records and awards tell us something of how his reputation has been attained and maintained, they do not effectively explain *why* he is venerated as an outstanding and uniquely Australian icon.

Bradman's heroism
'He's Out.'

These are the two words that appeared as a London newspaper headline banner during the 1930s Ashes tour. Clearly, the 'he' was Don Bradman, and the two words continue to be reproduced in books, exhibitions and films about him. Bradman's extraordinary popularity makes him the only one, the only 'he' to whom anyone talking about cricket could have been referring. Becoming this kind of hero requires the admiration of a large cross-section of a community, and in the case of the Don, of the nation. As the nation's ideal, Bradman represented the figure of 'Australianness' in the 1930s – the white heterosexual Protestant male, a family man and businessman who played sport at the highest level. In contemporary life, conservative politicians have continued to draw upon his legend to push their own agendas. Prime Minister John Howard, perhaps the most socially conservative politician in Australian post-war history, is very much a 'Menzies man', and like

Menzies, idealises Bradman as the quintessential Australian, however anachronistic that figure is to contemporary Australian life.
Despite the major shifts in the make-up of Australian society since
the late 1940s, Bradman remains – however nostalgically – very
much an idealised figure, and it is the complexity of his enduring
heroism that is addressed throughout this book.

Many books and videos have celebrated Bradman's heroism over
the years, but they have tended to be limited by commonly held
views on what Bradman did and who he was. They have concentrated on describing the events of Bradman's Test career between
1928 and 1948. Much of the literature tends to veer away from the
negatives, the critics and the controversies. As such, more appears
to have been obscured about Don Bradman than revealed. As one
thoughtful critic puts it – 'So much has been said and written about
Don Bradman over the years that ... the person has been lost
behind what others have thought'.[17] The man and the myth are,
therefore, inseparable and their indivisibility is largely the subject
of this book, which is not a conventional biography. It does not
cover the life and times of Bradman or attempt to find out what he
was 'really' like and log his strengths and failings. Moving between
the figure of Bradman, the cultural setting of the sport that he
played, and the wider national culture, I suggest that Bradman is
both an emblem of Australian culture and a shaper of it.[18] His
complex mythological character and the ways that it has been
constructed and used are the focus. There is plenty of evidence
to suggest that people's connections to popular representations of
Don Bradman are deeply emotive. We need only consider the actual

and media 'turn out' to his various memorial services to make this clear. Bradman is, therefore, a complex cultural symbol, and there are many different ways of understanding him: the relentless run-machine, the nation-builder, the unseen hero living in retirement (see Chapter 2); the boy from the bush (see Chapter 3); the brave fighter facing up to bodyline bowling (see Chapter 4); the businessman and administrator, the trademark (see Chapter 5); the apolitical sportsman (see Chapter 6); and the devoted husband (see Chapter 7). All of these have had different effects at different times, and all of these aspects of 'The Don' deserve attention.

The mass of Bradman materials has never been systematically assessed. Books and articles tell us 'what happened': Bradman's adventures in England, on-field feats and off-field activities. Fine writers such as Neville Cardus, Irving Rosenwater and R.C. Robertson-Glasgow paint absorbing pictures of the contests, scores, period and personalities. However, there is no in-depth synthesis and reading of these and other available sources – magazines, newspapers, images, museum displays, memorabilia, programs, songs, videos and documentaries. In order to understand Bradman's cultural significance properly, we need to carefully analyse these materials.[19]

Also, this book is primarily concerned with the contemporary fascination with Bradman's heroism, and explains this with reference to historical accounts. In building my analysis I have used the biographies, autobiography and cricket histories that review Bradman's life, and then compared these with many of the most recent books, reports and accounts in order to see how the past informs and shapes the present and vice versa.[20]

This book is not just about a cricketer who became an icon: it is also about Australian culture and nationalism. It investigates what Bradman means and represents and what these meanings and representations say about Australia, helping us to understand how Bradman's heroism informs and constitutes the nation's culture as much as reflects it. Those who would claim that an icon such as Bradman simply reflects the Australian character ignore that people also live and act through what they see in the mirror.

My concern here is with the function of Bradman within Australian culture. This emphasis is driven by both practical and future agendas. Particularly as no one has yet attempted this type of project, it had to be kept within manageable limits. In terms of future studies, I hope this volume fuels examination of Bradman in other cultural settings, especially in Commonwealth nations where cricket is a popular and established sport. Throughout the book, I make repeated references to the Bradman myth. I do not claim that accounts of Bradman's career have been falsified, but rather show how his story has been constructed in quite specific ways. The concept of myth signifies that a heroic image of Bradman has been generally accepted as categorically true, while at the same time it ignores the more critical accounts of his career and significance (see Chapter 4).

Connected to the issue of myth is the way I use the name Bradman and 'the Don' interchangeably throughout the text. It is possible to conceive that the name Bradman once simply referred to the man. 'The Don', however, is a much larger character, a mythical cricket and Australian legend who moves in many different directions and on many levels throughout the nation's popular culture. Understood in this fashion, the man and the myth are one and the same. The usage of Bradman's popular moniker is also indicative of his prominence in the Australian collective conscience. When I have spoken or written of the Don, most people have correctly assumed that I am referring to Sir Donald Bradman. Only one person has admitted believing that I was speaking of someone else (he thought I was referring to Don Burke!). 'The Don' could refer to the head of the famous Italian-American crime syndicates, another position with a powerful mythology built around it, but one that evokes a uniquely American story. In Australia, 'the Don' is a special part of the national nomenclature, with Carroll postulating that its appeal lies in it being 'rich with associations of chivalry, but also informal, intimate'. It is a nickname that creates a sense of familiarity and closeness – he is one of 'us'. The Don also manages to avoid the prospect of calling him Sir Donald, maintaining a distinctly Australian flavour that avoids the trappings of English pomp and formality that accompanies the knighthood he received in 1949.

In studying a popular hero in this way, my intention is not to 'tear down' and discredit Bradman's character. I am not, as John Birmingham stated, 'looking for a loose thread to pull in the hope that the entire tapestry will unravel'.[21] Rather, this book is an attempt to introduce some balance to the mountain of nostalgic dedications and hagiographies that are available on Bradman. Critical analysis and debate can bring a long overdue perspective to Bradman's place in Australian culture and history and I strongly believe that this approach is as respectful of Bradman's memory as any tribute.

CHAPTER 2

LOOKING FOR HEROES

Always you look for heroes. Always the people look up to see something that represents them, that is larger than they are ... He didn't seem to have any other credential but his ability and that was sufficient to make him a great hero and a great success, and therefore, a great inspiration.[1]

Although referring to American baseball's Joe DiMaggio, this statement could also be applied to Don Bradman. Sport, with its supposed level-playing field and strong nationalist qualities, is highly conducive to the creation of heroes. Don Bradman's heroic reputation has expanded over the years, in contrast to the diminution of the significance of many other historical figures after one or two generations. The challenge is to work out why Bradman is unique in this respect.

The production and reproduction of Bradman's iconic standing is a key focus of this book. We see it in his insertion into national myths (Chapter 3); in his role in dramatic historical events such as the 'bodyline' Test match series against the English in 1932–33 (Chapter 4); in his function as both a heroic symbol and an economic signifier (Chapter 5); in the use of Bradman in Australian politics and political representation (Chapter 6); and in how he has been viewed in terms of notions of nationalism and masculinity (Chapter 7). This chapter aims to establish a baseline for the broader themes and analyses presented in the following chapters by directly addressing the question of why Bradman holds such a place in the Australian popular imagination.

Since cultural meanings change constantly, no explanation of Bradman's heroism can be definitive or exhaustive. The objective of this chapter is to provide some compelling arguments on how and why Bradman is understood as an Australian hero, and more generally, to integrate these arguments into selected wider social, cultural and historical processes. Issues covered include the importance of cricket in the formation of Australian nationalism, Bradman's role as a nation-building figure, the use of statistics as a measure of sporting achievement, his heroic status in an age of media celebrity and scandal, and the nostalgia that informs the collective memory of the Don.

Cricket and nationalism

If the Don is to be understood as a peculiarly Australian icon, some account must be made for the role of cricket in the construction of Australian nationalism – why is it that cricket lends itself so well to the nationalist impulse and the creation of famous men such as Victor Trumper, Dennis Lillee, Steve Waugh and Bradman?

Bill Mandle has convincingly argued that it was not only the bush, goldfield or city that contributed to the formation of Australian national identity/ies, but also sport, and cricket in particular.[2] Over the course of the nineteenth century, cricket helped to 'invent' Australians for an English audience, which was important given that Australia was England's senior 'white' colony.[3] Cricket also helped Australians to form their own identity in relation to their colonial forebears and the world. The relationship between the two countries incorporated both opposition and accommodation (discussed further later in this chapter): Australia willingly and enthusiastically competed *against* England, but also undertook 'civilised' pursuits such as cricket that announced that it was *part* of the Empire.

Cricket became Australia's national game during the nineteenth century and into the twentieth. A popular pursuit, it was played in both city and regional centres and in all states. No other sport carried the 'moral and even spiritual connotations' that cricket did within the British Empire.[4] Football in its many variations, swimming, rowing, tennis and athletics were certainly vehicles for imperial and national pride, but cricket most clearly announced the imperial bond and offered the first chance for a nascent Australian nation to match itself against England. Cricket was also a sport thought unparalleled in teaching social lessons of discipline, self-control and decency.[5] Further, in an age influenced by the theories of Darwin, cricket was used as a guide with which to measure the racial progress of the English in the antipodes. Not surprisingly, when Australian teams started recording victories against English XIs from the mid-1870s, the consensus was that progress was moving along at a healthy rate. These victories also spurred on an emergent nationalism that, Mandle argues, 'was the best example of Federation yet'.[6] As an already established and popular expression of nationalist sentiment, cricket was ready to create national heroes and icons even before Federation occurred in 1901.

In the 1890s a distinctive Australian nationalism developed. It was then that the characteristics were formed of a particular 'Australian type', a mythical figure defined by a masculinist, Anglo-Celtic and intensely nationalistic character and who has an ongoing resonance within Australian culture.[7] The 'type' was put to test in cricket and sculling, measured in the military theatre of the Sudan and the Boer War, and appraised at Oxford and Cambridge. In cricket, Mandle describes the emergence of a less deferential and more independent Australian attitude, especially given the success of home teams over the English. This is also when the 'barracker' emerges:

> As the superiority of Australian cricket became more manifest, there arose the terror of touring sides, the Australian 'barracker'. In the 1890s he became a factor of some importance in the game. 'Overstrung' and 'peevish', he indulged in 'loud-voiced satire and banter', but, more than that, his 'spirit was fiercely partisan, and the Australian sentiment comes out on top with a decidedly anti-British flavour, expressed in bloodthirsty Australian patois'. So hostile did the barracking become that A.E. Stoddart was forced to comment adversely upon it at the close of the 1897–8 tour, 'We have been insulted, hooted at, and hissed in every match and on every ground without exception', he claimed.[8]

Australia was successful on the field, and its crowds were willing to aggressively support their own in competition against the English and other countries.

From the turn of the twentieth century, the nationalist inclinations of the 1890s continued to flourish. Plum Warner, the leader of the 1903–04 English tour of Australia, thought the behaviour of Australian crowds disturbing. A confronting experience in Ballarat led him to make the unusual suggestion that some boisterous young men in the crowd should be caned in order to discourage them from growing into barrackers.[9] On the field, records indicate that Australian cricket had little wariness of the British lion and emphasise the ascendancy of the younger nation. At the end of 1899, England had won 26 Test matches to

Australia's 20 (11 Test series to Australia's 6). However, from 1901 to 1926, the year of the series prior to Bradman's debut in the season of 1928–29, Australia registered 27 victories to England's 16 (7 series wins to England's 5). Warwick Armstrong, national captain from 1920 to 1921, captured an assured and assertive attitude in Australian cricket and culture. He led Australia to its first ever 5–0 series whitewash against England and presented 'a masterful, almost aggressive authority against the English cricketing establishment'.[10] Standing at about six foot three inches (approx. 191 cm) and weighing over 120 kilograms, 'The Big Ship', as he was known, represented an unapologetic, successful and independent national spirit that had been germinating for more than half a century.

The nationalist trajectory created the preconditions for the emergence of a hero whose image and appeal were widely embraced. By the late 1920s Australia was no longer willing to stand idly in the shadow of England, and Bradman capitalised on this nationalist impulse. Through him, Australia declared itself internationally and continued constructing its own distinctive history and culture.

The Don as 'nation-builder'

It is often said that Australia has little raw material to fashion a history – no great wars, distinctive military figures, or larger-than-life political heroes. The eighteenth and nineteenth centuries offered up motley convicts, some pioneering explorers and notorious bushrangers, but nothing that openly announced an Australian identity to the world. Processes of nation formation are especially pronounced in settler societies like Australia, unlike many European countries with comparatively lengthy histories, dense mythologies and 'the stories, the tunes, the images and the names of heroic ancestors' that gives their national identity/ies the appearance of naturalness and authenticity.[11] In working to form a uniquely Australian identity, both war and sport have supplied popular national mythologies and iconography. The Anzac experience of World War I has been constructed as a bold statement of sacrifice and courage, with this baptism by fire announcing Australia's arrival on the international stage. Simpson, the man with the donkey, possibly 'the most iconic figure in Australian military history', is a character through whom the 'Anzac spirit' has been personified.[12] It is not until Bradman in the 1930s that another person makes such a resounding, unequivocal and widely publicised statement of Australian competitiveness, success and independence to the world, or at least to the Empire, which constituted the parts of the world that mattered to many Australians of the time. The Don's domination on the international cricket field has been adopted as an idealised expression of Australian resilience and identity, particularly during the Depression of the 1930s and the years surrounding World War II. He offered the comfort of reliability, success and symbolic redemption in times of economic, political and military uncertainty, conflict and crisis, both nationally and internationally.

Donald Horne's *The Lucky Country* showed that Australians' attitude towards the expression of national independence is not straightforward.[13] On the one hand, the community deifies those who symbolise a defiant and independent Australian character. On the other hand, the Union Jack has pride of place on the national flag, the Queen of England is on the country's coinage and, as the 1999 Republic referendum attests, the head of the British monarchy is considered appropriate as the Australian head of state. The Australian mindset appears 'trapped between the aspiration to independence and the comfortable dependence upon Britain'; the dynamic of opposition and accommodation continues.[14]

A similar ambivalence has been observed in the case of Bradman, who led Australia to repeated and resounding success over English sides, but who also had a great fondness for England, its people and royalty.[15] Some commentators attribute the Don's legend to his performances against the English team of 1932–33 and their 'bodyline' bowling tactics (see Chapter 4). As Wright notes, these performances became tied up in the colonial relationship between the two countries:

> ... England's body-line tactics in 1932–33 struck so deeply at the core of Australia. Devised and implemented to stop Bradman from making his match-winning centuries, it was a negative philosophy born of defeatism ... Its employment by the patrician Jardine was interpreted as a symbol of Britain's determination to keep Australia under her dominion. In that series Don Bradman transcended the cricket field and entered the consciousness of the young nation. He became Australia.[16]

Yet no matter how much it is claimed that the Don's role in the bodyline series was an expression of an independent Australian identity, the statement unfolded through cricket, a game originating from and inextricably bound to British culture. Despite the tactics of English captain, Douglas Jardine, no one in the settler society challenged cricket itself. Although increasingly independent, Australia, like many other Commonwealth countries, accepted the legitimacy of the British game. It is argued that this awkward alliance of independence and dependence actually helped to bolster Bradman's popularity. He is shown to demonstrate to the British how the game *should* be played, not in a defeatist or negative way as Wright suggests, but in a positive and determined fashion. From an Australian perspective, Bradman mastered the master's game.

He signified an independent national identity without the turmoil of a radical rupture in the prevailing political and cultural order. This aspect of Bradman's heroism is particularly appealing, as through him Australia saw itself as symbolically appropriating the form of the dominant British culture, cricket, and making it its own.

Bradman is far from a radical or revolutionary. He is a benign figure whose name rarely features in open and/or hostile political disputes, and he is definitely not a lightning rod for activism or dissent. Significantly, this benign characterisation allows the Don to be cast as an all-embracing and popular national hero. For instance, despite invitations from both sides of Australian politics, he refused to join either party, a rejection that is often cited as proof of his apparent political impartiality (although it is clear that Bradman had conservative leanings; see Chapter 6). Following from this benign characterisation, the meanings associated with Bradman and cricket, with its white, masculinist character and history, are mainly socially conservative. This conservatism implicates Bradman, as a standard-bearer in the national sport, in a reading of Australian history and nationalism that is largely celebratory, egalitarian, mono-cultural, and that presents itself as apolitical. Of course, none of this invalidates enjoyment, amazement or pride in Bradman and his feats. But the apolitical appearance of the Don and his sport does tacitly legitimate a 'mainstream' nationalism and political order.

The context for the attraction that this mainstream image and Bradman's heroism holds for many Australians includes the pressures, constraints and discontents experienced in an age of globalisation. Communities anxious about the present and their future are inclined to look to the past. Some political groups have managed to maintain relevance and occasional dominance in

Australian politics by declaring a preference for a return to a less globalised culture (even if not an economy). As an emblem of a seemingly unified and triumphant Australian history, Bradman answers such expectations. He represents a past in which certainty and stability in economics, social relations and family life appear to be assured. It is a past that stands in sharp contrast to today's globalised world where the techno-economic imperative guarantees uncertainty, fragmentation and instability.

'You keep coming back to the numbers' – 99.94

Just as figures drive global money markets, so too do numbers dominate the telling of the Bradman story. As biographer and friend of the Don, A.G. Moyes, states, 'The immensity of ... [his statistics] is staggering! How can we place anyone before him?'[17] As a measure of achievement, statistics are the lifeblood of cricket and fuel debates over the best players of and between eras. According to *Wisden Cricketers' Almanack* editor, Matthew Engel, statistics are fundamental to the traditions and history of cricket in that they create a sense of order and capture a moment.[18] Bradman also found statistics valuable in the analysis of his batting performance and for the best part of the twentieth century, these statistics have kept him permanently in the public eye.[19]

The Don's admirers naturally stress statistics as a measure of sporting achievement and transcendence. His famous Test average of 99.94 runs per innings is well ahead of any other batsman before or since – the averages of other Test batting champions, such as the West Indian, Sir Garfield Sobers (57.78 runs), South African Graeme Pollock (60.97 runs), and Australian Greg Chappell (53.86 runs), are well below Bradman's average. In 1998 now retired Australian captain, Mark Taylor, equalled Bradman's highest Test score of 334 runs against Pakistan, but did not pass this figure out of 'respect' for the Don (Taylor later admitted he did try to pass the 334 run mark but failed).[20]

The Bradman Museum in Bowral, New South Wales, opened an exhibition in August 2000 comparing the achievements of the Don to nine other champions of world sport, including gymnast Nadia Comaneci, athlete Carl Lewis, Michael Jordan and Muhammad Ali. Sports historian Charles Davis has also compared Bradman to other international sports stars. Both the exhibition and Davis' study seek to show that statistically no other athlete dominates an international sport to the extent that Bradman does cricket.[21]

Despite their importance to fans and their usefulness for measuring success, sports records are an abstraction according to some commentators.[22] Statistics appear objective, exact, value-free and permanent. They do not, however, account for sport's social history. No allowance is made for variables such as weather, conditions and opposition. Without contextualisation, records artic-ulate the promise of a 'level playing field' and defy argument as they somehow 'speak for themselves' over time and across space. For many people, an average of 99.94 runs is incontrovertible proof that Bradman was the best batsman ever. Those who argue that other players have been as good as Bradman at different times and/or in selected capacities and/or under certain conditions, find it nearly impossible to overcome the authority of the Don's statistics. For example, C.L.R. James made the case that the West Indian George Headley, another champion of the 1930s, was a superior batsman to Bradman on wet wickets, and Jack Fingleton made a similar case about Trumper.[23] While their cases were acknowledged, they could not overcome the hurdle presented by Bradman's numbers: 'Figures can lie, but in cricket, taken in the large, they tell the truth, and in his [Bradman's] case defy all argument.'[24]

A focus on productivity and performance measurement is particularly useful in making sense of Bradman's heroism and the time in which he played. During the interwar years, modernising Western industrial economies were characterised by a push towards 'positivistic, technocentric and rationalistic' social orders.[25] The Australian economy, for instance, experienced a manufacturing production increase of 70 per cent from the start of World War I to the Great Depression; in the 1930s it more than doubled despite the Depression,[26] and technological and industrial innovations unfurled in the transport and construction sectors.[27] Communications technology was also developing, and radio broadcasts, particularly of the cricket, led to large increases in the sales of radio sets. By 1934, over one million wireless receivers were licensed – and able to bring descriptions of Bradman's batting to ever-increasing audiences.[28] Given the emphasis on production and technology, Bradman's relentless run accumulation captured and celebrated the overall mood of social development. He was not alone: Bill Ponsford, another Australian batsman of the 1920s and 1930s, also compiled large scores. Nonetheless, it was Bradman who possessed the potential to fulfil the modernist project of linear progress towards an ideal goal, in cricket symbolised by the 'perfect' average of 100 runs per innings. Bradman's 99.94 run average, falling so tantalisingly short of the target, is an interesting number not only for its immense and unprecedented scale, but also for its imperfection and reflection of human fallibility.

Bradman embodied the modernist faith in improvement and progress, which is reflected in the mechanistic way that his batting was often understood. Descriptions of his batting include: run-machine, automaton, business cricketer, adding machine, machine-like, flawless engine, mechanically faultless, functional, computer type approach and workmanlike. According to Harriss, Bradman's choice and caution in shot-selection conveyed a desire for efficiency by the calculation of risk and reward.[29] Bradman was sometimes criticised for sacrificing the style and grace that characterised batsmen of the 'golden age' of cricket – the late Victorian years up to the start of World War I. In that era, gentlemen-amateurs such as Englishman W.G. Grace, C.B. Fry and Ranjitsinhji, and the Australians Trumper and Charlie Macartney, held sway with their 'chivalry', 'style' and 'art' as batsmen. Bradman symbolised the arrival of a new era, the 'efficient age', in which science reigned over the aesthetic and in which the sporting body became 'an extension of the technical spirit'.[30] He was a mechanical spirit in a mechanical age:

> It was Bradman ... who transformed batting from an art to a science. The striking feature of the literature on Bradman is that he was noteworthy for the sheer enormity of the runs he accumulated rather than for the style or brilliance with which he batted.[31]

In contemporary Australian society, the figures are still to the fore in the Bradman story. The spotlight remains on the 99.94 average that is almost interchangeable with the name Bradman (there is even a baseball cap available with his average emblazoned on it). Increasingly, social and political activity is measured and managed according to the logic of the market and 'economically rational' outputs and returns. In this atmosphere, the relevance of Bradman's statistics as a cultural marker of success has grown, not stagnated.

Batting on in an age of celebrity

To understand why the heroic stature of Bradman has expanded rather than fallen in recent times, longevity, reputation in retirement and celebrity status must be considered. Beginning with retirement, Holt points out that people like their sports heroes to maintain an image of respectability and athleticism after their playing days are over as it allows their reputation to be 'assiduously polished'.[32] Bradman maintained an air of decency and moral rectitude for fifty years or more from the end of his playing career until his death. There were no bouts of alcoholism, ugly public divorces or family feuds played out in the media. Unlike former Test teammates such as Leslie 'Chuck' Fleetwood-Smith, who for many years was a divorced, homeless, alcoholic sleeping under bridges along the Yarra River in Melbourne,[33] or Sid Barnes, who committed suicide in 1973, Bradman appears to have had no dark side. Of course, if there had been personal scandal during Bradman's career, the media of the time may not have revealed it as quickly or with the same enthusiasm as the tabloid media today. After his career, Bradman also did not do or say much that could provide evidence of a scandal, though he no doubt had flaws that were not revealed either due to a reluctance to tarnish his reputation, a perceived lack of public interest or the possible threat of libel. The less titillating or exciting features of Bradman's life – devotion to his wife Jessie, his record as a straight-laced cricket administrator, his privacy and restraint – actually worked to maintain his heroism. In terms of lifestyle and public presence, he stood out for not standing out.

The Don's longevity must also be acknowledged. Bill Brown is now the only surviving Test player who played alongside Bradman in the pre-World War II era. By outlasting most of his contemporaries, the Don projects most clearly in the collective memory. The Bradman Museum and Bradman Foundation have also vigilantly protected his name and reputation (see Chapter 5), and most of his biographies painted the (then) 'living legend' in glowing terms.

Bradman's critics have, inadvertently, fortified his heroism. Fierce opposition provided the impetus for a community of 'true believers' to consolidate around various figures throughout history such as Winston Churchill and Martin Luther King.[34] A similar case, albeit to a lesser degree, may be made about the Don. A band of commentators have staunchly defended the Don's reputation against fellow Test players, particularly Bill O'Reilly and Jack Fingleton, who have been trenchantly critical of Bradman over the years. Defenders have included biographers Moyes, Page, Williams and Perry who have often concluded, rightly or wrongly, that criticism is a result of jealousy, envy and resentment. Loyalty to the Don was possibly further augmented by his sensitivity to criticism, a theme that ran throughout his autobiography, *Farewell to Cricket*, and was on display in 1995 in his letter to *Wisden Cricket Monthly* refuting points made by Gideon Haigh in an article detailing O'Reilly's grievances with the Don.[35] In Haigh's article, written from O'Reilly's oral history recordings held by the National Library, it is claimed that Bradman's personal animosity towards Clarrie Grimmett was the reason that leg-spinner was not selected for the 1938 Ashes tour, which signalled the end of his Test career. Bradman is also condemned for his failure to attend the Australian Board of Control's (now the Australian Cricket Board) carpeting of four Catholic members of the Australian cricket side in 1936–37 despite being team captain. Bradman strongly refuted both claims and asserted that the article had sensationalised O'Reilly's version of events and grossly defamed him.

The question asked of those considering the relative merits of Bradman and his (seemingly few) detractors is: Who should be believed? The world's greatest cricketer, or players who stood in his shadow? While criticism may be legitimate in some cases, it is arguable that Bradman's heroism is so well established, so entrenched, so sacred, that any criticism of him is almost automatically considered profane and actually further solidifies the worshipful mindset of the Bradman 'true believers'. With O'Reilly and Fingleton dying before the Don, they were denied the last word. O'Reilly at least appears to have recognised the inevitability of the majority judgement when he observed that 'the world frowns upon those who spit on statues'.[36]

Another key reason that Bradman stands out as a hero is that he appeared to represent the 'real' and 'authentic' in a contemporary media culture that features image manipulation and superficiality. He was far more than a 'human pseudo-event' who is famous for being famous, such as Mark 'Jacko' Jackson or Dannii Minogue. Bradman would never have garnered publicity by a one-off appearance on *Neighbours* or *Home and Away*, or tested his wits as a celebrity contestant on *Sale of the Century* or similar television shows. In a culture in which the fan–celebrity relationship can be intense, yet shallow and unpredictable, Bradman's public image has both stability *and* depth. Furthermore, as a national hero the Don seems to transcend the contested and delicate politics of identity that, according to some, makes it difficult for people to know whom to admire in contemporary culture.[37] The case of Ian Roberts who openly 'came out' as homosexual in the fiercely heterosexist context of Australian Rugby League stands in sharp contrast to icons like Bradman, that unifying national figure who was neither controversial nor confounding.[38]

The Don's heroic 'authenticity' is consolidated by the visual and audio images of his career that were produced by less complex and profuse media between the 1920s and 1940s. A limited number of media representations of Bradman's playing career exist, especially from that early period. The lack of footage and recordings can be explained by a failure of government and industry to recognise the need to collect such material until the 1970s. This shortage helps to construct nostalgia around the black and white photographs and films, the crackly audio recordings and their subsequent reproduction.

The romance of listening to descriptions of Bradman 'flaying the Poms' on the wireless is especially appealing in the current era. The mid-1930s was regarded as the start of Australian radio's 'golden era', reflected in fondly recalled tales of synthetic broadcasts of Test matches from England. Commentators in a Sydney studio would simulate the call of the action, including sound effects, by inventing sometimes fictitious details to complement the sparsely worded descriptions cabled from England every five minutes. These broadcasts had, as revered cricket commentator Alan McGilvray termed it (with a decidedly postmodern inflection), 'a touch of science fiction ... It was good fun and it was good radio. Sometimes we all lose our perspective and are prone to shut out our imagination in the pursuit of truth and reality.'[39] In contrast to today's media, which is characterised by pastiche and technology-driven colour and special effect presentations in any number of formats, the simple technology of the past paradoxically produced broadcasts that seem more 'real'. The imperfections of the old film and radio recordings make Bradman's image unique.

The scarcity of moving images of Bradman from his playing days, not to mention his reclusive lifestyle afterwards, actually adds to the estimation of his heroic symbolism. Transmission over the world wide web of tens of millions of images, 24-hour free-to-air and pay television, and worldwide DVD and video distribution now provide consumers with an excess of images. For almost any noteworthy event, person or place, a profusion of footage is available, preferably from different angles, in colour and with digital sound (or maybe footage is required *before* the event, person or place can be considered noteworthy). Celebrities like Madonna, Tom Cruise and Pamela Anderson, or Kylie Minogue, Mel Gibson and Nicole Kidman have a huge media presence. By comparison, we have a small range of images of a nimble-footed smiling Don from his playing days and beyond.

Unlike the fame of 'here now, gone tomorrow' celebrities, Bradman's heroism is generally acknowledged, his achievements are exemplary, his respectability is unquestioned, and the images we have of him do not seem ambiguous or crassly manufactured. In an age of multimedia and celebrity, what Bradman does not represent, as much as what he does, constructs his iconic standing.

Biographical understanding and cricket scandal

Bradman's biographers present him as a man of few words who shunned the public spotlight. His undemonstrative personality and his reluctance to enter the public domain strengthened his heroism: 'Bradman's phlegmatic personality, like a vacant block, proved ideal for bearing whatever constructions were imposed upon it, and he was so neutral that the common man … could identify with him.'[40] This personality was on display in his autobiography with its straightforward prose and minimalist detail. It was a writing style reminiscent of the laconic, no-nonsense manner that is seen as characteristic of many older Australian men. This personal style allowed biographers, the media, and people such as Australian Prime Minister John Howard to construct Bradman's reputation with little fear of open interference, contradiction or comment from the man himself. However, he did not completely maintain his silence, especially when the name O'Reilly was mentioned. He also wrote exclusively for London's *Daily Mail* newspaper as a cricket correspondent during the 1953 and 1956 Ashes series, capitalising financially on his reputation on these occasions.[41] Nevertheless, as journalist Peter FitzSimons maintains, the Don's profile was:

> low enough that we Australians are able to visit upon him pretty much any kind of personality traits we like – to best suit whatever we think the most admirable – for the most part unfettered by the reality of what he is actually like.[42]

With constant reiteration, Bradman's heroism has assumed an established character that is difficult to refute. Once again, in a media culture featuring endless public comment, interviews, appearances, and media releases, Bradman was comparatively mute. He fiercely guarded his personal and family privacy, and made limited public statements after his retirement from cricket administration. Even when administrating he kept his comments to a minimum. Cricket commentator Peter Roebuck sums up a common perception of the Bradman mindset:

> he led a simple life, kept his dignity, avoided the back-slappers, was not drawn to the celebrity trail or exploiting his name ... Rather, he demanded the privacy to which he was entitled, lived in a modest neighbourhood and kept the world at bay by just rejecting its intrusions.[43]

The silence of Bradman was indeed 'golden' as it stood in contrast to the powerful promotional machine that is part of contemporary media, and worked to create an idealised image of humility and selflessness. The less he said the more secure his heroism became as he was known to be involved in cricket for the 'right' reasons, not for publicity or fame, but for the love of the game.

The air of reverence around Bradman works to make the time in which he played appear as a mythological golden age, especially given the scandals and problems that have engulfed international cricket since 2000. The problems have included overt sledging, bouts of spitting by bowlers in the direction of the batsmen, and ball tampering. A national newspaper published photographs of Australian batsman Ricky Ponting after he was punched in the face following alleged drunken behaviour. Australian leg-spinner Shane Warne, one of *Wisden Cricketers' Almanack*'s best five cricketers of the twentieth century, was alleged to have been involved in a dispute with teenage boys while on tour in New Zealand and was then accused by a British tabloid newspaper of attempting to engage in phone sex with a British woman. Most serious of all is the 'Hansiegate' betting scandal. Former international captains, South Africa's now deceased Hansie Cronje, India's Mohammad Azharuddin and Pakistan's Salim Malik, have received life-bans for alleged match fixing.

These nefarious activities have severely damaged the reputation of cricket worldwide, prompting the International Cricket Council to take action. An anti-corruption unit headed by former Commissioner of the London Metropolitan Police, Sir Paul Condon, produced a report that included various recommendations designed to stamp out match fixing. Irrespective of possible solutions, the cumulative effect of these problems is dismay for cricket followers, which leads to an idealisation of cricket's past. As ethics commentator Simon Longstaff states: 'cricket has gone to the dogs. How that comparison must hurt former greats such as Sir Donald Bradman, who helped develop a game that was, at one time, synonymous with the ideal of decency and fair play.'[44] Steve Waugh concurred with Longstaff when he called upon the Don's memory to be used as an inspiration to shield cricket's image in the face of scandal. John Howard said that match-fixing allegations were a challenge to the 'very fine' qualities of cricket and to the 'very values personified by Sir Donald'.[45] Warwick Franks, editor of *Wisden Cricketers' Almanack Australia*, expressed a similar sentiment:

> an important component of cricket is a sense of morality,
> unfashionable though the word is in these post-modern times. Part
> of this component is a specific sense of a code of behaviour which is
> separate from what is legally enforceable – for example, the fact that

a bowler will generally not Mankad a batsman without first warning him. Its other part is a general approach which is reflected in the expression of something being 'not cricket', a notion that there is an agreed ethical standard which imbues the game itself and is at the heart of what makes it worthwhile and satisfying as a sport.[46]

Bradman actively reinforced cricket's preoccupation with moral rectitude by invoking Lord Harris' famous 1931 letter to *The Times*, which stated that cricket 'is more free from anything sordid, anything dishonourable, than any game in the world'.[47] Bradman has come to symbolise the integrity, honesty and fair play of cricket's past posed against the vice, corruption and moral stain affecting cricket now. To even contemplate that Bradman might have been involved in corruption such as match fixing is thought humorously absurd. The more scandalous cricket becomes, the more heroic Bradman becomes. It does not matter that betting and scandals predate Bradman's career. For example, claims persist that former Australian captain, Herbert Collins, was involved in an illegal wager that changed the outcome of a Test during the 1926 Ashes series, while a definite attempt to affect play via a bet is on record as having occurred during an 1875 match between Victoria and New South Wales.[48] Despite such incidents, for the media and the public, it is nostalgia for the mythical golden age of the Don that forms the moral framework that condemns current cricket players and officials for befouling the formerly lofty and unsullied standards of conduct.

Conclusion

In the construction of Bradman's public persona, his playing record is said to speak for itself and his importance as a symbol of national pride and independence is largely unquestioned. As James avows, those things we take for granted are the most enduring.[49] Additionally, while an increasingly pervasive media erodes the boundaries between the public and private spheres in its promotion of the cult of celebrity and its search for scandal, these boundaries stayed firmly in place in Bradman's case, and, with his decency and public quietness over many decades, helped to augment the public's fascination with him.

The Don managed an unusual feat, which I argue is among his most exceptional: his popularity and heroism were expanded by a *lack* of personal exposure. The further he drifted away from the public, the media and the cricket community, the more adulation for him intensified. Yet, while he fenced off his private life from the public, other people and organisations promoted his name and image on his behalf. He is relentlessly promoted, celebrated, protected and regulated through the Bradman Museum and the Bradman Foundation, the media, book publishers, national leaders and the sporting community. This is the most impressive feature of the Bradman story – he was not required to take part in it any more. The strength of his heroism is self-perpetuating and a seemingly 'natural' feature of Australian popular culture.

A theme of this chapter has been the role of nostalgia and the ways in which it shapes the Bradman myth. The Don repre-sents certainty and substance in the face of uncertainty, scandal and superficiality. He is a hero from a time that appears simpler and more attractive:

> ... he was the link to what many like to think of as a purer, better time. A time when doors were left unlocked, when a long walk in the evening – rather than an hour in front of the television – was a preferred pastime. That was the time of our youth as a nation and of course we remember it fondly.[50]

Moreover, he is seen as a 'real hero' in a postmodern age where the status of the 'real' is often in question. In short, there is little ambiguity or contradiction in the popular image of the Don. Agents such as the media and publishing industry also attempt to benefit from and perpetuate the 'antipodean Golden Age' glow that surrounds his career.[51] Such nostalgia is not limited to Bradman. Various Australian media and political forums emphasise a similar perspective; examples include the (nuclear) family, law and order, rural life, and the notion of a golden age of sport free from drugs, corruption and controversy. The concept of a golden age makes a simple solution to current difficult social problems appear possible and counters the uncertainty of the future, despite the impossibility and impracticality of returning to the past.

CHAPTER 3

THE BOY FROM BOWRAL

Sir Donald's supreme mastery of the game of cricket marked a stage in the growth of Australia's nationhood. The 19th century had been full of achievement, from the brave explorers to the innovative pastoralists, from the politicians who fashioned a new democracy to the writers who first gave expression to our national identity.
Sir Donald was a worthy heir, therefore, to an established tradition of achievement by one's own efforts.[1]

Sports heroes often tap a vein of populist sentiment and appeal to ideals of national and/or regional character. The cultural meanings associated with Donald Bradman indicate that he has captured this sentiment. He is seen as a nation-building symbol and a worthy successor to the pioneering explorers and pastoralists upon whom the Australian legend was founded. Such symbolism signifies that Bradman is understood through the frame of Australian national mythologies.

Bradman's biography evokes the Australian mythological characters of the white bushman, sportsman and soldier. In this chapter, I focus on the first two of these figures. In explaining the Don as uniquely Australian, it is crucial to recognise that his country upbringing and an accompanying rural-nationalist narrative are a powerful part of his popular appeal. The tale runs: simple country lad excels in the meritocracy of sport, goes on to become a national hero, but never forgets his country roots.

The Don emerged from the town of Bowral in New South Wales. As a 19-year-old he was selected for the state side, before making his Test debut the following year in 1928. In the course of his quick rise, he was dubbed the 'boy from Bowral', a nickname he happily wore and that stayed with him after his retirement from Test cricket in 1948. When he was 81, he was referred to as the 'wonderful boy from the bush' in a *Sydney Morning Herald* editorial on the 1989 opening of the Bradman Museum.[2] Similarly, he has been described as a 'bold, exuberant country lad' who took on the cricketing world and who never forgot his decent and honest 'small town, family values'.[3]

The popular picture of the Don's boyhood is of happiness, freedom, fishing, shooting, exploring and good-natured sporting competition.[4] For instance, the well-received 1984 *Bodyline* television mini-series showed the Don living a carefree childhood in Bowral (see Chapter 4). An image of Bradman as a boy hitting a golf-ball with a cricket stump against the base of a water tank is ingrained in the Australian memory. This simple exercise, invented by a mere child, is said to have created his wondrous skills with the bat. Current media-generated panics over children spending too much time inside playing computer games and watching television question the ability of today's young to be as inventive. This bat and stump exercise is also a metaphor for the simplicities of country life, which are more than enough to produce success and, as a by-product, modesty and an undemonstrative strength of character. Bowral is, as Roland Perry puts it, a 'Huck Finn Heaven' that represents a sense of community, certainty, comfort and security.[5] It is a seductive vision, but one in need of de-mythologising.

Bowral is located in the Southern Highlands of New South Wales, about 75 kilometres south-west of Sydney, and in 1996 had a population of 8,761 according to Australian Bureau of Statistics figures. Historically, Bowral is characterised by the influences of Protestantism, British-derived traditionalism and conservative political dominance.[6] The conservative roots of the town run deep and, according to Masterman-Smith and Cottle, in the 1970s resulted in occasional hostile actions towards those representing a left-wing viewpoint during election campaigns.[7] In its early history, dairy farmers, cattle graziers, market gardeners and brickworks were the mainstay of a small economy. Nowadays, Bowral sells its 'parks, gardens and English-type countryside' as tourist attractions, and is a weekend and holiday arcadia for Sydney's wealthy.

In August 2000, Bradman reminisced about his country boyhood in a speech delivered on his behalf by his son, John, at the inaugural 'Bradman Oration' in Melbourne. Sir Donald wrote of 'humble days', growing up without television and radio, and of his mother, Emily, preparing the evening meal while his father, George, bowled to him in the backyard.[8] The location of the Bradman Museum, not in a state capital or the national capital, but in the country town of Bowral, underlines this rural nostalgia. The pervasive sense of 'country', the 'rural' and the 'bush' that resonates strongly within Australian history also resonates within accounts of Bradman's life. Indeed, it is the myth of the Australian legend, or as Mandle pinpoints, the 'mystic appeal of the boy from the bush' that plays a fundamental role in the Don's continued popularity.[9]

My aim in this chapter is to critically evaluate the rural nostalgia that shapes stories of Bradman. In doing this, two prominent interrelated themes within Australian history – the bush myth, and the cultural, historical and geographical divide between the rural and urban – are drawn upon. In the concluding section, attention is directed to the ways in which biographers and others have selectively constructed Bradman's popular image, and in this process, reinforced the revered position of the Australian legend in the national consciousness.

I argue that Bradman's rural upbringing is a, if not the, determining element that connects the Don's biography to dominant Australian national mythologies. The reason for this is Bradman's incompatibility with other popular cultural myths. For example, Bradman as 'digger' – personifying the nexus between sport and war – is an unlikely image given his undistinguished career in the Air Force and then the Army during World War II (see Chapter 7). And it is virtually impossible to cast Bradman as the 'likeable larrikin' or 'lovable rogue' as during his playing days he had a reputation as a teetotaller, non-smoker who was both frugal and monogamous. Bradman was also a confirmed Anglophile with a love of England and its people, making it difficult to suggest that he craved 'sticking it up the Poms' in the way an 'ocker' Aussie might. Thus, if seeking to appreciate Bradman as a specifically Australian hero, biographers and the media usually focus on the boy from Bowral story.

The power of the Australian legend

Russel Ward's seminal study, *The Australian Legend*, situated the 'noble bushman' of the nineteenth century as the archetypal Australian male.[10] Ward's tough and taciturn ideal man has been fairly attacked for promoting a constrained form of Australian cultural identity with little empirical basis. Nevertheless, the legend remains one of the most dominant historical formulations of Australian identity in circulation.[11] It has, for example, been a regular and

prominent feature of Australian film since the early twentieth
century. It has been an extensively used motif in advertising and
media discourses selling 'typically' Australian programs and
products.[12] Samples include Australian television's *Blue Heelers*,
the *Bush Tucker Man*, and *SeaChange* (with its theme of escape
from the hectic and stressful city to the nourishment and spiritual
regeneration offered by country coastal living), country musicians
such as Lee Kernaghan and John Williamson, as well as the annual
Tamworth country music festival, the ABC radio program *Australia All Over* hosted by 'Macca', clothing items such as Drizabone
overcoats, Akubra hats and R.M. Williams boots, beer advertisements such as Victoria Bitter's 'As A Matter-of-Fact I've Got One
Now', and the Toyota work truck 'bugger' ads. In these examples a
'national essentialism' is displayed showing 'real' Australia as the
rural and the pastoral.[13] The legend may be a social fiction, but it
is undoubtedly popular.

Bradman has been inserted into similarly 'typical' representations of what it is to be Australian. Historian Manning Clark
believed 'he had the daring and the pluck of the bushrangers
and the explorers'.[14] This chapter's opening quotation from *The
Australian* added Bradman to the list of achievers who are said to
have forged the national character. The *Sydney Morning Herald*
editorial on the opening of the Bradman Museum speaks of
Bradman's career as 'a testament to Australian nationalism' and
'egalitarian mateship'. The *Daily Telegraph* stated that the very
sound of his name is 'like a whiff of clean country air'.[15] Derriman
writes that the Bradman family 'were essentially "bushies"'.[16] Steve
Waugh considers Bradman to be a 'little Aussie battler', while
Ashley Mallett believes the Don to be 'as Australian as the Holden
car and kangaroo'.[17] In calling upon the supposed down-to-earth
and resolute values associated with country life, it was stated in
response to his death:

To many contemporaries, Sir Donald represented the mythical values of an Australia anchored in the bush, one that treasured the practical and the resourceful, was self-taught, took quiet pride in achievement and never, ever cashed-in.[18]

Bradman made an appearance in two episodes of *Ginger Meggs*, Australia's most popular comic strip ever. The Don was the first to appear on a series of 1997 postage stamps titled 'Australian Legends', which were reissued shortly after his death. In 1999, Ray Martin's television summary, *Our Century*, and Peter Luck's *This Fabulous Century*, located Bradman as part of a uniquely Australian history. These examples highlight that journalists, players, biographers, cartoonists and merchandisers help to create a generalised 'common sense' view of Bradman, and that his heroism acquires abundant cultural power from the modelling of his life and experience in line with a mythical universal Australian experience.

In 1995, Sanitarium used Bradman as the image of Australianness. The Australian-owned company's high-profile television advertisement and package display campaign for their breakfast cereal, Weet-Bix, presented Sir Donald and Weet-Bix as '100 per cent Australian icons'.[19] Marketing manager of Sanitarium, Neale Schofield, stated of the campaign:

Our view is that it's important for Aussie kids to have Aussie heroes rather than American heroes like Michael Jordan. The reason Jordan and others like him are so revered is that they've been hyped up.

We've been negligent in not celebrating our own heroes which is something the Weet-Bix campaign will help to rectify. You just can't invent heritage, substance and integrity – and Bradman and Weet-Bix have that in spades. He should be recognised for what he is, the world's greatest sportsman.

The ads are about digging deep and the determination to succeed,
which is an aspect of the Australian character that today's young people
will recognise just as well as yesterday's. That's why Bradman is such
a special role model.[20]

Schofield communicates a strongly expressed nostalgia for a
homogeneous Australian culture of substance, integrity, determination and success. The campaign plays off our 'real' hero,
Bradman, embodying legitimate 'traditional' Australian national
identity, against an alien, hyped-up and illegitimate global
commercial and media culture that has induced Aussie school-
children into believing that a 'false' idol, basketball's Michael
Jordan, is their hero. It also helps to demonstrate that what is
viewed as 'Australian' is constructed from existing myths of
national identity, and that these are partly brought into being and
stabilised by reference to opposing national and cultural identities.
Bradman is a symbol that can be used to perpetuate a traditional
Australian character, as he is a white Anglo sportsman who
emerged from a country town to become a national and international champion.

Modelling Bradman as the universal Australian man endows his
heroism with a dimension that reaches beyond cricket audiences.
The boy from Bowral story and the surrounding country imagery
are pivotal in constructing this appeal and continue to have marked
meaning, given how various rural interest groups have claimed
ownership over images of what it is to be 'typically', 'genuinely'
or 'traditionally' Australian. These groups appear to possess a
'countrymindedness' that only they have access to, and have emphasised and sometimes exploited the historical and cultural divide
that exists between a supposedly degenerate urban experience and
a healthy rural lifestyle.[21] This countrymindedness is often evident

in the homespun wisdom of federal National Party members like De-Anne Kelly and maverick independent Bob Katter when they comment on the problems experienced in the bush. The idea of the rural as 'real Australia' has been spurred along over the past seven years in national politics. When former leader of the One Nation party, Pauline Hanson, claimed to defend the 'battlers' in the bush, she used backdrops such as the Stockman's Hall of Fame in Longreach for policy launches. News reports and images follow the national leader, John Howard, setting out on country tours of white farming areas in an awkwardly worn Akubra hat, while steadfastly avoiding Aboriginal communities. Howard also couches his well-known affection for Bradman within a nationalist impulse for the bush:

> He ... represented ... a sense of Australianness that a lot of us would like to see in ourselves. He was essentially a boy from the bush. He gave a lot of hope and inspiration to people ...[22]

Critics may point out that it is easy to overplay the influence of these images in structuring national identity. They do not reflect the diversity and complexity of identities and practices that constitute the Australian community. However, it is a mistake to underestimate the power of images in influencing the perceptions of people in everyday life, notably in popular culture and politics.[23] Within many representations of Australia, it is white farmers, rural townsfolk, larrikins, ockers and battlers who are constructed as 'mainstream'. Conservatively aligned politically and culturally, this construction is set up as a legitimate expression of Australian identity that is placed in opposition to marginalised ethnic and indigenous identities. In the case of the bush, legitimation of a mainstream ascendancy is especially pronounced in setting up white farmers as the 'rightful' owners of the land and, in the process, suppressing or denying the ownership claims of traditional indigenous communities. The Australian legend and the imagery it inspires may be an invention with little empirical basis, but its impact in determining how many people understand Australian national identity and its influence on the writing of Don Bradman's popular story are strong.

In establishing the connection between the Don and the Australian bush myth, it is usually left unsaid that Bradman left Bowral at the age of 20 and never returned. Born in another New South Wales town, Cootamundra, he lived in Bowral for only around 17 years, a relatively short time period given that he lived in Sydney for about 6 years and then Adelaide for the last 67 years of his life. This is a potential source of disruption in the bush myth that helps to sustain Bradman's heroism. According to David Nason, for several years many Bowral locals felt little affection for the Don. Mac Cott, former editor of a local newspaper who has lived in Bowral since 1958, states:

> It might be sacrilegious to say it, but for many years there just wasn't any interest in Bradman around here ... Some of the older folk resented that Bradman went to live in Adelaide, but the main thing was that there just wasn't that feeling of a lasting legacy. That's why there was so much opposition to the Bradman Museum. The attitude was that he doesn't live here any more, so why bother.[24]

It is only since the 1990s that the town has actively reclaimed the Don as its own, especially as the tourism benefits of the Museum have become apparent. In turn, it is fortunate that the founding and popularity of the Bradman Museum helped the Don to symbolically re-embrace Bowral. It is difficult to imagine his story leaving the same impression on the Australian imagination if he was known as the 'Adelaide wonder'.

Visiting the museum

The centrality of rurality to the Don's story is evident when visiting the Bradman Museum, a destination that has played an increasing role in the promotion of Bradman in the Australian community since the 1980s. Visual images are important in the creation of a sense of place within specific spatial and cultural contexts, to the point that some places are recognisable and elicit an emotional response even if a person has not been there: 'there is a fondness because it is familiar, because it is home and incarnates the past'.[25] Nostalgia and myth are fundamental to such 'topophilic' reactions. In relation to Bradman, the country town of Bowral and its landscape are arguably an example of such a place. As the Bradman Museum world wide web homepage declares, 'When you visit the Museum you return to sacred soil.'[26]

During my visit to the Museum in 1998, the first thing I noticed was the picturesque Bradman Oval. A pristine white-picket fence, trees and the Players Pavilion surround the oval. There are no advertising hoardings or light towers. An old red wooden public phone box sits near the entrance. While I wandered around the ground, a father and his two sons played with a bat and ball near the boundary. The oval is across the road from the Don's former modest brown brick home that is distinguished only by a small sign. It would appear that all signs of ostentation have been carefully excised from this scene in line with the story of the Don's humble country childhood.

At the entrance to the complex, a large three-section federation green sign announces the Museum and details such as its opening hours. An unusual feature of the sign given that the Don was still alive at the time was the description, 'A museum of Australian Cricketing history commemorating Sir Donald Bradman'. The Bradman Foundation operates as a non-profit charitable trust 'whose objective is to foster and develop cricket'. Small landscaped grounds lead to the front door of the Museum, the buildings of which are painted predominantly cream with green eaves. Near the entrance is a plaque stating that the second stage of the Museum was opened in 1996 by avid Bradman fan, Prime Minister John Howard, in the presence of the Museum's now deceased patron, Sir Roden Cutler. Large stained-glass windows of a batter, bowler, fielder and wicket keeper situated above the front door create an atmosphere of almost religious reverence. Greeting the visitor just inside the door is the quixotic passage that closed the Don's autobiography, *Farewell to Cricket*:

> Without doubt the laws of cricket and the conduct of the game are a great example to the world. We should all be proud of this heritage which I trust may forever stand as a beacon light guiding man's footsteps to happy and peaceful days.

The Museum's well-structured exhibitions begin on the ground floor with an introduction to Bradman and his wife Jessie; a chronological sequence follows, setting out the history of Australian cricket, including indigenous participation and women's cricket, and a wider social history. For instance, an unexpected feature was a first edition copy of Germaine Greer's *The Female Eunuch*. There is also a theatrette in which old newsreels of the Don are screened on a continuous loop.

At the top of the stairs it is possible to test your skills with a stump, golf ball and replica tank stand. In the softly lit 'Bradman Gallery' are Bradman bats, blazers and pictures, most encased in glass. Also on display is the sheet of paper on which country music star, John Williamson, wrote the original lyrics for 'Sir Don', his ode to Bradman that he played at the public memorial service in March 2001. The gallery is a sanctuary for the Bradman fan as these artefacts are 'vehicles of sacred contact': to be in the presence of an object that the Don touched is to be in his presence.[27] Adding to the atmosphere is a library where visitors can browse. Taken as a whole, the achievement of the Museum can perhaps be measured by comments in the visitors' book where several people who claimed to have little interest in cricket expressed their appreciation of the displays.

A consequence of the rise of the globalised consumer culture in which we live is an attraction to 'slow, quiet places' that appear to have been bypassed by the 'capitalist fast lane'.[28] The Museum is just such a place, with its atmosphere of reserved respect. Visitors can buy souvenirs from the Museum shop, enjoy tea and cake in the café and wander through the museum. Some people experience intense feelings during their visits, claiming to be 'all choked up … There's something about the ethos of cricket. It's quite inexplicable. Cricket somehow produces this response more than most other sports.'[29] During my visit, the reactions of visitors were generally positive. One female visitor exclaimed at her husband's excitement at being in the Museum, while a smiling father said to his young son, 'Tell us what year you're going to play for Australia.' Others obviously feel similar emotions given the number of people who pay to join the Museum's membership programs, 'Friends of the Bradman Museum' and 'The Bradman Legacy'.

The Museum is constructed as an 'island of tradition', at least by comparison to many other tourist destinations. It has none of the plasticity of *Warner Bros. Movie World* on the Gold Coast, the self-conscious rustic kitsch of *Old Sydney Town*, or the misplaced ambition of the defunct *Leyland Brothers* fun-park. It definitely lacks the garishness of American equivalents. Highlighting this deliberate contrast, Museum director Richard Mulvaney says of the Museum's soft-lighting and wood finish, 'No chrome or laminate for us.'[30]

The presentation of the Bradman Museum has similarities with the National Baseball Hall of Fame and Museum in Cooperstown, New York, a result of Mulvaney's 1998 visit to Cooperstown.[31] While the Bradman Museum is much smaller than its baseball counterpart, both are located in rural towns, nostalgically highlight the history of the sport and its great individual(s), and have exhibitions that direct the visitor to the souvenir shop. Both set themselves up as rightful defenders of their game's heroes in an aggressive contemporary marketplace where values such as honour, honesty and restraint are perceived to have given way to profit, greed and questionable taste.

During my visit, I also completed the Bradman Walk, a 1.7 km stroll around Bowral that visits the places in the town frequented by the young Don. Features of the walk include the two modest houses he used to live in, the oval he used to play cricket on (now Bradman Oval), the Anglican church his family went to, the public school he attended, the main street and the former real estate office in which he worked, and picturesque Corbett Gardens where the Don was received by the townspeople on his return from the 1930 Ashes tour. In its appearance Bowral connects with the myth of a romanticised country lifestyle and creates the impression that this is what rural Australia *should* be like, and a sense of place is constructed that is inseparable from Bradman's image and story.

The Bowral landscape that features on the walk presents a marked contrast to perceptions of a generally downtrodden rural Australia. Dennis O'Rourke's film *Cunnamulla* (2001), for example, controversially depicted alienation, poverty and social tension in a rural community. Wandering through the appealing streets and parks of Bowral makes it difficult to comprehend that about one-third of Australian country towns are in absolute decline.[32] Like Bradman, Bowral appears a winner. Concentrated mainly in the wealthy 'tourist zone', the walk bypasses evidence of the socially disenfranchised, working poor and unemployed that are part of Bowral's population.[33] To be fair, there should be no expectation that the walk should take the visitor into areas other than those that have direct relevance to Bradman's childhood. The point is that the walk, like the Bradman myth as a whole, is constructed to highlight the more attractive parts of the Don's story.

Making it against the odds?

A theme of Bradman's career stressed by biographers, cricket writers and journalists is that of an 'underdog bush cricketer making it against the odds'. Coming from what is described as 'underprivileged beginnings' and a 'humble country background', Bradman appears to have had remarkable early and continuing success.[34] With echoes of Jane Austen, Bradman said that he was 'the son of simple country parents, and without the benefit of wealth, power or influence, but with only the talents bestowed upon me by nature' with which to progress through to Sydney, state and international cricket competition.[35] This appealing image of the simple, innocent country lad taking on the assumed privilege of sophisticated city-folk taps into an Australian history that stresses the difference between city and country cultures.

An alternative to this 'underdog' narrative is worth examining, although it lacks romantic appeal: Bradman may actually have been well situated to capitalise on his sporting talent. His family and the community of Bowral were devoted to cricket, his uncles played in the town team and his father was involved in the administration of the Berrima District competition and the Bowral side. Bradman talks of the good values instilled in him by his parents and of his 'loving and self-effacing mother'.[36] His family appears to be 'ideal-typical Australians': clean living, morally upright and straightforward.[37] The president of the Bowral cricket club and long-time alderman and mayor, Alf Stephens, was a supporter of young Don and played a significant role in his development. As Bowral resident and Deputy Chairman of the National Council for the Centenary of Federation, Rodney Cavalier, states:

> It is hard to perceive what element of the Don's magnificent triumph was against the odds – he had inherited uncommon prowess in all games; his parents afforded him the discipline and character to explore that prowess to the frontiers of the possible. Don grew up in a loving home, where cricket was encouraged but kept in perspective, a view reinforced by siblings who made no fuss about their youngest. In the entire history of Australian cricket it is not possible to find another instance where the odds were stacked more decisively in anyone's favour.[38]

The key to the image of Bradman as a bush cricketer and/or battler hinges on an absence of formal coaching while he was growing up. He received, as Test teammate and champion leg-spinner Bill O'Reilly put it, 'the absolute minimum [coaching] – none at all. He went for cricket as a duck goes for water.'[39] Bradman too stated that he had never been coached. This image is perpetuated by stories such as that Bradman and his classmates used a tree branch as a bat in the schoolyard. He was not instructed as a youth on how to hold a cricket bat, hence his unorthodox grip. It is said that his family did not have the money for coaching books.[40] By his own choice he participated in little sport with children of his own age outside of school time, and this is seen to make Bradman's emerging talent all the more incredible.[41] It appeared Bradman was a case of country-bred immaculate talent: 'Greatness was born in him.'[42]

Again, there is an alternative to the 'immaculate talent' narrative, one that does not insist on a *total* lack of support and practice. For example, there are reports of Bradman being tutored in Sydney by the New South Wales coaches in 1928. He was not, however, formally instructed as a boy in Bowral. Accepting this, it is still necessary to recognise that Bradman's skills did not emerge without at least some help and limited resources. He is reported as practising regularly on the wicket at Alf Stephens' home, and on the half-wicket at the home of his uncle, Richard Whatman. His father used to bowl to him as a boy, and his mother, who had played cricket regularly with her brothers as a youngster, used to bowl left-handed to him when he was 9 or 10 years old. The Don also benefited from a regime of regular practice as shown by that famous exercise in developing ball-sense he undertook with the golf-ball and cricket stump against the water tank. Bradman stressed that 'there is no substitute for hard work and practice if you want to be successful' in his own coaching manual, *The Art of Cricket*, in 1958.[43] So while it can be said that Bradman was not formally coached when young, he was at least practised and had access to some support. This is not to say that Bradman achievements are not amazing, especially given the sparse resources he had at hand as a boy; only that he did not develop in a vacuum as some accounts infer.

The publisher of *Farewell to Cricket*, Tom Thompson, has thoughtfully questioned the theory of the Don's 'natural' development.[44] Thompson is co-authoring a history of Hurstville Oval in Sydney, home of the St George cricket team, the grade club that Bradman played for between 1926 and 1932. In describing Bradman's maturation as a batsman, Thompson makes the case that the Bowral years have been privileged over Bradman's experience at St George. He believes that St George represents a key period in the Don's cricketing development, explaining that Bradman told him on more than one occasion, 'Look at the record … I learnt everything at St George.'[45] It was here as a young man that he came under the influence of figures such as Ted Adams, Town Clerk of Sydney, Les Blackshaw, a former Hurstville mayor, and Dick Jones, captain of the first grade team. Thompson also names Frank Cush, who served for over 50 years as an office bearer at St George and was a chairman of the Australian Board of Control (1955–57). Bradman lived in the Cush household for a period until his marriage in 1932 and afterwards openly offered thanks for the help he received from Frank and his wife. Of these St George men that nurtured Bradman, Thompson writes that they had a great deal of influence in his development by teaching him about the values of cricket and business.[46] It was also the practical experience that St George offered on turf wickets, a different proposition from the concrete pitches of Bowral. Bradman declared to Thompson that it was 'The zing off the turf!' that helped him to make the decision to move from his home town.[47] While St George is mentioned in most of Bradman's biographies, it is curious that more has not been made of his time there because it appears to have been a critical period in his development. This lack of attention may be due to the possibility that a detailed account of Bradman's development in Sydney would disrupt the boy from Bowral story and its links to rural mythology.

The contradiction between the emphasis on the Don's 'natural' ability and the methodical features of his development hints at an unspoken worry: proper acknowledgement of hard work and practice may devalue the organic nature of his story. Yet, on these matters, Bradman expressed himself clearly:

> Blessed is the boy who finds himself possessed of these attributes as a natural gift.
>
> But like the boy prodigy who at, say, five years of age, finds himself able to play the piano, practice and more practice is needed to perfect his talent.[48]

He offered other similar opinions elsewhere in his coaching manual: 'I don't care who the player is or how great his skill, there is no substitute for practice'; and 'nothing produces efficiency like practice'. He also cited the case of Dr W.G. Grace who, he writes, 'worked just as hard learning cricket as he did at his profession. Very quickly I found that there was no Royal Road,' he [Grace] said.'[49]

Many of the popular versions of the Don's story have under-emphasised these unambiguous statements in favour of the 'boy genius' story. It makes for a better tale if the impression is that the lad from Bowral conquered the world with only his natural talent as a weapon.

Bowral and the bush myth

If critical analysis is discarded, the boy from Bowral story fits neatly into the Australian bush myth, and Ward's explanation that pastoral communities were in many ways defined by their 'distance and poor communications from the cities'.[50] Bowral was not, however, isolated 'up bush' in terms of either distance or communication.

The Bradman literature often represents the Don as 'the batting genius from the bush', 'the boy from the outback' who came from 'nowhere', creating the perception that he was straight off the Australian frontier – 'just a kid in from the sticks' as the Paul Kelly and the Coloured Girls song goes.[51] Yet it is difficult to think of Bradman as a 'real' bushman when he lived only a couple of hours train ride from Sydney. A railway station had been built in Bowral in about 1867, with the train daily transporting fresh produce to the Sydney markets. Bradman and his father travelled to Sydney to watch a Test between Australia and England at the Sydney Cricket Ground in 1920–21, and Bradman commuted between Bowral and Sydney every Saturday in the season of 1926–27 to play grade cricket for St George.

Word of Bradman's prowess had been reported in the city newspapers before he even arrived there to play. His 300 runs for Bowral against Moss Vale in the 1925–26 season Berrima District Cricket Competition final had been reported in the Sydney news-papers, not only for his score, but also due to the game lasting an almost unprecedented five consecutive Saturdays. Soon after, Bradman travelled to the city to trial before the New South Wales selectors.

The common image of Bradman's early years evokes a nostalgic and glorified view of rural life and the bush. The mystic appeal of the boy from the bush is strengthened when we are informed of Bradman's down-to-earth and solid family and moral values, and by anecdotes such as that he was out with his brother shooting rabbits when selected for his first international Ashes touring team in 1930. There is even a yarn about a young Bradman crossing paths with poet and writer A.B. 'Banjo' Paterson in a sports store.[52] Bradman is embedded in the imagery of the outback Aussie male: the bushman, jackaroo and grazier. These figures are thought of as stoical, self-reliant, admirable and courageous, and if imagined in a cricketing sense, in no need of coaching, coaching books, or proper equipment. Bradman's unprecedented achievements help contribute to a perception that there are 'many such potential champions hiding their lights under country bushels'.[53] In effect, Bradman serves as a symbol of a utopian rural lifestyle. The narrative of the boy from Bowral is of a nostalgic pastoral existence; a 'Huck Finn Heaven', of a child prodigy, and of a carefree, simpler, happier and easier time in an Australian bush that has experienced much recent hardship. The harder life appears to get in the bush, the more Bradman's story stands as a metaphor for those better times in the past – his heroism offers hope of a symbolic rural regeneration.

Conclusion

Bradman as the boy from Bowral is an image befitting a peculiarly Australian hero – a country-born and -bred, white, sporting male. Those promoting Bradman's popular biography have made effective use of the bush mythologies that feature in much Australian history. Most of this material lacks critical interpretation and there are certainly no accounts that hint at the other side of the bush legend: the sexism, racism and xenophobia.[54] There are no indications that Australia is one of the most urbanised countries in the world, nor is much made of Bradman having lived in Sydney or Adelaide for the last 73 years of his life, and not moving back to the country after his playing career was over. It also rarely mentioned in any detail that a city cricket club, St George, probably played a major role in his development as a cricketer. To many people Bradman remains the 'boy from Bowral'.

The boy from Bowral story cannot be reduced to a conscious attempt at manipulating audiences to believe that Bradman is an Australian hero. It can be partly explained by writers and producers concurrently performing the roles of critic, fan and cultural subject. Producers are often Australians creating material for a domestic market. They are unavoidably implicated in and/or may enjoy many of the national myths that they draw upon in shaping their biographical accounts. For example, Bradman biographers and cricket writers such as Moyes, Lindsay, Page, Perry and Mallett are generally open in their admiration of Bradman and his achievements and have varying degrees of emotional and/or physical investment in cricketing culture.

There is also no suggestion in this chapter that biographers, writers and others just 'make things up' to create a desirable image of Bradman. Rather, consciously or subconsciously, they overemphasise and/or embellish some parts of his biography and deemphasise and/or omit others in order to confirm the Don's status as an Australian icon. Examples of such selectivity have included an 'underdog' and 'battler' image that denies Bradman having any support as a young cricketer in the country and the implicit presentation of Bowral as part of the frontier despite its ease of communication with and proximity to Sydney. With a 'typically Australian' country childhood, Bradman becomes simultaneously both ordinary in his experience (as in 'one of us') and extraordinary in his ability, a hero with the common touch. This portrayal has been persuasive in creating a popular image of Bradman, yet it has served to sanctify history rather than explain it.

Bradman's story also highlights that the line between what is considered 'rural' and 'urban' is sometimes more imagined than real. Despite Bowral's close proximity to Sydney, some writers have constructed Bradman as practically a bushman. This suggests that notions of the 'bush' and the 'rural' are sometimes socially and historically constructed. But cricket writers are not likely to consider this point. The 'boy from the regions or provinces near Sydney' has none of the romance or appeal that the 'boy from the bush' does.

The sanctification of Bradman strengthens the Australian legend and national myths. An unrivalled sporting champion emerging from the bush rekindles many of the myths associated with the idealised character and lifestyle of rural Australia, particularly when these myths enjoy currency in contemporary popular culture, as shown by the examples of beer and truck ads, country musicians, the *Bush Tucker Man* and *SeaChange*. Such representations are further reinforced when conservative political figures such as Howard and Hanson openly favour a supposedly 'mainstream' Australian identity in which white farmers and townsfolk in the bush feature heavily.

CHAPTER 4

BODYLINE AND MYTH

Since the 50th anniversary of the bodyline Tests 18 months ago, there has been a great deal written and broadcast on the subject. For instance, there have been seven books, including a historical novel, published or republished in that time, and there is at least one new book about to appear.

Cricket enthusiasts consequently feel saturated by the subject. One senior cricket administrator told me the other day that he could not bear to see the word bodyline in print, much less watch the [mini-] series. This seems to be true of the survivors of the bodyline Tests, too. Sir Donald Bradman is known to be heartily sick of the affair, as well he might be after 51 years.[1]

In accounts of the 1932–33 bodyline Test cricket matches, the Australian team is represented as making a defiant statement of independence on behalf of the nation to the English who were intent on maintaining cultural dominance. This statement was played out through Bradman, who 'became Australia', with the series crucial to the construction of his popular heroism. He was pitted against the patrician English captain, Douglas Jardine, who is cast as a villain intent on winning by any means, and Harold Larwood, the supreme fast bowler who effected the method chosen – bodyline bowling tactics. The bodyline summer, and Bradman's role in it, has achieved such prominence in Australian history that it has taken on its own set of myths, even though Australia lost the series four Tests to one. Bodyline, in bringing 'honour to the nation',[2] is seen to have created a conception of an independent Australia that it is difficult to refute or challenge.

The exceptional character of the bodyline Tests is shown by their having been the subject of both a television drama mini-series and a novel, not to mention a flood of cricket histories. No other Australian cricket season has been the subject of such attention, and Bradman is in many ways the reason for this. The aim of this chapter is to investigate various reactions of viewers, reviewers and readers to those major portrayals of Bradman and the bodyline Test series that do not follow the conventions of the numerous popular histories. This survey indicates that popular myths are sometimes more important than notions of historical authenticity or accuracy in the reception of nationalist representations. The first subject of analysis is the 1984 *Bodyline* television drama mini-series and the second is the 1983 fictional novella of Paul Wheeler, *Bodyline: The Novel*.[3] The examination of these texts is followed by a brief consideration of how they have been constructed as fictionalised historical drama, as well as how the bodyline story parallels the Anzac legend.[4]

Myth and sport

Myths can give complex and sometimes confusing events particular meanings:

> A myth is not a total delusion or an utter falsehood, but a 'partial truth' that accentuates particular versions of reality and marginalizes

or omits others. Myths embody fundamental cultural values and character-types and appeal to deep-seated emotions. In the mythologizing process, events are drained of their historical 'truth' and repackaged in ways that serve the interests of powerful groups ... Critically, myths disavow or deny their own conditions of existence: they are 'authorless' forms of speech that derive from specific sites and power relations, but have become so naturalized that people are seldom aware they are being interpellated by them.[5]

Sport is a rich source in the creation of myths because of its nationalist character and because it provides an easily understood environment for the playing out of social dramas. It thus plays a key role in the legitimation of dominant values, identities and cultures. For example, sport serves to perpetuate myths involving the liberal-democratic ideals of fairness, justice and equality epitomised by maxims such as 'it's just not cricket' and a 'level playing field'. The Olympic Games carry several myths: the virtuousness of ancient Greek civilisation, the link between the ancient and modern genres of sport, and the so-called noble motives of the founder of the modern games, Pierre de Coubertin.[6] Another long-standing myth is the supposed creation of rugby union in 1823 by an English schoolboy, William Webb Ellis, when he is said to have picked the ball up during a game of soccer and run with it, thereby supplying the impetus for the creation of the ball-in-hand rugby code. These stories have been accepted as common knowledge, and like other culturally significant stories take on a life of their own as they pass into popular mythology.

This mythologising process has occurred in regards to the body-line Test series between Australia and England. There are more Australian accounts of 1932–33 than of any other cricket season. In nearly all cases, sympathy for the Don and the home side has accorded the bodyline Test series with such significance that it has acquired an openly nationalist character. The way the 1932–33 Tests are treated denies the possibility that the English tactics might have been legitimate – bodyline bowling was within the rules of cricket at the time – and those accounts that argue this counter position, such as Jardine's, are dismissed.[7] That the Australian team may have contemplated similar tactics had the team line-ups been reversed is rarely considered. England's bodyline tactics have been seen as dismantling cricket's traditional ethic of fair play, but the on-field sledging and intimidation of opponents by Australian teams since the 1970s is rarely viewed in the same light. In the bodyline Tests, Bradman and the Australians are the undoubted victims and are portrayed as courageous and defiant in defeat. This view of Bradman and the Australian team's performance has been emphasised to the exclusion of any alternative interpretation. The complexity of the bodyline Tests has been reduced, in a manner similar to the experiences of the Anzacs, to the simplicity of essences and has been thoroughly mythologised.[8]

The bodyline series and Bradman

The 1932–33 English cricket tour of Australia is regarded by many as one of the most controversial encounters ever staged in international cricket. Bill O'Reilly, for instance, called it 'the historic cricket event of the century'.[9] The 1932–33 series took place during a severe worldwide economic depression and in an atmosphere of diplomatic tension between the two countries over the issues of loan repayments and tariffs. The role of cricket in Anglo-Australian relations and the British Empire at this time is of great importance. For the many Australians interested in cricket, a Test match series against England was a cause for excitement, particularly with Bradman leading the Australian campaign.

Accounts of the Tests[10] inform us that the single-minded amateur English captain, Douglas Jardine, led his team to a 4–1 victory and in the process nullified the Australian team's chief weapon, Bradman. Victory was attained by bodyline tactics that were said to have been designed to limit the Don's run scoring ability, and to severely inhibit the other Australian batsmen. England's fast bowlers delivered the ball short, directing it at the batsman so he had to play it defensively off the body. A leg side field of six to eight men was then set for catches. The fastest and most accurate English bowler, Harold Larwood, ably executed Jardine's tactics, taking 33 wickets over the five Tests. Australian batsmen were regularly struck, and distress and controversy erupted. It was felt that the English bowlers were attempting to intimidate and hit the batsmen, not dismiss them, which was a gross betrayal of the accepted conduct and traditions of cricket. One of the umpires during the series, George Hele, expressed the fear that a batsman might be killed. The on-field controversy led to intense administrative and diplomatic exchange at the highest levels between the two countries (the Australian Prime Minister, Joe Lyons, even became involved), with threats made to cancel the tour after the Third Test, or as it has been called, 'the battle of Adelaide'.[11] The tour continued, but recriminations persisted long after. The significance of the bodyline series extends well outside of sport, as it is one of the earlier and best examples of sport and international politics directly and openly intersecting.[12]

Bradman's performance in the bodyline series has been the subject of conjecture. The preferred interpretation is that the Don's 396 runs at an average of 56.57 for the series is proof that he combated bodyline bowling, unlike most others who were soundly defeated by it. Arguments that he failed to bat in the team's interests and that he ignored his captain's orders on how to play the intimidating bowling are often disregarded. It has also been pointed out that though he scored more runs, he gave away his wicket at important times.[13] Bradman admits that no one mastered the English bowling that summer, although an average of 56.57 runs does indicate a degree of success.

A great deal of the off-field schemes and politicking during 1932–33 are left unexplained as a number of documents from the series held by national and state cricket ruling bodies have been culled, tampered with, or cannot be accessed. Historians are therefore unable to represent the entire episode by conventional methods, creating scope for a movie or a historical novel about the bodyline summer. National rivalry in the form of a sporting confrontation is excellent dramatic grist. A transcendent nationalism represented by Bradman, 'the legend', is squared off against the English enemy. While not the only person involved in events of the bodyline season, Bradman provides the clearest link to this history for Australian audiences:

> the bodyline series of 1932/33 had special significance. It was not only
> the Old Country determined to win in a way that was not cricket;
> it was young Australia coming to maturity and a new sense of
> independence. Leading the resistance, striking blows for Australia,
> was 'our Don Bradman'. The Bradman legend was created by
> bodyline bowling.[14]

In the Australian memory there is no bodyline without Bradman, as is indicated by the title of E.W. Docker's book on the series, *Bradman and the Bodyline* (1987). Bradman is the vital link between the past and present on account of his profile and reputation, with his heroism helping to stabilise and reinforce the mythical character of the bodyline summer.

Bodyline, the mini-series

The *Bodyline* mini-series is the only dramatic adaptation of the bodyline Tests to make it to screen, and its extensive use of nationalist myths helped ensure its critical and popular acceptance. Screened on Channel Ten in July 1984 over 10 hours on four consecutive nights, and costing an estimated $5 million, *Bodyline* won over audiences. One of the most successful locally produced dramas in Australian television history, it was watched by around 3 million viewers. In January 2000, according to ACNielsen, it ranked as the 21st highest rating program on Australian television since 1965.[15] The mini-series won its time-slot in Sydney, Melbourne and Brisbane, peaking at a rating of around 40. Channel Ten executives estimated at the time that the mini-series had achieved the network's highest recorded prime-time rating. *Bodyline*'s screening capitalised on renewed interest in the 1932–33 Tests coinciding with the 50th anniversary of the series (see Chapter 5). The series was produced by Kennedy-Miller, the same production house responsible for *The Dismissal* mini-series on the downfall of the 1975 Whitlam Labor government, as well as the movies, *Mad Max* and *Mad Max II*. Its production trumped a planned British film on the bodyline events by *Chariots of Fire* producer, David Puttnam. Kennedy-Miller continue to hold the rights to *Bodyline* and have not allowed it to be released on video or made it available to the general public, leaving open the possibility of its re-release in order to capitalise on the commemoration of Bradman.

The story presented in the mini-series develops the character of Jardine from his boyhood days as the son of the Advocate-General in Bombay, to his cricket at Oxford University, and on to his international playing career. As an amateur, he is depicted as aloof and imperious, wearing a multi-coloured harlequin's cap during playing scenes. He masterminds bodyline bowling while still in England

and prepares for its use in the coming Australian tour by recruiting fast bowlers. Emphasis in this recruitment is on professional paceman, Harold Larwood, who is presented as a sooty and poor Nottinghamshire coalminer. Played by Australian actor Hugo Weaving, Jardine is set up as a particularly ruthless character with his distaste for all things Australian made plain.

The character of the Australian hero, Bradman, is not developed in the same depth as Jardine, though the young Don is seen as experiencing a wholesome and happy country adolescence with his precocious talent made apparent by his performance against the men in a local district cricket match. His youthful enthusiasm and good character are evidenced by his loving relationship with a young Jessie Bradman. Jardine and Bradman set upon an inevitable trajectory of confrontation, played out in the bodyline Tests. A heroic Bradman and the courageous Australians surmount Jardine's tactics and Larwood's brutality by winning a moral and symbolic victory despite defeat on the field.

In the final Test match, Larwood is also revealed as Jardine's victim. When Larwood breaks down injured, the merciless captain refuses to allow his bowler to leave the ground until he finishes his over. Larwood stands at the crease and rolls his arm over, and the Australian batsman refuses to take advantage of the feeble deliveries, claiming the high moral ground. In the final scenes the morality tale is complete when Jardine receives a hostile and violent reception to bodyline bowling during a later tour of India and later again upon home turf when his tactics are roundly condemned as simply 'not cricket'.

Bodyline made Australian audiences feel proud of their Australianness. It employed to good advantage the technique widely used by Australian film-makers of drawing upon long-held nationalist myths such as the Australian legend and 'valorising those aspects of our national character which depart from English values and loyalties'.[16]

Bodyline sits alongside films such as *Breaker Morant* and *Gallipoli* in figuring Australia as the unfortunate victim of British indifference, incompetence or injustice. Focusing on the characters of Bradman, Jardine and Larwood, the mini-series contrasts the hero(es) and villain(s), the innocent and the guilty, the virtuous and treacherous, the powerful and the underdog. As was the horse in the film *Phar Lap* released a year earlier, Bradman is depicted as a hero whose very talent provokes attack and defeat.[17] A 1984 newspaper advertisement promoting the mini-series declared: 'Tonight Australia Needs A Hero. Bodyline: The day England declared war on Australia ... And tonight when Australia needs a hero, one man stands his ground' accompanied by a picture of actor Gary Sweet who plays Don Bradman.[18] Out of the many possible promotional messages, a nationalism–sport–war tripartite was chosen. This highlights not only the masculinist character of sport and war, but of Australian nationalism (see Chapter 7).

Judging by the ratings it achieved, the mini-series was successful in provoking a nationalist response among audiences. The exploitation of nationalist myths centring on claims to independence and the underdog status is blatant, as is the use of cultural stereotypes. A writer and director of the series, Lex Marinos, states:

> It was through people like Bradman that Australians started to express a different identity, Australia's changing identity. In the bodyline series you had aristocrats from England who played like convicts while the Australian team played the game the way it was meant to be played. It showed us how we wanted to be seen.[19]

Marinos' comment reveals that producers are partisan. Marinos not only appears to believe in nationalist myths, he actively perpetuated them through a television drama. Even if the makers of *Bodyline* did not necessarily believe wholeheartedly in these myths, they recognise their attractiveness to prospective audiences.

Nationalism is also a key reason for *Bodyline*'s favourable reception. Seven of the eight reviews of the drama that I found in Australian newspapers responded positively.[20] Reviews discuss the themes of sport and national identity, heroes, honour in defeat, anti-British feeling, and the colonials defying the imperial master. The mini-series is paralleled to the events of the Eureka Stockade, and the nationalist fervour generated by *Australia II*'s victory in the 1983 America's Cup. The drama is labelled 'intensely nationalistic TV', enjoyable despite occasional 'foolishly jingoistic' moments.[21] Reviewers also identify with the polarisation of the Australian hero and the English villain Jardine. Bradman's heroic status was re-emphasised and probably lifted by Sweet's portrayal of the Don, which is regarded as 'a handsome tribute' to a 'modest, quietly proud, troubled young man' and 'a man of rare and wonderful candor'.[22] The drama is framed in order that, 'We cheer Bradman and his brave laconic team', while 'We loathe Jardine and his careful clipped action.'[23] Journalist Garrie Hutchinson encapsulated the emotional reaction elicited by *Bodyline*, ending his review:

> It says something for the overall quality of Bodyline that I felt as if
> we had won in the end; I felt good, even though *we'd* lost the Ashes.
> Which is more than I can say when I watch a real Test match loss on
> TV.[24] (Italics added)

Overall, the reviews demonstrate that at some level producers, reviewers, and audiences all identified with and appreciated the presentation of Bradman and the heroic and nationalistic themes.

A note on *Bodyline* as television drama is required. Television critics, in their reviews, note features such as script, acting, sets, dramatic narrative and entertainment value, in contrast to sport journalists who are more likely to be concerned with cricket history and notions of historical veracity and accuracy. In explaining how the mini-series targeted the casual viewer, Derriman, a cricket historian and journalist, recognises that television's requirements are not those of the cricket aficionado.[25] *Bodyline* was not presented and sold as a rigorous historical documentary; it was sold as a television drama, as the *Sun-Herald* observed: 'No matter what the experts say, the bodyline [mini-] series will stand or fall as entertainment.'[26]

The success of *Bodyline* was not due to its attention to historical detail, but its ability to emotionally involve Australian viewers. There were, for example, undocumented or fabricated events and people: the Union Jack was not burnt by an angry Adelaide crowd; spectators did not sing the song 'Our Don Bradman' in unison; the narrator and Jardine's girlfriend, Edith, never existed; Larwood did not live in a slum in a coal town and had left the coalmines in 1922; Jardine never visited Larwood at his home; Bradman's wife, Jessie, never danced with Jardine; and a woman pictured in the Sydney Cricket Ground's Members' Stand seems unlikely as women were not permitted entry to the members' area at the time (it is worth noting that similar liberties with the truth did not prevent *Chariots of Fire* winning an Academy Award). A couple of the players from the bodyline Tests took exception to elements of the mini-series. Larwood, living in Australia, objected strenuously to his portrayal as a 'hateful' person, received abusive phone calls and had his lawyer look at the series.[27] O'Reilly called it 'a jumbled hotch-potch of anachronisms, untruths and impossibilities'. One Australian player, Leo O'Brien, liked the mini-series, but also noted 'gimmicky things ... you know, where they polished the whole thing up'.[28] Bradman made no comment (a consistent response from him). These inventions, objections or comments appear to have mattered little to audiences. If ratings are taken as a guide, many viewers took pleasure from the drama – indeed, historical inaccuracies or distortions are of marginal concern in the enactment and perpetuation of myth.

The *Bodyline* mini-series took the complexity of the Tests and its surrounding issues and reduced these to the simplicity of essences – Australia versus England and good against bad.[29] This confrontation is distilled into Bradman taking on Jardine and Larwood: 'Leading the resistance, striking blows for Australia, was "our Don Bradman". The Bradman legend was created by bodyline bowling.' The depiction of Bradman and Australia's courage and honour in defeat draws upon the Anzac legend and an idealised national character. In other words, it did not matter that the events of 1932–33 were 'drained of their historical truth and repackaged' in the television drama format. Rather, the repackaging served to create entertainment value and popularity. Such repackaging, however, can produce a different reaction, as occurred with Wheeler's historical novel.

Bodyline: The Novel

According to Lukács, the origins of the historical novel can be traced to the beginning of the nineteenth century.[30] Since the mid-1960s the impact of the historical novel has been most evident through the biographical novel and the advent of the 'new' journalism that is synonymous with Tom Wolfe and Hunter S. Thompson, and lately, Australian writer John Birmingham.[31] Examples of 'non-fiction fiction', or 'faction' as some clumsily label it, include Thomas Keneally's approach to the events of the Holocaust, *Schindler's Ark* (1982), and Don DeLillo's *Libra* (1988), a novel built around Lee Harvey Oswald and the Kennedy assassination. Other types of narratives also mix realism with fiction. Fiske argues that television news bears similarity to fiction in its construction as a text, and in its inability to give a 'full, accurate, objective picture of reality'.[32]

Paul Wheeler's *Bodyline: The Novel* was released in 1983, exactly 50 years after the 1932–33 series. Although a novella, it has the hallmarks of a historical novel: the significant historical events took place at least 40–60 years ago, documented events intersect with the characters' fortunes and historical figures provide direct links to history, with Bradman, Jardine and Larwood being the most important.[33] A characteristic of the historical novel, unlike most fiction, is that the outcome of the events in question is more or less known. The challenge for the novelist is to overcome the indeterminable aspects of the past – conversations, ethical and moral dilemmas, the feelings and emotions of those who lived or might have lived – in arriving at this outcome. The creation of a narrative 'during [a] historical cataclysm when its end was not known, histories without hindsight or foresight' is required.[34] The objective is to create a sense of *probability*, to install a non-literal truth that 'rings true' to the reader: 'This quality involves the degree to which an account of individual human actions or emotions is consistent with what we know about human ... behaviour in general. This means that it is not liable to empirical verification, but is judged subjectively.'[35]

The historical novel is a creation of an imagined, as well as a documented past. The author creates a past with the relation between the text and an external reality open to a much wider interpretation than conventional historical narratives allow. This subjectivity can introduce myth into the account. As naturalised 'truths', myths are stories that often ring true for particular people, groups and communities even though they may be difficult to support empirically.

The key character of *Bodyline: The Novel* is Jardine with his hatred and callousness towards Australians perhaps being more extreme than in the mini-series. His character is not well developed with the motives for his hatred not altogether clear. In one sequence Jardine complains, 'I dislike *everything* about Australians. I detest their false bonhomie and hearty handshakes, their excruciating slaps on the back.' In other exchanges Jardine bluntly refers to Bradman as that 'little bastard'. Yet, we learn little of Bradman's character either, which is disappointing given his centrality to the plot. This failure in character development also results in the contrast between the villainous Jardine and the heroic Bradman being underemphasised when compared to the clear-cut polarisation of the mini-series. The development of bodyline tactics is seen as an elaborate, sinister plot with a shadowy 'Mr Big' character, whose identity is never revealed, pushing Jardine, who is portrayed as a puppet of this 'greater power'.[36] The conspiracy is compounded by a member of the British government, J.H. Thomas, England's Dominion Affairs Secretary of State, encouraging Jardine to 'bend the rules' in an effort to beat these 'hoity toity buggers' (the Australians).

The image created is that of an English determination to maintain colonial dominance by any means. Descriptions of the cricket matches are similar to the available cricket histories, although conversations, exchanges and thoughts of participants are added. The main subplot is a failed romance between English cricketer, Freddy Brown, the youngest player in the tourists' squad, and an Australian woman who could not abide Brown's acquiescence to the English team's tactics. For Wheeler, her rejection of Brown is a metaphor for the Australian community's outrage at bodyline bowling. The novel closes with a 'mission accomplished' message from Mr Big to Jardine. Overall, the conspiratorial character of the story, combined with vague character development, makes for an uneven book. How then did reviewers respond to Wheeler's treatment of the bodyline controversy?

According to the seven reviews examined, Wheeler received negative critique in both Australia and England. His novel was thought of as 'lightweight reading', 'indescribably awful', 'disappointing', 'the oddest account [of bodyline]', soap opera and a 'potboiler' which featured a 'Mills and Boon subplot'.[37] Only one review had much positive to say about *Bodyline: The Novel*, calling it a 'rattling good yarn', but adding the qualifier, 'One has to take a lot of Mr Wheeler with a pinch of salt.'[38] The three English reviews were slightly more generous to Wheeler, although it would be exaggerating to claim that they were more than lukewarm. The largely negative reception to Wheeler's work may be attributed to two main factors. First, the book is occasionally poorly written with under-developed character sketches. This may be because the novel was to form the basis for the David Puttnam film script that failed to make it into production (Wheeler is a specialist screenwriter who has published the occasional novel). Second and just as vitally, unlike the *Bodyline* mini-series, though targeting a popular market, the book failed to appeal to celebratory national mythologies of either Australia or England.

Wheeler writes largely from the perspective of Jardine and the English team. While the Australian team is cast in a favourable light, the Australian nationalist imagination does not have much to grab hold of and the Don is not pictured clearly as a larger than life hero. As a result, the bodyline campaign reads like an unpleasant English conspiracy with the narrative failing to focus on the 'Australian fighting spirit'. Also, for the cricket buff, the details of exchanges do not always ring true. In one fictional exchange at Bradman's home, the Australian opening batsman, Jack Fingleton, and a sick Bradman discuss Jardine (he's 'a cold fish') and how to combat the bodyline tactics ('practise'). Anyone who has read of the antipathy between Fingleton and Bradman over the span of their careers would have doubts about this type of conversation taking place in Bradman's house as described. Wheeler may have been better advised to have a figure such as the respected Australian captain, Bill Woodfull, visit the Don. Woodfull is of course the man who uttered the famous words to the English manager, Pelham Warner, during the Third Test in Adelaide: 'There are two teams out there. One is trying to play cricket, the other is not. The game is too good to be spoiled ... It is time some people got out of it.'[39]

To this day it is not known who leaked Woodfull's comments to the press and Wheeler did not speculate about this mystery. Many have assumed it was most likely Fingleton, who made his living outside of cricket as a journalist. Fingleton, a staunch critic of the Don, accused Bradman of leaking the story, an accusation that Bradman strongly and consistently denied. The only other candidates appear to be Leo O'Brien, who was in the dressing room at the time, and Woodfull and Warner. The unresolved debate around such an event affords the historical novelist the opportunity to be provocative in constructing a scenario. Lamentably, Wheeler chose not to capitalise on the uncertainty and controversy of Woodfull's famed reproach.

For English reviewers, Wheeler provides next to nothing in the way of redemption from the events of 1932–33: bodyline tactics are presented as a dark plot, Jardine is outright and irrationally hateful in his attitude towards Bradman and the Australians, and is encouraged in his endeavours by a member of the British government. For English readers, Wheeler's version of the bodyline series offers no recovery of the English ideals of fair play or the traditional moral values and lessons of cricket and the importance of 'playing a straight bat'. Wheeler's failure to highlight either Australian or English cultural ideals and myths of national character helps to explain the unfavourable reception of the book.

As with the mini-series, those who played in the bodyline matches disapproved of the novel, although it was mainly the English players who were upset on this occasion. Many cricketers who had assisted Wheeler felt their trust had been betrayed.[40] Gubby Allen, a member of the English side who later became captain, pointedly distanced himself from the book after initially providing assistance. Larwood also dissociated himself from the novel, while former English spinner and later captain, Freddy Brown, was appalled to find his character engaged in a fictional romance.[41] These problems also explain why those members of the English cricket establishment who were invited failed to attend the launch of the novel. Reviews of Wheeler's book paid more attention to criticisms by former players than did those of the *Bodyline* mini-series. This can partly be explained by the fact that no player emerges from the novel with a better reputation than he had previously, which was not the case with the mini-series. The mini-series represented a brave and defiant Australian nationalism and reflected particularly well upon Bradman and the Australian players of the time, even if those still living did not approve of some of the dramatic licence and gimmicks. The English side generally comes out of *Bodyline: The Novel* looking either vindictive or complicit in the carrying out of reprehensible tactics, with the invented off-field relationships and exchanges only adding insult to injury.

The format of the historical novel also helps to explain the reception to Wheeler's book. Reviews of the *Bodyline* mini-series treated it as television drama *entertainment*, but Wheeler's book is regarded as being closer to 'real' or serious *history*. While reviewers generally acknowledged the fiction writer's imaginative licence, discussions of the documented histories of the bodyline series are rarely out of the picture. Occasional criticisms are made of Wheeler for writing weak history, which may reflect an assumption that the book's potential audience is intrigued more by traditional cricket history than by literary analysis. Davie and Hadfield believe the bodyline series dramatic enough without invention, and complain about Wheeler's embellishment and dramatisation.[42] Jones considers the portrayal of Jardine unrealistic with the man not coming close to the villain that appears in the novel.[43] Harris complains that unsupportable 'mysteries and passions' that never existed have been introduced.[44] At one level, of course, historical critique is unfair as Wheeler has written a novel, but the reviewers judge that Wheeler's narrative, in going well outside accepted historical understandings, fails a historical accuracy test. Perhaps the difference in the judgments on the mini-series and the book stems from expectations regarding the medium each was presented in. The written word has been a common vehicle for the presentation and dissemination of history for centuries. Historical television drama developed comparatively recently and is seen in a different light, closer to entertainment.

Bradman, Jardine and the rescripting of history

Two issues arise from the discussion thus far. The first involves the position of Bradman. Despite the argument that there is no bodyline without Bradman, he has occasionally not been the focus of my analysis. This imbalance can be partly explained by the demands of television drama and the historical novel. With a hallmark of historical fiction being that the outcome of events is more or less known, characterisation becomes central to the creation of drama, as combining historically documented *and* fictional behaviours has to be made convincing and compelling for the reader. The historically demonised character of Jardine, who one commentator described unkindly as a 'psychopath',[45] thus makes for a better subject to build a plot around than the comparatively remote Bradman, who for years had said as little as possible publicly and guarded his privacy. One reviewer commented disappointingly that the mini-series 'didn't face up to the Bradman enigma in as thorough-going a way as it did with Jardine. Bradman is as great a mystery now as he ever was.'[46]

The second issue revolves around the rescripting of history. As mentioned earlier, the national understanding of the events of bodyline cricket in 1932–33, particularly as depicted in the mini-series, bears similarity to the popular story of the Anzacs during World War I. To note that such a similarity exists is perhaps a travesty given the relative scale of events – a battle on the Turkish hillsides in which at least 7,300 Australians were killed as against the relative trifling of a home cricket series.[47] Yet, over many decades, the architects of national myth making – innumerable Australian historians, journalists, scriptwriters, film-makers and speech-makers – have rescripted both sets of events in remarkably similar terms. Arguably inglorious and comprehensive defeats have been transformed into glorious and heroic masculine defiance that ended in moral victory despite physically succumbing. Beneath this rescripting lies an anxiety about the emasculating effects of defeat, with the elevation of the losing protagonists on moral and symbolic planes acting to eradicate this unease.[48] By this eradication, debate over the possible causes of defeat or the worth of the cause being fought for is also short-circuited. National communities orchestrate such transformations because:

> defeat ... cannot be forgotten and a nation's people must find ways to redeem those who died [or lost] for their country to make defeat honorable. This can be done by honouring the individuals who fought rather than the country's lost cause.[49]

Bradman and Simpson, the man with the donkey, are honoured in this way. Both are examples of Australia announcing itself on the international stage in the first half of the twentieth century. Both appeal to an 'essential' nationalism that is defined by toughness and fairness, egalitarianism and mateship, courage and defiance. The popular versions of what happened at Anzac Cove and on the cricket fields of 1932–33 are deeply embedded in Australian pioneering and nation-building mythologies with the connection between nationalism, sport and war at the forefront. For example, in Peter Weir's film, *Gallipoli*, the principal character of Archie Hamilton is an athlete going off to war, whereas in *Bodyline* Bradman, Jardine and Larwood are athletes pictured as being at war. A similar parallel exists between the stories and photographs of Australian soldiers playing cricket at Anzac Cove during the World War I campaign and the visit in 2001 by the Australian cricket team, wearing slouch hats, to the same battleground. The Anzac and bodyline myths have also proven largely invulnerable to opposing voices that might seek to dismantle them.

Conclusion

The production of the *Bodyline* television mini-series and *Bodyline: The Novel* says much about the strength of the mythology and heroism built around the events of 1932–33. Over time, the boundaries between what is heroism (or anti-heroism) and super-heroism have been eroded. The choice of the bodyline Tests as the subject of a television drama and a novel over so many other possible events and people sees them transcend the strictly historical. What Bradman and the events of 1932–33 have come to *mean* in terms of cricket legend and national identity is now more important than whatever actually occurred.

If the bodyline Tests saw Bradman 'become Australia', in differing ways both the mini-series and novel acted to refresh the collective memory that this was so. According to O'Reilly, Bradman came out of the 1984 mini-series appearing more heroic than he did in 1932–33:

> Bradman emerged much more successfully from the film than he did from the real-life show 50 years ago.
>
> Our batting genius endured the kiln-heat of unplayable bodyline tactics with such obvious frailty that it took him 15 irksome months to regain his batting aplomb and the unblemished confidence of his teammates.[50]

Suffice it to say that the mini-series did not portray O'Reilly's version of events. Prior to the 1984 screening, the Don may have been a hero to many, but the mini-series introduced an almost superhuman Don to a very large new audience, the majority of whom were too young to have had any immediate understanding of Bradman's role in the bodyline Tests. The lack of close familiarity with Bradman among the public has had the inverse effect of increasing his heroism. The reduction of the Tests to, at best, the simplicity of partial truths, such as Bradman's heroism accompanied by the Australian team's bravery against English bastardry, tapped the deep-seated emotions of Australian audiences and helped to bolster the Bradman myth.

The impact of Wheeler's *Bodyline: The Novel* in buttressing Bradman's reputation and mythical notions of Australian valour in defeat was nowhere near as great due to its limited success and audience. Nonetheless, the novel did serve a similar function. Critics argued that Wheeler had contravened the details and spirit of the historical record, and in dismissing his book on these grounds, reiterated the popularised version of the bodyline story. By a lack of continuity with the popular historical record and the myths surrounding the bodyline Tests, Wheeler paradoxically reinforced them. Myths are resistant to disputation, and a challenge may see them further entrenched. Ultimately, whether the myths surrounding the bodyline Test matches are being reinforced or challenged, the naturalised power and stability of Bradman's heroism and of an idealised national character in the Australian consciousness are difficult to dislodge.

CHAPTER 5

AN INSATIABLE
DEMAND

*He gave hundreds of speeches, tens of thousands of runs, millions
of memories – all for free. A few weeks ago, one of his old cast-off bats
sold at auction for almost $50,000. It doesn't make any sense to
Don Bradman. He played just because he loved it …*[1]

The opening quotation is from a prelude to Don Bradman's final
media interview by Ray Martin on Channel Nine in 1996. The ex-
tract repeats a number of features of Bradman's popular story: it
intimates that he was an amateur who played only for the love
of the game and the pleasure he gave the cricket-loving people of
Australia; it also notes the value to collectors and investors of bats
he once used, and that is something he failed to understand. To say
that Bradman was totally unaware of the value of his persona, however, is a surprising claim given that Kerry Packer agreed to donate
$1 million to the Bradman Museum in return for the Bradman
interview.[2] Few other Australian sporting stars or celebrities have
attracted this amount of money for a single television appearance.
Nevertheless, Packer appears to have received value for money as
the interview attracted around 1.6 million viewers and was repackaged and replayed on the day that the news broke of Bradman's
death.

A key meaning associated with Bradman is that of financial accumulation, both in terms of his own career, media representations of him, and the 'Bradmorabilia' industry that is worth millions of dollars annually. Within popular culture, the Don exists at the intersection of the material, the cultural and the symbolic. The inseparability of Bradman the man, Bradman the product, and Bradman the hero captures this condition; this nexus has also assisted in elevating the Don from mortal cricketer to mythical hero.

The argument presented in this chapter is that the continuing production, sale and consumption of a wide array of Bradman-related products has become a self-perpetuating cycle that helps to affirm the commercial *and* heroic value of his name and image. An alternative view might be that the Don's commercial value is a reflection of his heroism: he is famous and historically significant so his heroism is financially lucrative when packaged attractively. However, this line of reasoning ignores that he is actually sold to the public as famous and historically significant. Over the last two decades in particular, a Bradman industry – made up of retailers, memorabilia producers and auctioneers, the Bradman Foundation, and the media, etc. – has emerged that anchors its marketing line on his reputation. In pursuing its own economic objectives, the industry serves to promote, stabilise and perpetuate his heroism and, in the process, ensure the popularity and growing value of Bradmorabilia. In summary, the industry ensures that the Don's symbolic value and his economic value complement and keep pace with one another.

The first section of this chapter looks at Bradman the player, businessman and administrator, and argues that much of the interest in Bradman and the associated commerciality is based upon a 'golden age' view of the 1930s and 1940s. This period is treated as an amateur age where men played for the love of the sport and little else – Bradman has said as much. The period can be interpreted differently, but those entities currently profiting from nostalgia surrounding Bradman have little interest in promoting an alternative view. Also briefly examined is Bradman's record as a cricket administrator and businessman after his retirement.

The second section deals with the increase in public regard for the Don over the past two decades. It suggests that a two-way exchange is at work: cultural codes are subject to economic practices, and economic practices are subject to cultural coding. Thus, Bradman's heroism influences the commercial value of his name and image and vice versa. Attention is also paid to the forces regulating the use of the Bradman name and trademarks.

The final section of this chapter investigates the burgeoning Australian auction market for cricket memorabilia and the importance of Bradman to this market. It then goes on to examine the development of world wide web auctions and the growing role of this online purchasing mechanism in the trade of Bradmorabilia.

Player, administrator and businessman

Among those who have portrayed the 1930s and 1940s as an amateur age that had 'hardly been touched by commercialisation' are Ray Martin and Channel Nine, Ronald Conway, and most significantly, Bradman.[3] In addition, the majority of Bradman biographies, cricket volumes and videos either only briefly address or bypass the issue of cricket commercialisation and earnings, leaving the impression that money was of little concern to the Don (or anyone else for that matter). Certainly, Bradman helped create this impression:

> ... in the days that I played cricket ... we were all amateurs. That
> is, the Australians were all amateurs. We didn't earn our living

playing cricket. We played cricket because we loved it, for the fun of the game.[4]

Yet, the rigid separation of amateur and professional players that prevailed in English cricket was not strictly defined or policed in Australia. It is undeniable that this regime rewarded Bradman with indirect and direct earnings from the game. For example, players received very small daily allowances when playing state and international matches, plus a baggage allowance when on tour. For a Test match in 1933–34 they could expect £30, but for the 1930 and 1934 Ashes tours a sizeable £600 plus expenses was on offer.

Bradman received money above and beyond these allowances. He agreed to move from Sydney to Adelaide in 1934 in order to play for South Australia and to take up a position with stock-broking firm Hodgetts and Co. As well as running the firm, Henry Warburton 'Harry' Hodgetts was a member of the South Australian Cricket Association's (SACA) Ground and Finance Committee. If cricket historian Chris Harte is correct, Bradman was practically a professional from 1934 to the start of 1940.[5] A deal was negotiated for Bradman that saw the SACA subsidise £500 of Bradman's declared £700 per annum wage as an employee of Hodgetts and Co. The New South Wales Cricket Association (NSWCA) queried this financial arrangement, as it contravened the amateur ethos. While the Don was not the only one on the South Australian books being paid to play, his arrangements appear unusual and there is no suggestion that the majority of players earned decent money from the game.

As far as indirect cricket earnings were concerned, Bradman was similar to the professional players of today. He endorsed bats, pads, gloves, boots, shirts and trousers, ties, hats, shoes, books (the first, *Don Bradman's Book* (1930), was released when he was only 22 years old), a car and automotive products, ice cream, lolly sticks for children, and a school of physical culture in Sydney. He signed employment contracts related to his cricketing profile with sports goods house Mick Simmons Ltd (1929). The £1000 from an appreciative expatriate Australian soap magnate, Arthur Whitelaw, that he pocketed in 1930 after scoring the then world record Test score of 334 runs against England at Headingley is well known. On the same tour he earned £500 from a series of fourteen 10-minute batting instruction performances at the London Palladium. The reception on his return from the 1930 tour was unprecedented: he was widely feted, honoured by public gatherings, and showered with gifts, including £100 from fans in Melbourne and a Chevrolet car, one of only six made in Australia, from General Motors.

A 1931 offer for Bradman to join the Accrington Club in the professional Lancashire League in England is of great importance in understanding how he estimated his self-worth.[6] An impressive remuneration package, the largest up to that time made to a cricketer to join the league, would have netted the Don over £1000 annually (around $50,000 today[7]), but would have spelt the end of his Test career. Acceptance of the offer would have been in breach of a contract that Australian players had signed prior to the 1930 Ashes tour and the Australian Board of Control indicated that his selection for the national team would not be approved if he joined Accrington. Much to the horror of many in the Australian media, public and cricket fraternity, Bradman seriously considered the lucrative offer and kept everybody in suspense for a month. The Don stated his position unequivocally:

> I consider it was a very handsome offer, and I must say I was greatly tempted by it. I don't think anyone could have blamed me if I had

then chosen to capitalize my cricket by accepting it. No one would criticize a singer for getting as much as he could for entertaining the public in his particular way.[8]

This statement is significant on two counts. First, it demonstrates that Bradman did not see himself simply as an amateur cricketer who was lucky just to play the sport he loved for his country. Second, and more pointedly, he saw himself as similar to an entertainer selling his skills and services in an open market and felt obliged to consider and/or capitalise on offers from entrepreneurs. As it was, Bradman capitalised on his 'entertainment value' by signing a three-cornered contract with Radio 2UE Sydney, the Sydney *Sun* newspaper, and F.J. Palmer and Son Ltd Retailers, worth more than £1000 a year. This contract had been organised to ward off the Accrington offer, but it led to problems. The Board of Control attempted to prevent him writing for the *Sun* in 1932, again claiming he was in breach of their regulations. After another potentially career-threatening waiting period, the *Sun*'s managing director, Sir Hugh Denison, agreed to release Bradman from his contractual obligations. By his actions and words, Bradman made it known that he saw business and cricket as inseparable.

The Don's popularity helped others to make money. For example, in 1930, people could buy the sheet music to the well-known 'Our Don Bradman' and the less successful 'Take Off Your Hats to Don Bradman', and then 'Mighty Don' in the late 1940s. In the early 1930s came an eight-and-a-half minute film, *Don Bradman in 'How I Play Cricket'*. His ability to attract paying spectators to Sheffield Shield fixtures was unrivalled. Cashman has calculated that between 1930 and 1940 average crowds were 14,557 on days Bradman did bat, 7,627 when he did not.[9] Upon hearing of the Don's move to South Australia, the NSWCA treasurer is supposed to have wept because of the expected fall in Sydney Sheffield Shield gate takings.

Bradman is said to have been conscious of his own worth, possessing an 'impregnable self-estimation – not arrogance, but a remarkable awareness of his entitlements ...'.[10] As early as his first Ashes tour, at a chance meeting with cricket writer R.C. Robertson-Glasgow, he let it be known that he was intent on financially capitalising on his success.[11] Bradman critics, Jack Fingleton and Clif Cary, have commented on his business acumen and ability to take advantage of his profile.[12] The Don's determination to achieve financial security took shape in the shadow of the Great Depression of the late 1920s and early 1930s. The Sydney real estate office in which he had worked as secretary, Westbrook & Deer, was closed down in 1929, which coincided with his signing for Mick Simmons. Rising unemployment and clashes between the police and the unemployed were indicative of the severe economic downturn in the Australian economy.

Selected commentators believed cricket in the 1930s and 1940s was a business. In *Bradman* (1948), Moyes notes the commercialised nature of cricket 'in this materialistic age', Page discusses those who expressed dismay at the 'commercialisation of cricket' in the 1930s, and Fingleton commented that in the same period, 'Big cricket was big money.'[13] Other sources trace the development of cricket's commercial characteristics. Between 1870 and 1910, W.G. Grace earned around £120,000 from the game.[14] Sport in Australia had become increasingly commercial since the 1850s with sponsorship and player earnings very much part of the game, one writer notes, while another argues that the fact that cricket in England was a business by 1900 influenced Australia.[15] In the 1939 *Wisden Cricketers' Almanack*, Bradman pronounced that cricket could not be dissociated from the 'cold, hard facts of finance'.[16]

The state of cricket at this time reflects Australia's status as a capitalist, industrial Western democracy, and rather than attempting to make out that Bradman was immune to commercial matters, it is more constructive to situate him within this market system.

The contemporary nostalgia for a 'pure' amateur age of Australian cricket supported by Martin, Conway, Bradman and others is undermined by historical and cricket studies proffering different interpretations. Even allowing that most cricketers did not make a living from the sport, their viewpoint ignores the game's long history of professionalism and commercialism. While economic conditions in Australian cricket during the 1930s and 1940s were not the same as they are now, these years form antecedents to today's game. The implicit denial of the existence of commercial and professional practices in Bradman's era allows the idea of a 'golden age' to surface, and this nostalgia connects with the heroic mythology and idealised nationalism surrounding Bradman that have worked to submerge the commercial character of his name and image. The Don is a measure for sporting integrity precisely because he is rarely thought of in terms of financial calculation.[17] The 'golden age' notion also implies that an unbridgeable chasm exists between cricket in the 1930s and 1940s and the highly commercialised contemporary game, instead of acknowledging continuities between these eras.

Bradman's involvement in the business world continued for over three and a half decades after his retirement from cricket. He was a successful Adelaide stockbroker until 1954 when he closed his firm, Don Bradman and Co. His firm had been set up in 1945 after Hodgetts and Co. declared bankruptcy with liabilities of £82,854 and 238 unsecured creditors. Bradman issued a statement denying any knowledge of the events leading up to the bankruptcy (see Chapter 8). After the later and less controversial winding down of Bradman and Co., the Don continued to take an active interest in the firm that took over his operation, Len Bullock and Co., and accepted directorships for many companies until 1984.[18] As a director, Bradman had a reputation for his cautious approach and good business skills. Banks, insurers and manufacturers also knew that his attendance as a director at private meetings was likely to attract influential cabinet ministers and VIPs.[19]

Throughout Bradman's playing career and afterwards, his energies were directed towards ensuring that his name meant business. In 1950 he expressed a strong faith in commerce and a preference for Australia to be a shareholder society. He believed, rightly or wrongly, that large companies were not run just by rich businessmen, but were actually owned mainly by small shareholders who were a 'vital necessity to the well-being and democratic progress of a country'.[20]

The Don's reputation as a shrewd businessman served him well as he became president of the Commonwealth Club of Adelaide. Having bought himself a seat on the Adelaide Stock Exchange in 1942, he captained the Exchange in a cricket match against a Taxation XI to celebrate his fiftieth birthday (he scored 85 runs). He was also a correspondent with the London *Daily Mail* during the 1953 and 1956 Ashes series. In arranging the 1996 Channel Nine interview, he is said to have got along amiably with Kerry Packer, a turnaround given that the two were on opposite sides during the World Series Cricket (WSC) imbroglio of the 1970s.

Outside of the business world, the Don enjoyed a long career as a cricket administrator. His connection with the game was unbroken from 1949 to 1986. Bradman served as a Test and/or state selector between 1936–37 and 1971–72, except for the 1952–53 season and the selection of the 1953 Ashes touring team due to the illness of his son. He held various positions at state and national levels, including as a member of the Australian Board of Control/Australian Cricket Board (1945–1953, 1953–1956, 1957–1980), which he also chaired from 1960 to 1963 and 1969 to 1972. Bradman's dedication to administration is summed up by his attendance at an estimated 1,713 meetings of the SACA between 1935–36 and 1985–86 – 'very probably another record'.[21] In terms of his impact on the game, his influence in the attacking style of play adopted by the Australian team in the famous 1960–61 Test series between Australia and the West Indies, featuring the tied Test in Brisbane, has been acknowledged.[22]

In later years, Bradman recognised the popularity and role of one-day cricket and claimed to accept the need for sporting professionalism. He stated that he understood the need for cricket to adapt to the contemporary social conditions and that he had no objection to night cricket, players wearing coloured clothing or the use of white balls. What concerned the Don was not change, but rather that as change unfolded 'we are able to preserve the underlying character-building edifice upon which the game was founded'.[23]

Bradman said he understood the commercial necessity of top-level cricket for gate money and media coverage, and that attractive play is required to maintain both. Yet as a member of the ACB in the years prior to the revolution of Kerry Packer's WSC in the late 1970s, he was intransigent in his refusal to increase player wages.[24] In holding down wages, he can be seen either as protecting the board's financial position or, more likely, as believing that cricketers should use their profile to earn money outside the game. Irrespective of his motives, as an administrator his resistance to increased player payments is at odds with his own determined pursuit of capital accumulation, as well as with those bodies that have used his name for the same purpose.

The explosion of Bradmania

A sharp upturn in community interest in Bradman coincided with two events: the 50th anniversary of the 1932–33 bodyline series in 1983 and the highly successful screening of the Kennedy-Miller *Bodyline* television mini-series in 1984. These events rekindled public fascination for the Don and stimulated a fertile market that has produced, among many things, a spate of books, videos and prints. Despite the arbitrary nature of choosing any year to commemorate an historical event, a 50th anniversary is considered especially meaningful.

The 50th anniversary of the bodyline season generated a surge in public and commercial interest in Bradman. For example, more new Bradman publications were produced in the years 1980–89 than in any previous decade and this escalation continued into the 1990s and the new millennium (see Table 4 and Figure 1 in the Appendix). Thirty new publications were produced after 1980, outstripping the 25 released in the previous five decades. Four new books on Bradman were published in 1983, the highest number in any one year and, in addition, Page's biography went into a second print run. Another four new books on Bradman and/or bodyline were released in 1984–85, plus the re-publication of at least another four, including Douglas Jardine's *In Quest of the Ashes* that had not been printed since 1933.[25] Riding the wave of a late 1970s–early 1980s publishing industry boom, commercial publishers capitalised on the renewed interest in the Don and added publications in the following years.

Further marking the resurgence of interest in the Don is the 1983 official proposal for a Bradman Museum to be established in Bowral. One of the current directors of the Bradman Foundation, Garry Barnsley, suggested the idea to Wingecarribee Shire Council after his attention was captured by Page's *Bradman: The Illustrated*

'The Don' refers to more than one man, but he is a powerful figure either way.
A Courier Mail *newspaper cartoon commenting on corruption in international*
cricket. (Neil Matterson)

Readers awoke on 27 February 2001 to an avalanche of newspaper dedications
to Bradman following his death. (News Limited)

Bradman's funeral procession through the streets of Adelaide on 1 March 2001.
Sir Donald's son, John, leads the procession. (News Limited)

A statue of Bradman is lowered onto a podium alongside other Australian icons.
This cartoon appeared in the Daily Telegraph *newspaper following Bradman's*
death. (Warren Brown and the *Daily Telegraph*)

An illustration of Bradman dwarfed by his 'saintly' shadow. This image neatly captures the argument that Bradman the man and the myth are indivisible. (News Limited)

Former Test teammates Leslie 'Chuck' Fleetwood-Smith and Don Bradman during their playing days. As Chapter 2 explains, they experienced differing fortunes in their lives after cricket. (Photograph courtesy of the State Library of South Australia)

The Longest Odds ...

To even contemplate that Bradman might have been involved in corruption such as match fixing is humorously absurd. This cartoon appeared in reaction to the 'Hansie-gate' cricket match fixing affair during April 2000. (Reprinted by permission of Cathy Wilcox, *Sydney Morning Herald*)

Another cartoon commenting on corruption in international cricket. Bradman's 'sacred' baggy green cap is juxtaposed with the mobile phone that Hansie Cronje used to fix matches with bookmakers. (Cartoon by Peter Nicholson from *The Australian*)

The Bradman Museum at Bowral. (News Limited)

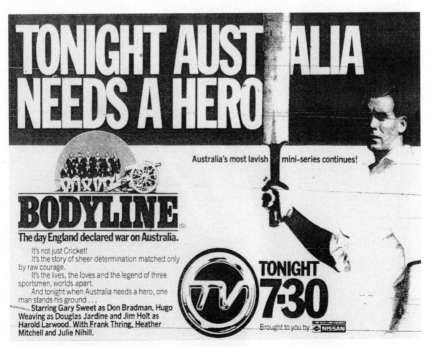

A 1984 newspaper advertisement for the Bodyline *mini-series featuring Gary Sweet as Bradman.* (Courtesy of Network Ten)

Champion Test leg-spinner and Bradman critic Bill O'Reilly. (News Limited)

Sir Donald Bradman and Channel Nine's Ray Martin. In 1996 Martin conducted Bradman's last major media interview. (News Limited)

CHAMPIONS OF ST. GEORGE

DON BRADMAN and JOLLEY'S

We can't all make centuries like Don, but what we do make will go further at Jolley's.

Jolley's Departmental Stores Ltd.
290 FOREST ROAD, HURSTVILLE.

An advertisement from the 1930s highlighting the use of the Bradman name for commercial promotion. This advertisement also highlights the link between Bradman and the Hurstville area of Sydney where he played grade cricket for St George.

Bradman featured in a Peters ice-cream advertisement during his playing days.
(News Limited)

Biography, released to coincide with the 50th anniversary of the bodyline summer. The idea for the museum struck him when he realised that the only landmark in the town recognising the Don was Bradman Oval. After approval problems and local concern regarding possible environmental and property value impacts were overcome, Bradman opened the first stage of the Museum in October 1989, with a second stage unveiled by Prime Minister Howard on Bradman's 88th birthday, 27 August 1996. The Museum has played a significant role in magnifying the Don's profile. Museum director, Richard Mulvaney, states:

> He's captured the public imagination and continues to do so 50 years after his last game. Those of us involved with the Bradman Museum feel some sense of guilt as through our energies Sir Donald has allowed himself to become much more a public figure in 1990s than he was prepared to do so in the 1940s … The more he's allowed himself to become part of the public domain, the more the public want to know about him.[26]

Since the early 1980s, Bradman products, from many different sources, have mushroomed. Prices range from a few dollars for souvenirs such as stickers, placemats and fridge magnets through to thousands of dollars for big-ticket items such as signed limited edition memorabilia and prints. For example, $4,950 will purchase a limited edition bronze bust of the Don. Many products are of a high quality, but some items arguably cheapen the Bradman name and have tenuous links to the Don or cricket – Bradman bears, stress balls, neoprene sunglass cases and macadamia chocolates. There has also been a marked increase in audio-visual products. The videos, *Bradman 87 Not Out, Bradman, The Bradman Era*, and a newly released copy of the 1934 film, *How I Play Cricket*, plus an eight-hour audiocassette interview by Norman May with Sir Donald, *Bradman: The Don Declares*, are on sale. Fans can buy a compact disc, *Words from the Don: A Collection of Speeches by the Great Sir Donald Bradman*, and the audiocassette of Sir Donald's speech at the opening of the Bradman Museum in 1989. Mirroring the two Bradman songs of the 1930s are the 1987 Paul Kelly and the Coloured Girls single, 'Bradman', and the 1996 John Williamson song, 'Sir Don', which the Bradman family liked because they believed it had a 'touch of Waltzing Matilda' about it.[27] Bradman's classic coaching manual, *The Art of Cricket*, is now available both as a book and an interactive CD-ROM. Another 50th anniversary, this time of the Bradman-led 1948 Australian Ashes squad – the Invincibles – led to a documentary video, *The Invincibles*, and a new book, *The Invincibles: The Legend of Bradman's 1948 Australians*.

The product and the image

The proliferation of Bradman products reveals a far-reaching commercialisation process that is of significant cultural consequence. As culture 'has become a product in its own right', previously autonomous or semi-autonomous areas such as sport, art and heritage have been increasingly drawn into the spheres of the state and the demands of the market.[28] What is striking in the case of the Bradman myth is that it runs counter to the argument that commercialisation attacks tradition. Rather than attacking tradition, the industry built around Bradman restructures and incorporates it for market demand. Bradman products transform the emotion, desire and nostalgia of the fan for a heroic golden age image of the Don into a rationalised value – an amount of money. 'Bradman' has become a product, and has been drawn into the cultural logic of late capitalism.[29]

The producers of Bradman-related products fall roughly into two categories, although the demarcation between them is fuzzy. First are producers with a largely commercial motive. Breakfast cereals, stamp releases, sections of the commercial media and the mass of assorted Bradman souvenirs, memorabilia and products are primarily designed to generate a financial return. To appeal to the widest range of consumers, producers choose desirable nationalist and heroic representations of Bradman. While these images lack the critical cachet of biographies and documentaries, their repetition and banality work to ingrain the 'great (Brad)man' as a seemingly permanent feature of the Australian popular culture psyche.

The second category includes biographers, documentary makers and media commentators. These people attempt to present serious analysis while still trying to attract an audience. Over time many analysts, but not all (Gideon Haigh and R.C. Robertson-Glasgow being notable exceptions), have produced numerous sympathetic and heroic portraits of the Don that image him as a national icon. The outcome of these portraits is a robust 'naturalised' conception of Bradman as a glorious hero by virtue of their repetition and, more tellingly, the 'expert' status of the producers and the cultural and intellectual authority they hold.

Why fans desire Bradman products touches upon how 'admiring identification' is constructed.[30] The Don's exceptional performances are only the first part of the equation. For widespread consumer desire to be created and sustained, a mythical image that appears to transcend the strictly commercial must be legitimated. The heroic and nostalgic representations – books, videos, music, calendars, prints and so on – help to affirm his popularity. These items form a heroic frame of reference through which Bradman is read. These are commercially driven products 'more interested

in the symbols and the mood than in a detailed account'.[31] For
example, the limited edition bi-metal coin (costing $380) released
after Bradman's death came with an insert identifying the coin
number and a dedication that evokes an especially celebratory
mood:

> His legendary achievements on the sports field still stand far ahead
> of those of the many champions since, and his integrity and grace off
> the field have likewise seldom been matched. His life has been and
> remains a role model and inspiration for countless people in all
> walks of life around the world, from sports people to world leaders
> in politics and business.[32]

With products such as these and their associated sentiments
continually being produced, the glossy heroic image of Bradman
accumulates integrity, which maintains the consensus on who and
what Bradman was – a hero.

These products help Bradman's heroism assume a self-perpetuating character. Representations of and admiration for Bradman
begets fans, fans then serve to culturally embed Bradman's heroism, and his heroism begets retailers and manufacturers that sell
celebratory products to fans. The consumer is, in effect, purchasing
the '"aura" of symbolic meanings and values' contained in the
Bradman image and 'sealed' in the product.[33] Given the saleability
of such items, it is little wonder that the market appears un-
interested in producing items that posit alternative critical interpretations of the Don. As his name and image were increasingly
packaged and consumed, Bradman the man, the living being, became almost indistinguishable from this commercialisation. Whatever Bradman actually thought and felt was gradually subsumed by
the hero-worship and nostalgic sentiment that we associate with
the Bradmorabilia market.

The Bradman Museum

Sports museums are most commonly dedicated to a sport, a club's history, or a nation's sporting history; the Bradman Museum is unusual in that it is dedicated to an individual. Another smaller Bradman collection is on display in the State Library of South Australia in Adelaide. These public displays are testimony to Bradman's popularity, but they also operate in a commercial realm. Sports museums 'cater to the nostalgia market and have, almost without exception, institutionalized the concept of a golden age in virtually every sport'.[34] Despite an apparently non-worshipful stance, Mulvaney does admit that 'a pilgrimage mindset' has started to grow around the Museum site:[35] 1,000 people visited the Museum to mourn the Don's passing, and some 75,000 visited in the 1996–97 financial year.[36]

The sense of reverence and tradition elicited by the Museum is particularly advantageous in an era of 'excessive' and 'cynical' commercialism. Whereas management mega-agencies and agents promote other famous personalities, Bradman's major public representative is a Foundation that honours his legacy and built a Museum in his name. The Bradman Museum is run by a public company limited by guarantee, operating under the name The Bradman Foundation which, in 2001, had a board of seven men. Among the seven are Ian Craig and other former Australian Test representatives, Alan Davidson and John Benaud. The board operates on a rotational basis. Established in 1993, the Foundation's function is to run the Museum and its membership programs. It organises and funds activities such as coaching clinics, special matches on the Bradman Oval and the Bradman Scholarship scheme for young cricketers. The Foundation has also registered the Bradman name and associated trademarks such as 'The Don' in every cricketing country worldwide, in keeping with Bradman's own wish that his name not be exploited for unauthorised commercial gain.[37]

The Foundation licenses a range of Bradman products in the hope that they will help meet the costs of running the Museum and its activities. For example, in 1994–95 a 'most significant' sponsorship proposal was accepted from Sanitarium, the makers of the breakfast cereal Weet-Bix, to lend the Bradman name to television commercials and packet displays.[38] The cards and posters produced as part of this deal now fetch hundreds of dollars at auction, particularly if signed by Bradman. Other examples include the 1996 initiative of the Royal Australian Mint to produce 500,000 Bradman $5 coins, the 1997 release of Bradman stamps and philatelic products, and a deal with Dunlop Slazenger to produce a range of 'Bradman' cricket equipment.[39] In recent times, Elite Sports Properties has been appointed to manage the Foundation's range of merchandise and licensed products, and will work to access wider markets and product endorsements. Also, only a couple of days before the Don's death, it was reported by the *Sydney Morning Herald* that the Bradman name was to appear on a new range of pens, stationery, glassware and towels, with the intention of developing these products for the Indian and South African markets.[40]

A string of illicit attempts to cash in on the Bradman name demonstrate its value. The Foundation's legal representatives have had plenty of work to do in protecting the Bradman name against unauthorised use and the trademarks against infringement. Permission to use the trademarks is occasionally granted to those not associated with the Foundation – the State Library of South Australia has permission to sell a range of products associated with its exhibition. Another example of a successful application was the registration of a 'Sir Don' cherry (as in the fruit).

In 1992, Powers Brewery produced a limited edition of 100 cases of 'Bradman's Bitter Ale' for the Queensland Cricketers'

Club to be sold to the public for $44 each. Bradman's lawyers intervened, as permission to use the Don's name and image on the beer had not been given.[41] The stock was destroyed with only two or three cases having been sold, and in June 2000 'Simply Cricket', a Brisbane auction house, had to withdraw two of the remaining bottles of the Bitter Ale from sale.

Again in 2000, a widely publicised threat of legal action was made against an Adelaide restaurateur, Lyn Mounsey. She planned to call her establishment Bradman's Café/Restaurant as it is located on the renamed Bradman Drive. She received a letter from Bradman's lawyers that demanded she deregister the name because they wanted to avoid 'any association between the name "Bradman" and the production, promotion or sale of alcohol, and this conduct represents a grave abuse of our client's reputation and standing'.[42] A fair compromise was reached when Mounsey agreed to rename the dining venue Bradman Drive Café/Restaurant. An adult shop on the same drive, wishing to call itself Erotica on Bradman, was indirectly prevented from using the name by government intervention. The Foundation also refused permission for the museum of the Don's birthplace at Cootamundra in New South Wales to use the name, 'Bradman's Birthplace'.[43]

Significantly, just two days prior to Bradman's death, a settlement was reached with New South Wales based property developer, Bradman Corporation, after the Foundation had taken the first ever Federal Court action against entrepreneurs for 'illegally incorporating, trading or threatening to trade under the name'.[44] Representatives of the Bradman Corporation and its related companies agreed to cease trading under the name within two years, and handed over the Internet domain name bradman.com.au to the Foundation. Papers lodged during the court case stated:

The Australian public ... regard Sir Donald Bradman as an Australian hero, icon and idol ... and they would regard the name Bradman appearing in relation to the supply of goods and services ... as having qualities of uniqueness, excellence and perfection which the public associates with Sir Donald Bradman.[45]

Court action and the other problems mentioned prompted an unprecedented intervention by the federal government in October 2000. Following dialogue with Bradman's family, Prime Minister Howard announced that amendments would be made to Corporations Law Regulations preventing companies from registering the word 'Bradman', or variations of Sir Donald's name, unless they can establish a valid connection with the family or with the Foundation. Bradman joined members of the royal family, and the words Anzac, University and Commonwealth on a select list that cannot be commercially exploited, an unparalleled privilege for a private citizen, whose name was registered as a trademark. Asked whether this intervention by the government was unusual, Howard responded directly:

Well it is unusual, but he is an unusually special figure in Australian history, not only our sporting history but our cultural history. The Government took the view that there was a very strong potential for people to commercially exploit his name, to suggest a connection which didn't exist, and following some representation from his family I considered the matter and the Government decided that we should provide protection through the Corporations Law which means that people can't use the name in circumstances suggesting a connection that doesn't exist or hasn't been authorised.[46]

The government's action, however, has not halted attempts at profiteering. The sale of private letters written by Bradman is proving an ongoing difficulty for the Foundation. In November 2000, a Sydney bookseller, Paul Feain, intended to sell 35 of Bradman's private letters written between 1994 and 1998 for around $20,000. According to newspaper reports, the deeply personal letters included details of the Don's sorrow at the loss of his wife Jessie to cancer in 1997. Following public and media pressure, Mr Feain withdrew the letters from sale and publicly apologised for the incident.[47]

Trouble flared yet again in July of 2001 when two letters written by Bradman rebuking former Australian captain Greg Chappell for his role in the WSC controversy in 1977 went to auction. The surprise conclusion to this sale was that a bidder calling itself 'Some Australians Value Ethics' (SAVE) paid $18,800 for the letters and then returned them to the Foundation and Bradman family. In an invocation of the moral framework described in Chapter 2, one of the anonymous businessmen who funded the successful bid contrasted his admiration for Bradman to the 1981 Australian underarm bowling incident, which occurred under Chappell's captaincy, in a one-day match against New Zealand:

> Bradman is one of the few heroes we have in Australia and he set an example in his day. Now Chappell was in a similar position to Bradman and yet Chappell created in 1981 the most shameful act in Australian sporting history with the underarm bowling incident, which was quite legal but outside the spirit of the game.[48]

The more sordid cricket becomes, the more heroic and superior Bradman and the time in which he played appears.

Despite these difficulties, the Bradman trademarks, in concert with effective financial management and sponsorship, have put the Foundation in a strong position. Apart from a first-year deficit in 1993, profits after tax have been consistently in the hundreds of thousands, varying anywhere from over $90,000 in 1994 to $1,400,919 in 1996.[49] By 2000, the Foundation's net assets had grown to over $5 million, a sizeable increase on the 1993 figure of $1.3 million, especially considering that the Museum receives no ongoing government grants.[50] In the course of building and developing the Museum, the Foundation was sponsored by prominent members of the Australian business community, which brought cachet and capital to the Museum.[51]

The cost of running the Museum is sizeable, with operating expenses close to $1.5 million annually. The maintenance of the picturesque Museum facility and Bradman Oval are significant ongoing expenses as are the scholarships, cricketing clinics and other charitable activities. As mentioned earlier, each year the Museum conducts coaching clinics for junior cricketers, with matches featuring both local and international touring sides on Bradman Oval. It also organises charitable activities benefiting young cricketing talent, such as the annual Bradman Scholarship scheme. The Bradman Scholarship is awarded to a young cricketer who has achieved on the cricket field and who has a promising academic record at the tertiary level. These activities help to fulfil the Museum's aim of assisting young people, sponsoring youth cricket and promoting the game generally. Upon Sir Donald's death, the Museum also took responsibility for the Bradman Memorial Fund, a charity designed to provide opportunities for people in need.[52]

In raising revenue, the Bradman trademarks are extremely valuable as the public's appetite for Bradmorabilia is unremitting. The Foundation's combined income from sales and royalties has shown a generally consistent and impressive upward trend, growing from over $200,000 in 1993 to more than $1.5 million in 1999.[53] The average spending of each visitor increased from $7.05 in 1997/98 to $9.97 in 1998/99.[54] These figures compare to the 1997 Australia-wide museum average of around $1.20 per visitor. Online sales through the Museum website are expanding significantly, generating close to $30,000 between autumn 2000 and summer 2001.[55] Garry Barnsley explains that:

> The licensing and merchandising revenue generated by the Bradman legend is a vital supplement to the other conventional income streams that sustain the activities of the Foundation. The public's profound respect for Sir Donald, and everything that he epitomises, is reflected in the insatiable demand for products bearing his name – as much as by the public's continuing support for the Museum reflected in visitation figures.[56]

Mulvaney is of a similar view to Barnsley, commenting in the *Financial Review* shortly after Bradman's death, 'We believe it [Bradman] is the most marketable name in Australian history.'[57] Of course the Foundation's expenditure is often charitable, helping aspiring young cricketers along the way with scholarships, for example.

However, the issue has been raised as to whether merchandising exploits the Bradman name. Haigh, for instance, has pointed out that in some cases Sir Donald Bradman may be reduced to Sir Donald Brandname.[58] The use of the Bradman name on some products – drink bottles, macadamia chocolates, fridge magnets and stress balls for example – may cheapen it, but account must also be taken of sports museums being situated at the intersection of history, nostalgia and the marketplace. Museums cater for people seeking to affirm their devotion, even though the object they purchase might have little correspondence to the past. Fans enjoy the material form and they often wish to affirm their admiration and feelings.[59] As 'chunks of meaning', the products provide a way for people to stake a claim in Bradman.[60] In other words, this is not a straightforward case of a producer duping unwitting consumers into buying things they do not want. People invest financially and emotionally in these products because they provide a physical symbol of their feelings. Owning a Bradman product allows the individual to feel included in a wider community that idolises the Don.

The auction market and going online

The sports memorabilia retail and auction market experienced a pronounced upsurge in the late 1980s and 1990s. The retail side alone is estimated to be worth around $30 million annually.[61] Bradmorabilia is a key feature of this market. Supply is plentiful as Bradman signed bats, posters and the like for 70 years or more, creating a possible pool of over one million objects from which to draw. This ready supply of Bradmorabilia appears to have done little to dampen demand:

> Never before – in any field of collecting memorabilia or more
> generally in the art market itself – has the life, career and death of just
> one man played so central a role to the very existence of a collectable
> market. Bradman's life and career remain for many the central
> inspiration for collecting cricket memorabilia.[62]

In other words, it is the heroic quality of the Bradman name and image that forms the very basis of this market, and following his death the value of his signature increased by between an estimated 20 to 50 per cent.[63]

Established auction houses such as Christie's, Phillips International, Sotheby's, and Lawson's deal in cricket memorabilia, or 'cricketana' as some refer to it. These houses also operate on the world wide web and compete against Internet-dedicated operators. In Australian sporting memorabilia auctions, Bradman-related objects have proved very popular, reliably fetching good prices. Among cricketers, only Victor Trumper, W.G. Grace and Garry Sobers appear capable of attracting similar money. The highest price achieved for a Bradman item is $74,750 for a life-sized bronzed sculpture of the Don, with Bradman bats attracting prices of close to $50,000 (see Table 5 in the Appendix). Although not for sale, the 'holy grail' of Bradmorabilia, his 1948 Invincibles baggy green Australian cap, is insured for $153,000 while on loan to the Bradman Museum. After Bradman died, the value of this cap may have been overtaken by the bat he used in his final innings, with a representative of Christie's auction house speculating that people might pay up to $500,000 for it.[64] Such speculation buttresses both the economic and symbolic value of the Don by helping to ensure a supply of buyers and onlookers when an item is up for auction. The considerable sums paid for Bradmorabilia are not, however, the largest values placed on Australian sporting memorabilia (in 1999, Phar Lap's 1931 Cox Plate sold for $420,500).

Cricket lends itself well to the auction market. It has a long, rich history and is a popular viewer and spectator sport nation-wide, creating a large pool of possible buyers. The prominence of statistics in the game helps to capture notable achievements, which in turn assist in the creation and valuation of memorabilia (a similar phenomenon is evident in American baseball). The market is generally broken into two categories: authentic memorabilia – clothing, equipment, etc. used by the player in question; and commercially produced commemorative items. Among the latter, auto-graphed, limited edition, fully endorsed items are more valuable as their worth generally appreciates. The value attributed to bats and alike used by famous players can be gleaned from the prices listed in Table 5 (see Appendix), and also by moves such as the federal government's use of cultural heritage laws in 1998 to forbid a collection of Trumper memorabilia being exported from Australia. A growing realisation of the value of cricket memorabilia appears to have flowed from the Marylebone Cricket Club Bicentenary auction in 1987, with a Cricket Memorabilia Society formed two years later.

The assignment of value to specific objects at auction is loosely based on its association with the 'great and good': 'by reason of antiquity, scarcity, previous ownership, use or a special factor such as an important innings'.[65] Bradman's value is virtually assured because of his heroic reputation in Australian culture and because he played numerous significant innings during his career. The move into cricketana of prestigious auction houses such as Christie's, Lawson's, and Phillips International, which previously dealt mainly in fine art and antiques, has served to regulate the criteria for valuing items and increase their market worth. Prior to a major 1997 Christie's cricket auction valued at between $400,000 and $500,000, Christie's historical documents specialist, Michael Ludgrove, highlighted the changing character of the memorabilia market:

> I think in the past, sport memorabilia in general has been relegated to a share which is outside fine arts. This sort of sale has a much different image now in this glossy Christie's catalogue. So the message is, it's going to become much more collectible from an investment point of view rather than just the passionate, enthusiastic swap-card collector market.[66]

Tory Norton of Lawson's confirms the altered character of the 'popular culture' market of cricket memorabilia following the entrance of 'high culture' art and antique auctioneers. She says that Lawson's began to deal in cricket memorabilia in the late 1980s – early 1990s after recognising that people outside their normal target groups wanted to purchase items. With these companies dealing in cricket memorabilia, the stature and value of the market have been boosted, as the enthusiast-cum-collector now has to compete against the investor at auction.

Bradman's commercial value is now self-sustaining, and the media have performed – and continue to perform – a critical function in creating that situation. The electronic and print media publicise large or record prices achieved at auction for Bradmorabilia. These reports lead to stories about growth in the sports memorabilia market. The well-publicised $48,000 paid by Kerry Packer in 1996 for a Bradman bat is thought to have lifted the cricketana market to another level. Values continue to grow – since Bradman's death Packer's bat is thought to be worth closer to $100,000.[67] Even smaller cricketana auctions such as one held in Brisbane in February 2000 received coverage on local Channel Seven and ABC television news. Reports and stories of these sales provide opportunities to again mention or display images of the Don, further impressing him on the minds of viewers and readers. This process has contributed towards the naturalising of Bradman's worth and reputation, and sees the media acting almost as a sales agent for upcoming auctions by highlighting how much people are willing to pay for a piece of the Don.

Journalist Michael Reid supports the argument that the media play a principal role in the cricket memorabilia market: 'Sporting memorabilia, as an accessible area of international collecting, have been propelled into the popular consciousness via the saturation of the sports media.'[68] In Australia, Channel Nine has played a principal role, especially given its captive audience of cricket followers. During the 1990s, Test and one-day broadcasts increasingly featured products such as limited edition framed photographs, special edition books and statuettes, including one titled 'Bradman – The Cover Drive', that could be purchased through Channel Nine's *Wide World of Sports*. It is reasonable to suggest that these items and their cost, usually between $150 and $1000, aided in awakening the public to the value and desirability of these items. Nine helped auction houses to establish a larger cricket and sporting market for their catalogues. Stephen Moyle of 'Simply Cricket', a newly established cricket memorabilia auction house, believes:

> It is the media driving the popularity of cricket memorabilia. Channel Nine has been central to this as they are selling a lot of products. It is profit driven and Channel Nine really got the ball rolling.[69]

Channel Nine cricket commentator, Tony Greig, who also markets cricket products for the network, agrees:

> Because of this exposure I think it is fair to say that the reaction you have received from memorabilia merchandisers is correct. We have now got to a stage where we have to be selective with the product we put to air and are finding the manufacturers of such products are plentiful. It is also worth mentioning that the advent of internet trading, especially through companies like eBay, would have created some extra interest in these products.[70]

The dominance of Bradman in cricket memorabilia sales is distinguishable by more than just media coverage. Bradman items at the 'Simply Cricket' Brisbane sales I attended in February and June of 2000 ranged from signed and limited edition prints, posters, photos, cards, envelopes, bats and mini-bats, a tankard, a jug, a glass bowl, plates, badges and a 500-piece 'Bradman. The Man. The Legend' jigsaw puzzle (the catalogue describes it as, 'Unusual... but Bradman!'). The auctioneer's line, 'It's a Bradman piece ladies and gentlemen', revealed that Bradmorabilia is keenly sought. Just to watch people's interest rise when a quality Bradman piece was put under the hammer was anecdotal confirmation that the Don's reputation needs little or no explanation. By my calculations, of the combined 248 items up for sale at the February and June events, 48 were specifically dedicated to Bradman. The next closest player was former Australian captain, Allan Border, with a total of 11. Also by my calculation, the average price achieved for a Bradman piece was approximately 30 per cent higher than for other items. Even allowing for the varying quality of the objects for sale and the unpredictable levels of competition between buyers, on average, Bradmorabilia still easily eclipsed the value of all other player-specific pieces.

A similar dominance of Bradman-associated objects is evident when examining the online auction market. A survey of cricket items listed for sale on four of Australia's most popular world wide web auction sites, SOLD.com.au, eBay Australia, Stuff Auctions and GoFish, revealed a huge gap between Bradman-dedicated items and those of other cricket players, the closest being Australia's top wicket taker in Test cricket, Shane Warne (see Table 6 in the Appendix).[71]

In a pattern similar to unauthorised attempts by companies to use the Bradman trademarks, the allure of the Don is demonstrated by the production of fake Bradmorabilia that is then sold through online auction. The Foundation has taken action against those perpetrating this fraud, leading to arrests and seizures in both Melbourne and Canberra.[72] In one case, Sir Donald had personally signed 26 cricket bats and 29 wall plaques not knowing that the items were to be offered for sale over the Internet and in retail stores. A week after his death the value of the Bradman name was underlined by the theft in the Hunter Valley of New South Wales of 10 Bradman signature bats, which were valued at between $3000 and $8000 each prior to his death. Publicising this type of incident reinforces the value and profitability of the Bradman name. As for the problem of fakes, Mulvaney states that the online auction market has opened a 'whole new marketplace for these people to offer their products' and that over the past three years illegitimate sporting collectibles have reached 'plague proportions'.[73] The Bradman Museum is said to be working with the Australian Cricket Board, the Australian Federal Police and marketing bodies to halt such deception. A former police forensic examiner and signature expert is now working for the Museum providing authentication of Bradman signatures.[74] Overall, the need for such measures further distances the nostalgic idealised image of Bradman from the perceived immorality and corruption of the present day.

Conclusion

Desire for products associated with the Don maintains momentum. Possibly the most curious items come from a Bowral woodcrafter who made a 'Bradman bed' worth $1,500 and other furniture pieces from the wood-paling fence that once surrounded one of Bradman's boyhood homes. Such items are produced and sold due to Bradman's enormous marketability, which in cricketing terms is unparalleled. This marketability is structured through an image of a golden age where Bradman stands above all others. Bradman is a measure of sporting integrity precisely because he is rarely discussed in terms of financial calculation. Yet, other interpretations of the Don tell us that he was at the vanguard of commercial self-promotion and professionalism during his playing career. He may have played for love, but love is not the only thing that cricket helped him to accumulate. That commercial development from Bradman's playing career to cricket today might be continuous is an unappealing notion. Rather, it is the idea of a rupture between then and now that fuels the mythical and heroic integrity of the Don and the 1930s and 1940s. The Bradmorabilia market not only draws on and lives off such nostalgic yearning, it actively produces it.

Bradman's image is protected and regulated by various groups and individuals, including the media, souvenir producers and sellers and the auction industry, for example. They help to create a two-way process in which cultural values and beliefs centred on Bradman's heroism work off economic processes and vice versa. Cumulatively, these elements form a self-perpetuating commercial network that helps to construct, stabilise and propagate the mythical proportions that Bradman's heroism has assumed within Australian popular culture.

CHAPTER 6

POLITICAL CONNECTIONS

He [Bradman] is the greatest living Australian without any argument...[1]

Bradman appeared to be an apolitical figure by making little if any comment on politics, his silence reinforcing the principle that sport and politics should not mix. Yet heroes have a political character with or without their consent, and one of Bradman's keenest admirers, Prime Minister John Howard, has repeatedly highlighted the relationship between sport, politics and heroism. Howard's heartfelt tributes to Bradman have included the bold statement above, the Australian Cricket Board's inaugural Sir Donald Bradman Oration in 2000, opening a new stage of the Bradman Museum, and leading the singing of 'Happy Birthday' to Bradman for his 90th on national television. Upon hearing of Bradman's death, Howard was noticeably upset and penned a dedication to the Don that appeared in many newspapers.

Howard's consistent and effusive praise has boosted Bradman's profile and drawn attention to the political character of Bradman's heroism. This chapter investigates the political meanings of his heroism by noting the political, social and biographical similarities between Bradman and Howard. These aspects are then placed into the wider historical context of Australian social conservatism as manifest in the Liberal Party. Howard names as his other Australian hero the country's longest-serving Prime Minister and a founder of the Liberal Party, Sir Robert Gordon Menzies.[2] Bradman, Howard and Menzies share a belief in the virtues of an Australian brand of social conservatism, and a key theme of this chapter is how the symbolism of Bradman, and cricket as a cultural form have been used to maintain this tradition. A brief genealogy of how cricket and social conservative politics have dealt with the issues of the republic, race, multiculturalism, women's affairs and South Africa is also presented.

In this chapter, I look at the political character of Bradman's heroism and the ways in which it has been used. My aim is to politicise a sporting icon who is popularly viewed as apolitical. The Don is presented as a standard-bearer of achievement in Australia and his name does not feature in political disputes, thus allowing him to appear as a hero for *all* of us. Stripping away this apolitical visage is important as it is through figures such as Bradman that the political character of social life – 'of authority, legitimacy and power' – is played out.[3]

I am not saying that Bradman and cricket are only of interest to the right wing of Australian politics. Many politicians from the left, including former Labor Prime Ministers Bob Hawke and John Curtin, and former Labor leader and Menzies rival, Herbert Vere Evatt, have played cricket and/or been high-profile spectators. Former Opposition leader Kim Beazley and leading Labor senators Robert Ray and John Faulkner are also passionate about the game. As with John Howard, who attempts to fashion himself as 'an average Australian bloke' – an ironic stance given his extraordinary position of power – these male politicians' appreciation of the game involves both their personal and public lives and undoubtedly appeals to some voters.

Though the bipartisan interest in cricket is acknowledged, perception of the era in which the Protestant and Mason Bradman played arguably differs between the Liberal and Labor parties. Labor's origins engender a historical sympathy for the Irish-Catholic community, whereas the Liberal Party possesses a Protestant heritage. Conflict between the political ascendancy of Protestant groups and the chiefly Catholic working class of Irish background had unfolded in Australia almost since European settlement.[4] This conflict is mirrored in the administration of Australian cricket where Protestant and Mason administrators dominated the sport during Bradman's time (the national team was not captained by a Catholic between 1888 and 1949, the year after Bradman's retirement).[5] The Australian cricket community into the 1950s and 1960s is said to have been socially conservative and drawn to the 'the Liberal ethos of free enterprise and moral decency'.[6] Given the traditions of the Labor Party, and Bradman's own conservatism (see next section), it is little wonder that the Don and his era are not overly romanticised by the left. The Liberal Party and Howard are far more likely to idealise these years. It is argued that Howard's love of Bradman and cricket is of greater consequence than simple political popularity: Howard views the game as compatible with the conservative tradition and authority he is part of and supports.

Discussion of the 1930s and 1940s sectarian divide in politics, cricket and Australian society continues today, and the carpeting of four Catholic members of the Australian team in 1936–37 for failing to support Bradman's captaincy is regularly cited as evidence. Derriman, Haigh and Mallett have recently discussed the religious divisions within the cricket community.[7] After the Don's death, it was pointed out on ABC television's *Lateline* program that Bradman was a Mason who was part of a Protestant community.[8] In the case of Howard, Gerard Henderson, social commentator, Liberal Party historian and former Howard political adviser, describes John Howard's mother, Mona, as discouraging her sons from mixing with Catholics, and, at the time, she was far from alone in this attitude.[9] Despite such attitudes having dissipated, Howard once explained the support for an Australian republic by Nicole Feely, a former chief-of-staff, as being due to 'the Irish blood in you coming through', while Paul Keating's former advisers were described as 'Irish Labor bang-em-on-the-head types'.[10] There is no suggestion here that Howard is anti-Irish-Catholic, as his comments are more jocular than hurtful. The point is that similar sectarian-political viewpoints, experiences and traditions inform Bradman and Howard's biography.

Bradman and John Howard

Bradman quietly declined offers to join either side of Parliament. Yet despite the Don's lack of political statements, there is some conjunction between him and Howard. A commitment to conservative politics, Protestantism, the monarchy and business features in both men's lives. Bradman had 'strong, mostly conservative political opinions' and was 'conservative by nature in business, politics and cricket'.[11] For example, in the late 1940s Bradman admitted sympathy for the cause of the Liberal Country League in South Australia and, as a successful stockbroker and a member of the Adelaide Stock Exchange, he expressed a commitment to free enterprise, thus securing his place in the business establishment.[12] Bradman's patron and long-term friend during his childhood years in Bowral, mayor and alderman Alf Stephens, was a local conservative political leader for many decades. This patronage is in line with the historical development of Bowral as a whole, which is dominated by the influences of Protestantism, conservatism and a British traditionalism (see Chapter 3). Bradman's Protestant-Anglican experience also parallels Howard's Protestant-Methodist upbringing.

Howard would have enjoyed the Anglophile viewpoints in Bradman's autobiography.[13] The Don also briefly met another of Howard's heroes, Winston Churchill, on a train platform in 1934. Bradman's volunteering for the defence forces during World War II indicates his commitment to the preservation of Empire. This commitment would have impressed Howard whose father, Lyall, and grandfather, Walter, were both Empire loyalists and served in Europe during World War I. Pro-imperial values were held by the majority of the Australian cricket community, and probably helped to cement the friendship between Menzies and Bradman. Given this convergence in beliefs and values, Howard's idolisation of Bradman, a conservative who was a flag-bearer in Australia's summer sport, comes as little surprise.

John Howard is a 'self-confessed cricket devotee', or 'cricket tragic' as former Australian captain, Mark Taylor, famously called him. The roots of Howard's devotion to cricket lie in his childhood and his subsequent political and cultural worldview. In the 1950s, Howard lived in Earlwood, a lower middle-class, Anglo-Celtic suburb in Sydney. He played in the Canterbury Boys High School Second XI as an enthusiastic player of average ability.[14] During his youth, cricket exemplified Anglo-Australian imperial ideals and loyalty to the British Empire. Howard says he was very comfortable in that world, where he felt 'that everybody was about the same'.[15] Given this comment, it is also fair to say that a limited cultural and social experience insulated him from the social poverty, racial divisions, industrial disputes, and the sometimes bitter religious and Communist/anti-Communist divisions of the 1940s and 1950s.

Howard's nostalgia for the 1950s is linked with his faith in social conservative values and tradition. Australian social conservatism, particularly within the Liberal Party, emphasises tradition, continuity and a residual paternalism, combined with the notion that individual initiative produces social and economic advancement. These attitudes are encapsulated in values and beliefs such as individual responsibility, free enterprise, anti-collectivism, 'family' values and the monarchy. These values also help to explain Howard's ambivalence towards multiculturalism and Aboriginal rights, his opposition to republicanism and dislike of feminism:

> It's not that John Howard is intent on returning Australia to the 1950s. He knows that this would be impossible. It's just that Howard feels more comfortable with the Australia of the 1950s – and with its predominant views on monarchy, family life and the like – and the absence of public discussion on homosexuality, euthanasia, Aboriginal reconciliation or heroin trials. For John Howard is a genuine social conservative.[16]

The case put here is that Howard's hero-worship of Bradman and his public affection for men's cricket and its history runs deep, and was not just manufactured for political gain. The personal, social and political dimensions of his devotion to cricket are indivisible, and support a social conservative political vision underpinned by a sympathy for a British derived, pro-imperial Australian past. Cricket, its history and Bradman provide a connection between 'the chains of private meaning and association which links … [Howard's] … personal history and experience with the public political language, the points through which personal emotions and desires can flow through into the public ideological forms of the day'.[17]

Howard has appropriated the Don – 'he is the greatest living Australian' – not just because cricket is popularly regarded as

Australia's national sport, but also because cricket's history and many of Bradman's beliefs and values are reasonably consistent with Howard's social and cultural agenda. Moreover, Bradman is a powerful political symbol for the very reason that he appears to transcend politics. Howard can identify with him without the difficulty of having to deal with any formal acknowledgement of the Don's political loyalties.

A principal text linking Bradman and Howard is the inaugural Sir Donald Bradman Oration, staged by the Australian Cricket Board in August 2000. Both the electronic and print media widely publicised the oration. In a pedestrian speech, Howard repeated many of the dominant and worn interpretations of the Don: he had an unparalleled record, was an inspiration in difficult years, possessed a virtuous character and always accepted the umpire's decision. His abiding adoration of Bradman was on public display:

> ... a man representing many of the values, much of the character
> of his countrymen. Even now, in another century, in a world scarcely
> recognisable to that in which he played, the name Bradman resonates
> with meaning – talent, determination, commitment, fair play, honour.[18]

Howard finished his address by opining that if Sir Donald's example is used for inspiration, any dream can come true. This idealistic endorsement of Bradman confirms Howard's deeply felt personal affection. Howard also revealed his enthusiasm for reflection upon Australia's glorious past, as represented by Bradman; his reluctance to reflect on less flattering episodes, some of which he has dismissed as 'black-arm band' history, is well known.

Howard's oration is built upon figuring Bradman as a sporting exemplar and an Australian role model. On both counts, his analysis is superficial at best. His claim that the Don is a sporting exemplar is based upon a few random quotations and a reading of Bradman's coaching manual, *The Art of Cricket*. He believes Bradman's example as a captain and leader is his legacy, ignoring that Bradman's tenure as captain was not always a harmonious affair and that especially prior to World War II, he did not always have the respect of all those playing under him (see Chapter 7). As an Australian role model, or as Howard puts it, 'a man representing many of the values, much of the character of his countrymen', Bradman is an unusual choice: Bradman's extraordinary success unavoidably placed him above his fellow players and outside the egalitarian ethos and levelling tendencies at the centre of traditional conceptions of 'typical' Australian masculinity (also see Chapter 7). Perhaps it is more Bradman's background as a cricket playing, Protestant, socially conservative businessman and servant of Empire that attracts Howard. Given the close convergence in both men's values, Bradman is the type of man the Prime Minister *would like to think* represents *the* Australian character, despite evidence to the contrary and the multiplicity of ways to enact 'Australianness'.

In pursuing a popular image over the past few years, the Prime Minister has not restricted himself to following only cricket. He follows St George in rugby league, has been seen at the Davis Cup tennis and international rugby fixtures and was a self-appointed chief national 'cheerleader' during the 2000 Olympics. Such use of sport and the nationalist fervour it generates aims to create an image of the Prime Minister as an 'everyday Aussie bloke' for political gain. But Howard's enthusiasm for cricket is deeper than this: 'Nothing will shake my love of cricket. Nothing.'[19] This investment is as much about his preference for and preservation of a conservatively aligned way of life as it is about the spectacle and drama of athletic competition.

The Menzies tradition

To understand the place of cricket in Liberal social conservatism, an examination of Australia's longest serving Prime Minister, Robert Gordon Menzies (1939–41, 1949–66) is useful. Menzies is considered to be the Liberal Party's only hero.[20] He is credited with being a founder of the party in 1944 and enjoyed a reign as Prime Minister during the 1950s and 1960s that coincided with unparalleled economic prosperity and stability. Each year of Menzies' second period as national leader saw average weekly earnings rise by 4 per cent in real terms, while unemployment remained steady at between 1 and 3 per cent between 1950 and August 1965. Menzies stood for anti-Communism, business and individualism. His electoral popularity was built on appeal to and elevation of the middle-classes, those he named, in his famous 1943 address, 'the forgotten people', a catch-cry that corresponds to 'Howard's battlers', and 'aspirational' voters. In the 1950s, Howard's parents and the four brothers, a firmly Liberal, middle-class and small business family – 'frugal, hardworking and home-centred' – typified 'the forgotten people'.[21] Certainly, the satisfaction that his father Lyall took in Menzies' election victory over Ben Chifley's Labor government in 1949 had a lasting resonance for John Howard.[22]

Menzies' favourite recreation, some have said 'obsession', was watching and following cricket.[23] He wrote about the game (even in verse), was a trustee of the Melbourne Cricket Club and often addressed Test dinners. He was friends with many cricketers, with the stand-out among them being Bradman whom he regarded as the 'undisputed master batsman of my time' and as 'a highly intelligent man in anybody's language'.[24] Menzies also founded the annual Prime Minister's XI fixture. Cricket expressed his imperial outlook and was central to his devotion to British institutions; in the 1963 *Wisden Cricketers' Almanack* he wrote that, 'Great Britain and Australia are of the same blood and allegiance and history and instinctive mental processes' and also stated that cricket 'was a unifying factor' for the Australian populace.[25] Menzies also resolutely believed that sport and politics should be kept separate, though cricket for Menzies did have a political function, and he used it as a diplomatic tool in relations between Commonwealth nations.[26]

Menzies' friendship with Bradman is significant – the Don was the focus of whatever 'unifying' effect cricket might have had, first as a player, then as an administrator. Menzies even sounded Bradman out about being the Australian High Commissioner in London. At Menzies' request, the Don made his final playing appearance in the 1963 Prime Minister's XI match, a return to the cricket arena that one journalist compared to 'a reappearance of Michelangelo in the art world or Keats among the poets'.[27]

While there has been debate over whether John Howard is faithful to Menzies' brand of social liberalism, there is no doubt that he believes he is continuing his example. Donald Horne once described Menzies as a 'frozen Edwardian' and on occasion it has been possible to conceive of Howard as a 'frozen Menzian' in his social outlook. He has physically affirmed his idolisation of Menzies by having the former Prime Minister's desk moved into his office in Parliament House. Of the Menzies years, Howard states: 'I think of the Menzies period as a golden age in terms of people. Australia had a sense of family, social stability and optimism during that period.'[28] Howard's use of the past tense signals that he believes Australian society has, to some extent, lost these qualities. This unease may have been part of Howard's motivation for inviting the Australian people after his 1996 election victory to feel 'relaxed and comfortable'.

For Howard, cricket is another appealing part of the Menzies years. His lauding of the Don and his friendship with Mark Taylor follows Menzies' example. During Taylor's reign, Howard made the incredible statement: 'I really have regarded being captain of the Australian cricket team as the absolute pinnacle of sporting achievement, and really the pinnacle of human achievement almost, in Australia.'[29] Upon Taylor's retirement, Howard commented that he deserved to be thought of alongside Bradman as a great national captain and contributed the foreword to Taylor's autobiography.[30] Trips to England on political duties that coincided with the cricket were a feature of the Menzies' years – and Howard emulated him, visiting London in June 1997. With the second Ashes Test featuring on the official itinerary four out of the seven days, the visit was adversely received at home.[31] Unlike Menzies, Howard was attacked for giving the impression that he was indulging his love of cricket under the guise of looking after the nation's interest. While Howard may feel a keen affinity for his political hero's example, there is no guarantee that the media and public feel the same way.

The Empire and 'minority groups'

Resistance to an Australian republic has been a defining feature of John Howard's political career. During the 1987 federal election lead-up, he was introduced at a major policy address as the leader who 'believes in the values of Middle Australia – God, Queen and country'. In 2000, he declared that 'most Australians still regard our relationship with Britain as the most important'.[32] His monarchist beliefs were openly displayed during the campaign leading up to the unsuccessful 1999 Australian Republic referendum. While constitutional change was at issue during the referendum, so was the preservation of the social conservative tradition. The Menzies era was pro-monarchy. Bradman was unwilling to publicly declare an opinion on the prospect of a republic, but it is almost certain that he had sympathies with the monarchy. He thought meeting the royals a 'red letter day', and while attending the Silver Jubilee of 1948 in London felt his 'heart swell with pride' at the singing of 'God Save the King'.[33] A year after his retirement and with much publicity, Bradman proudly but modestly accepted a knighthood, which among other things he considered to be a royal tribute to cricket and its role in Empire.[34]

Throughout the Bradman and Menzies years, mostly Protestant white men ran cricket. The sport exemplified pro-imperial deference with its popularity firmly rooted in Commonwealth nations, where it remains. Loyalty to imperialist institutions and traditions in Australia was maintained through various mechanisms, not least the White Australia Policy. This legislation, designed to maintain Anglo-Celtic uniformity, was partnered by Menzies' belief in the right of British imperial rule over 'lesser' races,[35] and the treatment of Australian Aborigines in cricket was in line with such attitudes. The man Bradman deems to have delivered the fastest bowling stint he ever faced, Queensland Aborigine Eddie Gilbert (who played from 1930 to 1936 achieving a bowling average of 18.22 runs per wicket), had to sleep in a tent in the State Cricket Association secretary's backyard during the season. By instruction of the Protector of Aboriginals, he would then return to Cherbourg Aboriginal Settlement at Barambah.[36] Sadly, in 1948 Gilbert was admitted to Goodna Mental Asylum. He suffered from congenital syphilis and died thirty years later out of the sight and regard of the cricket community. The discrimination experienced by Gilbert and other Aboriginal players is symptomatic of the sense of white supremacy upon which the British Empire was built.[37] Into the 1950s, Haigh points out the continuing contradiction in Australian race relations during the West Indian cricket tour of 1951–52:

> Despite the results, it was not an unhappy tour, and the West Indies were well liked. Australians might have barely acknowledged their

own black population, denied them the vote and broken up their
families, but they saw nothing incongruous about applauding a
coloured cricket team.[38]

A decade later, the attitudes within the cricket establishment
and among the game's followers had not changed. With the White
Australia Policy still firmly in place, around half-a-million people in
Melbourne warmly farewelled the 1960–61 touring West Indian
team led by Frank Worrell, but there is little evidence that administrators, including Bradman, displayed much interest in increasing Aboriginal involvement in cricket. Despite this earlier lack of
interest, an attempt to start balancing the ledger was made immediately after Bradman's death, with a special 'Bradman Memorial
Fund' set up to encourage participation in cricket among dis-
advantaged groups including indigenous communities.

Both Bradman and Menzies thought cricket an almost peer-
less medium for generating goodwill between nations.[39] However,
its role in fostering understanding between different sections of
Australian society is less than outstanding. Despite comprising the
first Australian touring side to England in 1868 and being reasonably well represented in Australia's football codes, indigenous
Australians have rarely featured in cricket. Of the 7,076 Australian
male cricketers listed in first-class records between 1850 and 1987,
only ten are Aboriginal.[40] One man, Jason Gillespie, and only one
woman, Faith Thomas, have ever been selected for Australia. Few
Aborigines are found in cricket crowds at major grounds. ACB
Chairman, Denis Rogers, admits to being troubled by his sport's
lack of Aboriginal representation; the previous failure of ACB
officials to reach out to indigenous sportspeople prompted the
formation of an Aboriginal Cricket Working Party in 2001 to
develop the game in indigenous communities. A similar lack of

Bradman endorsed various types of playing equipment in the course of his career. He is pictured here with a 'Don Bradman' Sykes brand bat in 1932.
(Hood Collection, State Library of New South Wales)

A 2001 Christie's memorabilia auction. Auctioned items included Bradman letters and a cricket bat used during the bodyline series of 1932–3. (News Limited)

A newspaper cartoon suggesting that those seeking to cash in on the Bradman name are going to almost absurd lengths. (Warren Brown and the Daily Telegraph)

Australian Prime Minister John Howard leads the singing of 'Happy Birthday' to Sir Donald Bradman for his 90th on Channel Nine's The Midday Show *with Kerri-Anne Kennerly in 1998.* (News Limited)

John Howard openly acknowledges his personal and political admiration for former Liberal Prime Minister, Sir Robert Menzies. (News Limited)

Menzies looks on approvingly as Bradman breasts the tape in a foot race. The occasion is a track and field meeting in 1940 that took place while Bradman was enlisted in the Army. (La Trobe Picture Collection, State Library of Victoria)

A poppy seller smiles as she pins a poppy on Bradman in the late 1920s or early 1930s. (Hood Collection, State Library of New South Wales)

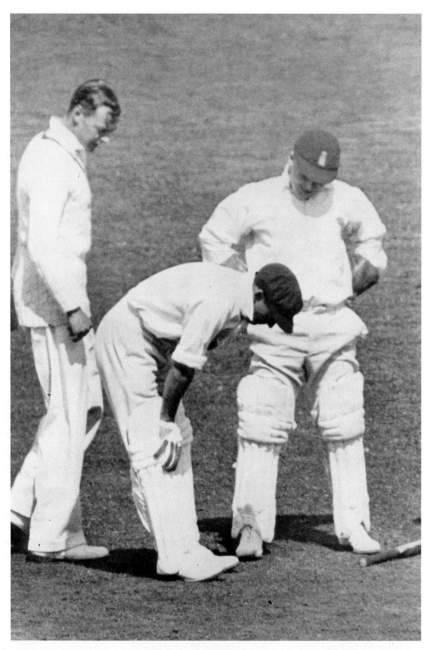

Bradman tries to recover after being hit by fast bowler Harold Larwood at the Oval in 1930. As Chapter 7 outlines, this is the match that Bradman referred to when testifying to his physical fortitude and denying claims that he was frightened of bodyline tactics. (Photograph courtesy of the State Library of South Australia)

The 1932 wedding of Don Bradman and Jessie Menzies at St Paul's church in Burwood, Sydney. (Hood Collection, State Library of New South Wales)

An unfamiliar sight. The provocative headlines advertising the feature articles written by David Nason that appeared in The Australian *newspaper on consecutive days during November 2001. (*The Australian*, 16 Nov. 2001;* The Weekend Australian *17 Nov. 2001)*

representation is found with Australians from non-English speaking backgrounds (NESB). Roebuck reminds us:

> Cricket is still struggling to reach beyond its confines ... still the game is mainly Anglo-Saxon. For a long time this has been the game's main limitation. Apart from a few dubiously treated Aboriginals in decades past, and some sons from families of European origin, cricket has been unable to convince new communities that it is a game worth playing.[41]

Additionally, despite having played Test matches since 1934–35, women have endured constant media and public prejudice against their participation.[42]

A lack of appeal to so-called 'minority groups' such as Aborigines, Australians from NESBs and women may prove a problem for cricket as the nation's cultural composition continues to shift. Proportionally, Australia has more migrants than any other nation in the world except Israel.[43] While in 1945, 90 per cent of the population was Australia-born and English speaking, by 1994 40 per cent of the population were immigrants or children of immigrants, half of whom were of non-British origins.[44] Cricket and its heroes such as Bradman may be marginalised if it remains a sport played almost exclusively by Anglo-Celtic males. 'Everybody appears about the same' in cricket by the very lack of indigenous players, Australians from NESBs and women. But there may be signs of change: a small group of media commentators noted that Bradman's passing marked the closure of a white, male-dominated, mono-cultural era in cricket that poorly reflects the heterogeneous character of contemporary Australian society.[45]

The Don is a symbol that can be used and/or manipulated in order to invoke an imagined common Australian culture as he *appears* to represent a unified national identity, with his apolitical character central to the implication that he is a hero for 'all of us'. Unfortunately, neither Bradman's representation nor national identity exists outside of or prior to culture and politics; rather they are the very inventions and products of history, culture and politics.[46] In other words, any symbolic national unity that Bradman is seen to produce can only ever be partial, incomplete and contested. Does Howard recognise these limitations of Bradman and cricket in representing the nation? It is arguable that the Anglo-Celtic complexion of Australian men's cricket and its history captures what Henderson terms is Howard's 'denial of difference', his desire for cultural homogeneity, for 'one nation' as Howard himself terms it.[47]

South Africa

Cricket's status as a mainly white cultural practice in selected nations is best captured by the case of South Africa and its former apartheid regime. This example intensifies focus on the social conservatism of Bradman and Menzies and their conviction that sport should be an apolitical activity. It also shows that while Howard disapproved of apartheid, he once subscribed to his heroes' view on sport and also was against trade sanctions being imposed on South Africa.

In his 1970 book, *The Measure of the Years*, Menzies vehemently argued for the separation of sport and politics and, on this basis, maintained that sporting competition with South Africa should continue. For his stand, Menzies has been seen as both a 'man of his times' and 'not a man of, but terribly behind the times'.[48] From a contemporary perspective, in dogmatically defending the principle of national sovereignty and in spite of his belief that apartheid would fail in the long term, he appears to defend South Africa's former political system as a legitimate form of government. He believed apartheid to be a 'rude word' that simply means 'separate development'. We are told that Dr Vorster, the former South African president, is no racist – this being the president who oversaw apartheid's imposition and declared that his country's cricket relations with the world were to be white relations. Menzies derided anti-apartheid protestors who concentrated on '*sporting* activities' (original italics) and claimed that they 'discriminate in favour of the Communists', and that protests served to strengthen white South African attitudes. In line with his defence of Australian contact with South Africa, Menzies threatened to pull Australia out of the Commonwealth if any of the coloured nations attempted to engage his government over the White Australia Policy.[49]

The break in sporting contact with South Africa that Menzies feared occurred in September 1971, when the proposed 1971–72 season cricket tour of Australia by the Springboks was cancelled. The central character in this decision was the chairman of the Australian Board of Control, Sir Donald Bradman. Like Menzies, Bradman had difficulty in seeing that politics are not restricted to formal party and parliamentary affairs, and he maintained his belief that sport and politics should be isolated from one another. The tour's cancellation came in the wake of the United Kingdom Cricket Council withdrawing its invitation for South Africa to tour England in 1970 and an occasionally violent and controversial 1971 South African rugby tour of Australia. The white South African Cricket Association (SACA) had invited the South African Cricket Board of Control, an alliance between Africans, Coloureds and Indians, to nominate two players for the Australian tour. The South African government vetoed any such selection, leading Bradman to claim that they had politicised sport. Cabinet Papers from 1971 reveal that, in making his decision, Bradman had sought formal advice from the federal government, led by Billy McMahon. McMahon sent a message to the South African ambassador expressing concern and disappointment at the South African government's action, but he also advised Australian organisers that he had no objections to the tour going ahead. Despite McMahon's stance, Bradman announced the tour's abandonment. In a lengthy prepared statement, he said:

> Our board has not introduced politics into sport. I don't think it can be denied that the South African Government has ... While there was substantial evidence that very many Australians felt the tour should go on, the board was equally made aware of the widespread disapproval of the South African Government's racial policy which restricted selection of South Africa's team ... There could be no doubt the tour would set up internal bitterness between rival groups and demonstrations on a large scale would be inevitable.
>
> The police would be called upon to provide massive and prolonged protection at matches and elsewhere ... The Board wishes to commend the South African Cricket Association and its players for their courageous stand against their Government's apartheid policy in cricket.
>
> It earnestly hopes that the South African Government will in the near future so relax its laws that the cricketers of South Africa may once again take their place as full participants in the international field ...[50]

As the editorial in the *Sydney Morning Herald* on 9 September 1971 emphasised, the tour was cancelled for practical reasons, not political or moral ones. The cancellation was not read as a sign that Bradman and the board concurred with the anti-apartheid protestors, 'a small but ruthless minority' as the *Herald* labelled them, although it should be noted that Bradman had corresponded with organisers of the Anti-Apartheid Movement before making his decision.[51] The consequences of the decision were felt immediately as it left South African cricket internationally isolated, and later led to rebel tours of the Republic.

Bradman's sporting and racial idealism is open to challenge. It is impossible to cordon off sport from politics, whether under the apartheid regime or at any other time.[52] To claim, as Bradman and the board did, that the South African government had politicised sport in 1971 is to distort history. Between 1888 and 1970, South Africa played 172 Test matches, all of them against only three white nations – Australia, England and New Zealand – as South Africa had declined to establish cricket relations with the West Indies, Pakistan and India.[53] After being expelled from the Imperial Cricket Conference in 1960 on becoming a Republic, South Africa had continued to play against only Australia and England. Disputes in relation to apartheid also occurred within the wider international sporting community. In 1970, the Republic had been expelled from the International Olympic movement, although a poll revealed that 68 per cent of white nations supported South Africa's participation.[54] These interplays between sport and politics make it difficult to understand how Bradman or anyone else could claim that South African cricket or sport generally had enjoyed immunity from politics prior to 1971.

Another issue arises out of Bradman's statement regarding the 'courageous' anti-apartheid stand SACA was said to be taking. The 1971–72 tour impasse was certainly the first time that the Republic's white cricket community had decided that merit should be the sole criterion for selection of the national team.[55] While this move was significant, the idea that SACA was anti-apartheid is debatable. SACA may have had no race bar in its constitution, but since the end of the nineteenth century it had practised a segregationist policy. Even by the 1980s, SACA was not one of the sport organisations at the forefront of reformist multiracial sport and did not condemn apartheid. SACA's 1971 stand had more to do with the white community wanting to maintain international contact than with humanitarian issues and racial justice for the majority of the Republic's population. As Booth points out, the black population still endured wholesale unemployment, substandard living conditions and housing shortages, deficient health services and poor education.[56] Possibly due to a lack of exposure to such circumstances, Bradman's visit to South Africa in 1974 had little impact on his views. The Don's audience with President Vorster was devoted solely to trying to sort out the cricket dispute.[57]

In 1975, Howard's position on sport and politics was in line with that of Bradman and Menzies when he spoke in federal Parliament of his disappointment at the then Labor government stopping a South African cricket tour. By 1988, and as demanded by the rest of the Commonwealth, Howard had changed tack in declaring Liberal Party support for the Commonwealth Heads of Government 'Gleneagles Agreement' (signed in 1977 by the Malcolm Fraser-led Liberal government), which deterred sporting contact between Commonwealth nations and the Republic. Howard had shifted position on sporting boycotts, but he never relinquished his belief that economic sanctions against South Africa were unjustified; he opposed sanctions on the grounds that they were 'at least as likely to strengthen the hand of the present South African Government as it is to weaken it'.[58] In 1999, however, on a visit to South Africa, Howard acknowledged that trade sanctions against South Africa 'probably' had an effect in its dismantling.[59]

Howard mimicked Menzies on trade, but not on sport policy. Such selectivity was necessary – to disapprove of the Gleneagles Agreement would have been to go against international opinion and could have made the Liberal Party irrelevant in regards to the South African issue. Despite this, and in a vein similar to both Bradman and Menzies, Howard failed to acknowledge that formal trade links with the Republic under apartheid granted legitimacy to an anti-democratic and racist system of government. As one-time Labor Minister for Foreign Affairs, Bill Hayden, pointed out in 1984, the Republic's government had greeted Liberal policy on South Africa as 'a welcome development'.[60] Neither sport nor economics can be separated from politics: sporting boycotts did work, and by Howard's admission, economic sanctions probably had an effect.

Conclusion

The Australian social conservative tradition encourages the idea of distinct areas of social activity. For example, the actions of Bradman, Menzies and Howard indicate that sport and politics (and trade) should be kept separate from one another. This is a difficult position to sustain. As with any social institution, sport and its heroes are political entities whether they choose to be or not. Bradman and the images associated with him contain political meanings that are mainly socially conservative. He played a sport that is an almost exclusively male game and that connotes values that evoke an Australian past in which a mono-cultural masculine privilege and Empire held sway. As Australia's most celebrated cricketer, Bradman cannot be separated from this history and its associated values.

It will be fascinating to see what the long-term effect of John Howard's championing of the Don will be. By Howard's association, he has revealed that the Don is not an apolitical icon, but is rather a figure with distinct political meanings. The question that will be answered over the next ten years is whether Bradman can continue to appear to transcend politics, or whether Howard has devalued Bradman's heroism by marking him as a standard-bearer of social conservatism. My feeling is that some political partisanship has been introduced into the Don's image, but that once Howard departs from the political stage, the all-embracing apolitical appearance that has long sustained the Bradman myth will again hold sway. This image will persist as it best satisfies the interests and desires of the Bradman industry, the Foundation and the Museum, the media, publishers, and the many Australian people who wish to read about triumphant – not politically partisan – Australian heroes.

CHAPTER 7

NEVER QUITE TYPICAL

For the great irony of his beatification is that he was never, as one might imagine, an acme of Australian-ness ... Where the archetypal Australian male is hearty and sanguine, priding himself on good fellowship, hospitality and ability to hold his alcohol, Bradman was private, reserved, fragile of physique and teetotal. Where the traditional Australian work ethic has been to do just enough to get by, Bradman was a virtuoso who set his own standards and allowed nothing to impede their attainment.[1]

Bradman certainly didn't fit the Keith Miller 'Jack the Lad' image – and didn't even smoke, or drink or gamble, or play up – like so many of his Aussie team mates ...[2]

There are tensions between the received view of 'typical' Australian masculinity and Don Bradman's behaviour. In line with Australian national mythologies, a sporting hero is most likely a white male who is independent, courageous, hardy, bold, good humoured and who possesses a strong sense of mateship, especially given that within these mythologies it is men who represent the 'national type'. As with most forms of exemplary masculinity, however, the distance between the ideal representation and the lived experience is most likely unbridgeable.[3] In the case of Bradman, the opening quotations indicate that although he is an Australian hero, he is far from the mythical universal Australian man.

Quintessential Australianness invokes images of the tough and masculine white bushman, soldier and sportsman, and Bradman's story encompasses all three. These images capture the gendered foundations of nationalism and leave no doubt that the Australian character is masculine. Once again, Russel Ward's *The Australian Legend* is a principal source in the propagation of this gendered nationalism. Ward's influential reading of the Australian past is conservatively aligned and features stories of the white community's struggle and achievement. The legend is masculinist, mono-cultural and largely positive, and Bradman is implicated in these reductive and narrow configurations of gender, cultural and historical identity.

Bradman's biography neither neatly fits nor lives up to the valorised standards of mateship and physicality usually associated with 'typical' Australian masculinity. As a sporting hero, he might be seen as typical, but he neither drank, smoked nor gambled, was not generally a 'mate' with those he played alongside and did not have a hardy physical constitution – in short, 'The man usually hailed as representative is never quite typical'.[4] Those who situate the Don as an 'acme of Australian-ness' choose to overemphasise and embellish selected dimensions of his behaviour and/or to underemphasise and omit others, and I intend to outline some of these. Then I explain how the construction of Bradman's popular image and masculinity intersects with the revered position of the Australian legend in the national consciousness. This argument is set out by investigating key issues in the Don's story, and concludes by showing how his story fits generally into the wider context of Australian masculinities.

This chapter searches for gaps and tensions in Bradman's heroism. In reading against the grain of Bradman's iconography it is the issue of gender that is of particular significance, not only because of the gendered foundations of history and culture, but because Bradman's sanctification has taken place in and through a privileged and masculinist sphere of Australian culture, sport.

The Australian masculine ethos

This chapter returns to many of the nationalist discourses discussed in Chapter 3. As well as linking the national character with rural life in Australian popular culture, Ward's Australian legend has helped to define a detailed, distinctive and enduring Australian masculine ethos. This ethos was developed from Ward's laudatory interpretation of the nineteenth-century bushman, and in particular the cheeky, resourceful larrikin who became the basis for a mythic 'national type'.[5] Ward's familiar description states that:

the 'typical Australian' is a practical man, rough and ready in his manners and quick to decry any appearance of affectation in others. He is a great improviser, ever willing 'to have a go' at anything, but willing too to be content with a task done in a way that is 'near enough'. Though capable of great exertion in an emergency, he normally feels no impulse to work hard without a good cause. He swears hard and consistently, gambles heavily and often, and drinks deeply on occasion. Though he is 'the world's best confidence man', he is usually taciturn rather than talkative, one who endures stoically rather than one who acts busily. He is a 'hard case', sceptical about the value of religion and of intellectual and cultural pursuits generally. He believes that Jack is not only as good as his master but, at least in principle, probably a good deal better, and so he is a great 'knocker' of eminent people unless, as in the case of his sporting heroes, they

are distinguished by their physical prowess. He is a fiercely
independent person who hates officiousness and authority, especially
when these qualities are embodied in military officers and policemen.
Yet he is very hospitable and, above all, will stick to his mates through
thick and thin, even if he thinks they may be in the wrong ...[6]

Despite possessing qualities such as loyalty and practicality,
Ward's model of masculinity is, for the most part, limited, though
this has not stopped the Australian legend from featuring in advertisements, television, music, film, politics and literature. As the
2001 release of the third film in Paul Hogan's *Crocodile Dundee*
series demonstrates, the hardy, laconic, no-nonsense Aussie male is
alive within the nation's imagination. Despite being dismissed by
critics as predictable and outdated, the film topped the Australian
box office on its opening weekend, taking over $2 million.

The argument can be made that in using 'typical' Australian
masculinity in analysis of the Don, the diversity that exists among
Australian men is ignored. For example, Connell's excellent life-
history essay on an elite level iron man highlights the contradictions
between the exalted masculinity that this man is seen as representing and the thoughts, feelings and experiences that he actually
has.[7] Yet the Australian legend is not drawn upon by advertisers,
television writers, politicians, etc., because most men 'live it' or did
so in the past. The legend is dominant because it is accepted by
many – consciously or subconsciously – as an identifiable
construction of Australian nationalism. The legend's masculinity
is part of the:

repertoire of representational codes, the discourses through which
Australians currently agree to represent themselves and their country.
Its importance is not finally as a reflection, or as a refraction, of the
past, but as a construction of the present ...[8]

The currency of the Australian legend is apparent in many of the dominant political themes presented throughout this book. Ward's imagined 'Australian man' appeals to a victorious and heroic national character. Through him, the Australian people are figured as struggling against the harsh realities of the frontier, winning through despite enormous odds. He seems to exist prior to and outside racial, ethnic and gender politics, helping to deny the legitimacy of such matters. As a result, there *appears* little possibility that the Australian people are anything but wholly unified and ready to stand as one. The legend also obscures that national identity, and, by default, gender is socially and historically constructed, contested, and mutable. In sum, Ward's model of masculinity is nostalgia writ large across the popular culture of the nation. Nostalgia is also the source of the legend's power – many men and woman immediately recognise the image and that provokes an assured emotional response.

In order to understand the gendered foundations of Australian popular culture, it is necessary to engage with the legend and with the notion of a 'typical' bloke that it inspires. The very point of such representations is to reify masculinity, to set up a 'natural' ideal, and to construct an identity that many people can accept even if they have never lived or experienced it.

Mate or individualist?

According to the Australian legend, a prominent trait among men is group loyalty. A good deal of Australian history has enshrined mateship as the core of national identity. An egalitarian, anti-elitist collectivism permeates the cult of mateship that sees the individual defer to the interests of the group. A similar rationale informs team sport whereby a member's interests are meant to give way to those of the team (e.g. 'there is no I in team'). For Bradman, this code posed an inescapable problem due to his batting dominance.

Because of his ability, the value of his contributions often out-weighed the rest of the side. Alan Kippax, former Test teammate of the Don and former New South Wales captain, asserts:

> If Don played for the West Indies they would be the leading cricketing country. If he played for New Zealand they would be the leading cricketing country. If he played for England they would be the leading cricketing country. If he played for South Africa they would be the leading cricket country.[9]

Bradman's supremacy was a source of consternation for some teammates who felt that, on occasion, recognition of their efforts was overwhelmed by adulation for the Don. In defence of his popularity, Bradman pointed out that it is no one's fault that the public 'pay homage to the individuals' in cricket.[10] Nevertheless, Victor Richardson expressed dismay that the performance of spin bowler Clarrie Grimmett on the 1930 Ashes tour was ignored as Bradman was feted above all others: 'We could have played any team without Don Bradman, but we could not play the blind school without Clarrie Grimmett.'[11] Compounding such opinions was a perception that in 1932–33 Bradman put his own interests ahead of the team, and did not follow the orders of his captain, Woodfull.[12] Bradman's determination to achieve huge scores ran counter to the levelling tendencies of the collective. His lack of compatibility with the purported Australian desire for equality followed him even after death:

> A curious aspect of the flurry of [media] supplements honouring Bradman was that in a nominally egalitarian society most of the supplicants tried to outdo each other in elevating the great man way above his team-mates. Arthur Morris was at the other end when Bradman made his final duck, sitting on a small matter of 196 runs,

and he was lost in the rush to puffment, both in 1948 and especially now. 'Not since Shakespeare,' wrote Peter Roebuck, 'has anyone been so far ahead of his colleagues.' Bernard Shaw protested about the 'Bardolatory' of Shakespeare, but that had nothing on the Bradolatory that followed the fading of the Don. In the land of Supplementaria, it seems, there is a god rather than a king.[13]

In becoming a hero, Bradman rose so far above the 'common ruck' that he challenged the very validity of egalitarianism.

Sticking with your mates is the basis upon which the Australian legend is built. The individualism of Bradman as a cricketer was exacerbated by his individuality off the field. He was not a mate – he lacked 'hearty masculine sociability' and tended not to make close friendships with other players.[14] He could seem 'blunt, inflexible and unfeeling' in the pursuit of his goals.[15] Saunders has suggested that Bradman was closer to an upright and staid gentleman than to a 'typical' Aussie sportsman.[16] One of the Don's teammates and most severe critics, Bill O'Reilly, said,

> He was a chap who found it terribly hard to mix in with the hoi polloi.
> He was never a fully fledged member of the team socially. He WAS
> the team as a player on the field, but off the field he disappeared, you
> hardly ever saw him … I would say up until he went to England in
> 1948 … Bradman had never made the slightest effort to be a real,
> hundred per cent team man … [he] wasn't a man's man in any shape or
> form, never was.[17]

Described variously as a loner, shy, and with an aversion to parties, Bradman resented those who questioned his behaviour:

> There were those who thought I was unsociable because at the end
> of the day I did not think it my duty to breast the bar and engage in

a beer-drinking contest. At least I made no attempt to interfere with the habits of others, and if I thought my most important need was a meal and a cup of tea, I had as much right to complain of their late entry into the dining-room as they had to complain of my absence from the bar.[18]

Abstaining from alcohol of course saw him missing 'shouts' at the bar with teammates. Nor did he appear to smoke, gamble or swear. In contrast, teammate Keith Miller was 'Australian in excelsis', with his love of a beer and a bet.[19] Bradman's lack of participation in pursuits such as beer drinking is said to have created an atmosphere of solemnity:

> There are humorously affectionate stories about most great cricketers, intimate, if somewhat apocryphal stories about them; of what
> Dr Grace said when Ernest Jones bowled a ball through his beard …
> of what Johnny Douglas uttered when second slip floored a catch. But there are no funny stories about the Don. No one ever laughed about Bradman. He was no laughing matter.[20]

If good-natured, irreverent and self-deprecating banter is the bedrock upon which the cult of mateship is erected, Bradman is the legend's 'other'.

The Don's masculinity has often been retrieved by biographers and journalists through examples of his competitiveness and 'hardness' on the field. The opening match of the first Test series against England in 1946–47 is sometimes used to highlight Bradman's steely resolve. According to the English side and their captain Wally Hammond, Bradman, when on 28 runs, was caught at second slip by Jack Ikin off the bowling of Voce. Bradman, however, stood his ground and was given not out by the umpire much to the astonishment of the fielders and the bowler. Bradman went to score another 159 runs. Hammond is said to have been furious at Bradman's refusal to walk; Bradman consistently maintained that he would have walked if he believed he was out.

Another great Australian, World War II hero, surgeon and sportsman, Weary Dunlop (1907–93), was, like the Don, from the 'old Protestant, imperialist, masculine Australia' and was never regarded as a 'typical' Australian male:

> ... Weary was emphatically not a 'mate'. He stood too tall to be considered an exemplar of an egalitarian virtue ... His heroism lay more in the capacity to inspire the practice of mateship among 'his' men than in his own identity as a mate. He expressed his admiration of the mateship demonstrated by others, but implicitly placed himself outside (or above?) the circle of mates.[21]

Both Dunlop and Bradman, despite their esteemed standing, set themselves apart from other men. This trait suggests that the relationship between Australian masculinity, leadership and heroism has a contradiction at its heart, as the man thought to be representative is never quite typical.

In fairness to Bradman, while he may never have been a 'mate', he was regarded differently by team members after the war. According to Mallett, as a youngster in the Australian team of the early 1930s, Bradman had a tendency to lecture his fellow players on the excesses of drinking and smoking.[22] Senior members of the national team did not take well to such admonishments – for example, Kippax, a graceful batsman and senior player, is said to have been 'no great fan of the younger star'.[23] The troubles of the 1936–37 season, when four teammates were called before the Board of Control for failing to support Bradman's captaincy, are further evidence of conflict. When combined with his self-deprecation and humour, Bradman was not only at odds with teammates but also with the popular conception of masculinity at the time.

After the war there was a distinct change in personal regard for Bradman. By the 1948 Ashes tour, with a side made up of younger men, the Don was far more at ease as a leader and possessed a more welcoming demeanour. Robinson, for example, reports that Bradman made life comfortable for new members of the side by having a quiet chat with them. Bradman's new approach was informed by perceived resentment towards him prior to the war:

> You've probably heard rumours about my relations with other players. I've been criticized a lot, but when I was a young boy from the country in a team of world-famous players they wouldn't speak to me. They seemed to resent me.[24]

As shown by the various dedications, particularly after his death, from Bradman's post-war underlings such as Sam Loxton, Neil Harvey, Bill Johnston and Arthur Morris, he is remembered warmly by some.[25] Loxton is most effusive when he says, 'We loved him because he was a great bloke'; yet it must also be conceded that this is an unusual comment coming from one of Bradman's former teammates.

Despite a warmer image as Australian captain at the end of his career, Bradman's reputation remained that of a taciturn disciplinarian demanding 'great exertion' from those under him.[26] Lindsay Hassett, the Australian captain appointed after the Don's retirement, was known for his liberal leadership and renowned humour. Some of the ex-servicemen on the 1950 tour of South Africa, such as Ken Archer, twelfth man in all the Tests, appreciated the 'life is for living and cricket is for fun' attitude that prevailed, which was a marked change from the Bradman regime.[27] In Bradman's eyes, a 'she'll be right' attitude was inappropriate as cricket was a serious business where winning was the only objective. On the field, 'near enough' for him and any team he led meant domination and victory – the undefeated record of the 1948 Ashes team served as testament to this attitude.

Overall, Bradman's status as the 'other' to the Australian legend is consistent with his background as an Anglican Mason who was descended from a respected free settler (his grandfather, Charles Bradman). Bradman's Protestantism is out of step with Ward's thesis that a mix of Irish Catholic, convict and working-class heritages helps to define the Australian character. Avoidance of alcohol and gambling and a well-defined work ethic are traits consistent with a strict Protestant upbringing. For the Don, hard work, discipline and frugality appear to have eliminated traces of moral waywardness, excess and laziness. In terms of morality, the Don appears to have identified with a Christian ethos.[28] His rejection of betting and so on was not in accord with the attitudes of some teammates, such as O'Reilly and Fingleton who might be described as Catholic larrikins and for whom drinking and gambling were entirely acceptable. This difference in values was no doubt the source of some unspoken (and spoken) resentment throughout the Don's career, especially when on tour.

Bradman's Protestant-derived work ethic is on display in his coaching manual, *The Art of Cricket*, with its many references to hard work and constant practice. His thrift resulted in complaints from fellow cricketers, especially given his resourcefulness in financial accumulation: 'He is the best batsman in the world ... but that is where he finishes. He did not spend twopence during the [1930] tour.'[29] Bradman knew his worth as a man and was determined to capitalise on it. As a reader of good literature and an accomplished public speaker, the Don is also unlike the legend's 'hard case' as he was not sceptical towards intellectual and cultural pursuits. In forming an overall picture of Bradman's habits, it is his individualism and taciturn self-expression that matches the Australian legend. In other ways, however, he is far from the mythical universal Australian man.

Sex appeal and 'knocking' authority

Accepting that Bradman does not fit the description of the 'typical' Australian male, how is it then that he can be credibly presented as a '100 per cent Australian icon'?[30] While Bradman's behaviour resisted the 'beer and a bet' description, at another level his image accommodates selected populist dimensions of Australian masculinity.

The Don's popularity among female spectators assisted in creating a nationalist response. As the prelude to Ray Martin's interview with Bradman stated, the Australian people of the time 'packed up their troubles and they went out to watch the cricket, especially the ladies', with an accompanying image of seven female spectators and a rather grave-looking man standing among them.[31] Perry writes that one cause of envy among the Don's teammates was that young women sent notes to him, while other writers have cited reports of women fighting and struggling to kiss or touch him.[32] There are reports of females who cared nothing for cricket attending matches just to watch Bradman. His popularity with English women was rumoured to be even greater than at home: 'When he came in there was a rush, especially of women, to pat him on the back. Although women are great cricket fans in Australia, I have never seen so many at a cricket match in England.'[33]

Estimates of the proportion of women spectators in 1930s Australian cricket crowds run at 30 to 40 per cent. However, it was not only Bradman's presence that led to increased attendance by women. The World War I effort had helped to loosen attitudes about 'appropriate' women's leisure practices, affordable gate charges prevailed, and, with alternatives limited, cricket was a favoured leisure activity.[34] Many women may simply have liked following cricket, a possibility that most writers fail to contemplate. Nonetheless, Bradman's drawing power is historically unparalleled and his 'sex appeal' to women contributed to this power.[35]

Bradman may have appealed to many women (and probably some men) because he adhered to the minimum cultural benchmarks of masculinity without embodying a threatening hypermasculine persona. For example, he was carefully and quietly spoken in public. Physically, he was not a large man, only 5' 6" (154.5 cm), but many regarded him to be handsome with sparkling eyes. Though short, he appeared very athletic, especially in his younger years, as his commanding batting and his agility and speed in the field indicate. He was not a physically imposing and expressive cricketer like Keith Miller 'who followed a bouncer with a smiling toss of his black mane'.[36] Bradman's comparative containment physically, emotionally and verbally is perhaps the key to his attractiveness. He was *not* intimidating, *not* macho, *not* overtly physically or verbally aggressive, yet was still sporty, successful and hence powerful.[37] He was a 'real' man without being a potentially dangerous one.

While Australian men are said to highly regard their mates and often enjoy each other's companionship over that of women, these relations are prescribed as heterosexual.[38] Suggestion of homosexual attraction and relations are often thought unacceptable, and where they have existed, they have often been explained away as being due to a lack of (white) women.[39] Bradman may not have generally been a mate among those with whom he played, but his appeal to large groups of women allows him to be presented as glorifying a hegemonic form of Australian masculinity – heterosexual, white, able bodied and sporting.

Another characteristic of the 'typical Australian' is hatred of officiousness and authority, and Bradman's confrontations with cricketing authorities have been used to show how he exemplified this attitude. The *Bodyline* television mini-series showed a heroic Bradman taking on an apparently unsympathetic and unfair Australian Board of Control. The Don has staunch defenders in biographers Page, Moyes and Perry who talk of Bradman's search for justice as he confronted administrative bulwarks, and who also hint at the resolute individualist ethos motivating the Don's actions. During his playing days, Bradman had three main disputes with the board. The first occurred in 1930 over a breach of contract after articles he had authored appeared in the London *Star* newspaper while he was still under contract to the board during the Ashes tour of England. The second came in 1932 as Bradman sought to honour a contract to write for the Sydney *Sun* newspaper against the board's wishes. The third was over the board's refusal to allow wives, at their own expense, to accompany players at the conclusion of the 1938 Ashes tour. The 1932 and 1938 quarrels resulted in threats of Bradman's cricket career in Australia being finished.

The paradox in using Bradman as a symbol of independence fighting an out-of-touch cricket establishment is that after retiring from playing he joined the establishment. Bradman's positioning within the cricketing hierarchy was established in his formative years – at 17, he was appointed honorary secretary of the Bowral cricket club. His administration career, which saw him ascend to the leadership of the board that he once so spiritedly defied, is characterised by a conservatism that usually saw him attempting to protect the Australian Cricket Board's power on issues of player rights and professionalism. For example, Bradman displayed particular obstinacy in the face of player wage demands during the World Series Cricket dispute of the 1970s.[40] Also, his position on South Africa and apartheid was hardly anti-establishment. In these cases, Bradman's attitude appeared as inflexible as those of the 'fuddy duddy' administrators it is claimed he faced as a player.[41] In understanding Bradman's relationship to authority, these examples serve mutually exclusive ends: he is used to embody a defiant Aussie spirit fighting officiousness and authority, at the same time as he personifies that very same authority's respectability and power. Thus, whether Bradman is viewed as 'knocking' eminent men, or being 'knocked' as an eminent man, depends on whose interests are at stake and what type of image of his heroism is being constructed.

Pain, injury and fear

The endurance of pain and injury are key elements in proving manliness. The Australian legend conjures up an image of men whose masculinity is affirmed as they endure hardship and stick together. It is not clear that Bradman lived up to these standards by his actions during the 1932–33 bodyline series, though it is worth examining Bradman's defence against this apparent failure as it tells us much about exemplary standards of Australian masculinity.

The tactics of the English cricket team during 1932–33 are well documented. Some of the Australians refused to bow to the English bowling, fighting back with aggressive, attacking batting that 'carried the fight to the enemy'. At different stages, Richardson took on fast bowler Harold Larwood in the manner expected of a 'larrikin', batting belligerently as if 'lion-taming'.[42] Stan McCabe similarly parried bodyline tactics 'and scruffed it as a terrier would a rat'.[43] Using an orthodox batting stance, Richardson and

McCabe, as well as Woodfull, Ponsford and Fingleton, took numerous blows to the body during the series. These tactics had little impact overall as Australia lost the series comprehensively. Nevertheless, by enduring a battering these batsmen 'proved' their masculinity. Larwood offered this opinion:

> Woodfull … also stood up to me, preferring to take balls on the body rather than make a stroke. Ponsford, Fingleton and Richardson behaved in a similar way. They had guts. Fingleton was probably the most courageous man I ever bowled to.[44]

Bradman did not follow such injurious masculine heroics. He often backed away as the bowler delivered the ball in order to make room to play an offside shot and also to avoid being hit. Unlike his bruised teammates, he was hit only once during the Tests, and although topping the Australian batting averages, faced fewer balls during the series than Woodfull, McCabe, Fingleton and Richardson (Bradman did miss the first Test).

A number of sources describe Bradman as variously ill at ease, rattled, nervous, jittery, on the run, lacking physical (if not moral) courage and backbone, and, most tellingly, frightened by the short-pitched bowling. These accusations created a perception that the Don's tactics placed self-preservation over the value of his wicket, working against the team's interests.[45] Rather than stoically enduring the criticism, Bradman made a statement complaining about the English tactics to Australian officials that was also released to the press. Such grievances about bodyline bowling occasionally resulted in the courage of the 1930s generation being compared unfavourably to the diggers of World War I, whose 'grin and bear it' attitude was by this time beginning to assume mythological proportions. A poem by J.C. Squire, titled 'A Whining Digger', from the *Evening Standard* in January 1933 reads:

Where is that tough Australian grin?
When comrades did you learn to faint?
Can you not take without complaint
A dose of your own medicine?

Finish this futile brawl to-day
We won't believe the paradox,
A whining Digger funking knocks,
Come on one up and two to play.[46]

For Bradman to complain was to contravene the masculine code of accepting ills without whining. Thankfully for the Don's reputation, his complaint was vindicated when the board sent the famous telegram deploring Jardine's side's tactics to the English cricket authorities during the Third Test in Adelaide, and then again later, when bodyline tactics were banned in cricket worldwide.

Of the 1932–33 series, Bradman said then, 'I would sooner return from Brisbane [the fourth Test venue] with a pair of "ducks" than a pair of broken ribs,' and added only in 1995, 'I had no desire to get hit.'[47] These feelings, nonetheless, did not prevent Bradman strenuously denying Larwood's claim that he was frightened.[48] An Australian selector also denied accusations of cowardice on behalf of Bradman (and Woodfull). Decades later, Larwood conceded that he did not believe that Bradman was frightened. These exchanges are instructive in outlining normative standards of masculinity in sport. Bradman openly stated that he had no desire to be hurt – an understandable motivation. Yet, when accused of being frightened, he offers an indignant denial. For an Australian male sporting hero to have their physical courage called into question is to strike at the heart of the exemplary masculinity that he stands for.

In salvaging his 'manhood', Bradman argued that his technique against bodyline bowling actually put him in 'graver danger' than the orthodox batting methods used by his teammates, as backing away from the wicket increased the likelihood of being hit by the ball.[49] These comments point towards an unhealthy notion that sportsmen are expected to put themselves in danger – any move to preserve their safety and bodily health in the face of physical attack equates with fear and cowardice. Seventeen years after the 1932–33 series, Bradman again sought to counter any accusations of fear of bodyline tactics. In his autobiography, he cited newspaper reports telling of his physical fortitude at the Oval in 1930 when he was hit in the chest and hand by intimidating fast bowling.[50] By redeeming his masculinity, he might then be included in narratives of 'hard cases' that endure stoically in the face of injury and pain. It appears that a national hero must adhere to masculinist benchmarks of valour; that is, suffer, emerge triumphant, or lose nobly in a style reminiscent of the legendary Anzacs without regard for the physical price that might be paid in the process.

Physical frailty, the defence forces and 'the best partnership of my career'

The smallest member of his family, the Don was not bronzed, burly, or 'slouching six feet or more in his socks' – not readily identifiable with that archetypal Australian hero, the digger.[51] Intermittent sickness and injury during his career increased the distance between Bradman and this hardy archetype. One of Bradman's most famous episodes of illness came at the end of the 1934 Ashes tour when his life was threatened by a bout of 'thunderstorm appendicitis' that caused a secondary case of peritonitis, resulting in rumours of his death. He missed the entire 1934–35 domestic cricket season as well as an Australian tour of South Africa while recuperating. During his career, Bradman's afflictions included a torn leg muscle, various ankle problems (turned, twisted, sprained and broken), recurrent fibrositis affecting mainly his back, chronic gastric problems, being run down, tired, and experiencing poor general health. His frailty was probably inherited from his mother who 'was never robust' (although frailty obviously did not affect his longevity).[52]

Bradman, with the onset of World War II, had another opportunity to fulfil the image of the Australian legend. Previously a private in the Illawara Regiment (New South Wales), Bradman volunteered for the Royal Australian Air Force (RAAF) in June 1940, his enlistment acclaimed 'as an inspiration to all sportsmen'.[53] He soon transferred to the Army due to an oversupply of RAAF volunteers.[54]

The mythological digger, in the writing of Charles W. Bean, was resourceful, brave, enterprising and had impressive endurance. Unfortunately for Bradman, it was the last of these that let him down. About one year after enlisting, and after three stints in hospital, he was invalided out of the Army and his post as a physical training instructor. The diagnosis was fibrositis in his back muscles. Physical frailty had counted against him and denied him the opportunity to be presented to the public as a dashing war *and* sporting star in a vein similar to other Australian players of the post-World War II era, including Hassett, Ray Lindwall, Arthur Morris and Ian Johnson. It was Keith Miller whose 'blithe spirit' as 'a dashing, fearless Mosquito bomber pilot' who best fitted the spirit of the Anzacs.[55] The popular story of Bradman therefore emphasised his strong moral commitment to the Australian defence cause in spite of his weaker physical endurance and resolve.

Part of the Australian legend's masculine character is a presumption 'of the superiority of male companionship over the marital'.[56] Ward explained that the wives and children of itinerant rural workers were viewed as encumbrances during the mid-1800s as employers did not want to feed extra 'unproductive' mouths who inhibited the mobility of the men.[57] These conditions helped foster the exclusive ethos of mateship, with women often portrayed as 'nags' and 'spoilsports' who shackled men into domesticity.[58] Bradman's lack of mates has already been covered. Also tied up in this mateship equation is the role of Bradman's wife, Lady Jessie Bradman (née Menzies), who passed away in 1997, aged 88 years after 65 years of marriage.

An endearing feature of the Bradman story is his life-long commitment to his wife, with their story together an ideal example of a traditional monogamous relationship. He was devoted to and in love with her – 'the best partnership of my life' – and said as much. This is an unusual proclamation from a man of his generation, which is often regarded for its aversion to overt displays of emotion and affection. The two first met as children in Bowral in 1920 when Don was 12 years old, adding to the romance of the small-town experience that is so central to Bradman's story. Don's mother and Jessie's father had gone to school together and were friends. As a result of this connection, Jessie boarded for a year with the Bradman family during the school week, as her family lived on a farm out of town and she was too young to travel to school by herself. Don and Jessie became good friends and walked to school together each day. According to Perry, by his late teens Bradman decided that he wanted to marry her but admitted to being too shy to ask.[59] Finally, the two announced their engagement in November 1931 before being married on 30 April 1932. The sad part of their life together came when Jessie was diagnosed with incurable cancer, an event that devastated Bradman, who wrote, 'I feel that my life as I have known it has ended.'[60]

In the course of his playing career Jessie appears a constant source of support, which Bradman always appreciated. She played a pivotal role in Bradman's major career decisions: 'Jessie's sound judgement and wise counsel were to prove invaluable.'[61] She was neither an encumbrance nor a deterrent to his cricketing adventures, accompanying Don on the privately run 1932 North American tour, their honeymoon, in the active capacity of team hostess. He said he would not have gone on the tour without her and both saw it is an opportunity to see North America. When her husband was away during the 1948 Ashes tour, Jessie acted as a deputy clerk in order to keep his stockbroking business running. Unlike some other married players on tour such as the Don's Test teammate Leslie Fleetwood-Smith, who was infamous for his 'wenching' involving up to five women a night, Bradman was not one to play up with other women when away.[62] Bradman also threatened to quit Test cricket over the board's refusal to allow Mrs Bradman to accompany him at the end of the 1938 Ashes series. For the Don, it appears that his wife came first and cricket second. Part of the reason that Bradman accepted his knighthood is that it honoured Jessie and recognised 'the vital role she had played in his life and career'.[63] Williams even devoted his biography of Bradman to her, writing 'For Jessie Bradman, an Australian heroine in her own right'.[64] Pronouncements of this type do not always fit well within the masculine domain of sport in which the 'missus' is often left to tend to domestic affairs at home while the men go about their public business.

Too much tenderness 'may be considered to unsex a man and to compromise his Australianness'.[65] Bradman not only disavowed 'typical' Australian masculinity by preferring the company of his wife to his cricketing mates, he also openly stated his adoration of her. In terms of Jessie's role, however, she should not be mistaken as transgressing 'normal' gender roles in the 1930s–1940s and beyond. She seems to have performed the supporting role of dutiful wife and mother to their two children, John and Shirley, and backed her husband in every way. Even so, until very recently it was unusual for an Australian male sporting icon to acknowledge warmly, openly and regularly the support and love of his partner.

Conclusion

Nationalist heroic myths have a habit of 'thinning out' the past, simplifying and accentuating selected events and behaviours, and jettisoning and glossing over others. In the creation of a popular and desired image of the Don, some parts of his story are stressed and exaggerated in order to fit the myth of the 'typical' Aussie male. In proving his 'Australianness', emphasis is placed upon Bradman's 'hardness' on the field, his heterosexual appeal, his 'knocking' of authority, and his forthright independence. Correspondingly, the features of his masculinity that do not neatly fit or contradict the myth are de-emphasised, bypassed or disputed, as in the case of his lack of mates, accusations of fear, and his authoritarian role as a cricket administrator. Where possible, these contradictions are transformed into positives on the grounds of moral worthiness, such as the Don being a non-drinker who was faithful to his wife.

In terms of gender relations in Australia, perceptions of Bradman generally serve to highlight that even celebrated male sports heroes do not necessarily fit cultural ideals of masculinity. Though men may function in a high-profile domain that celebrates tough and aggressive behaviour and a pervasive tendency towards male bonding, this celebration cannot obliterate other forms of masculinity. Bradman's masculinity has not so much been marginalised, but edited and then incorporated into dominant 'typical' Australian imagery. In other words, when an Australian sporting hero such as Bradman does not fit dominant conceptions of masculinity, a collective, albeit sometimes unconscious, effort is made to make him fit. Tensions situating Bradman as the 'other' to an exemplary Australian masculinity are thus neutralised, which helps secure his position as a national hero.

CHAPTER 8

CHALLENGING
THE MYTH

In December 2001 a controversy featured in *The Australian* high-lighting that the public remembrance of cultural figures and icons can become a fraught issue. It was reported that a member of the board of the Heide Museum of Modern Art, Janine Burke, was under pressure to resign after writing a critical biography of Albert Tucker, the famous Australian artist and Angry Penguin. It was alleged that Burke's book placed in jeopardy a $1.5 million gift to the museum from the late artist and his widow, Barbara, who felt 'very upset' about some of the views expressed in the biography about her husband and believed that it should be rewritten.[1] *The Australian* went on to explain that Burke refused to resign from the museum board, defending her right to 'dissent and scholarship', and despite a successful motion being passed for her to step down. The board's majority position was 'particularly conscious of the importance of securing the gift of significant artwork from the Tucker estate'.[2]

Many people, for different reasons, may have a vested interest in maintaining the perception of someone as a hero of their time.

When I examined the memorial issue of the Bradman Museum magazine, *Boundary*, with its heartfelt dedications to a 'great Australian', it reminded me that there have been few challenges to the Bradman myth and that these challenges have failed to dislodge the hegemony of the popular story. The power of the myth is such that 2001 will more likely be remembered for Bradman's passing than for the Centenary of Federation in Australia.[3] The Don's death does, however, mark a new stage in his remembrance. There may now be slightly more room to critique the Don, his life and what he means to Australian culture, but his iconic status will no doubt endure.

Those seeking to demythologise the Don face a considerable task. Popular hagiographies, members of the cricket fraternity, sections of the media, the memorabilia industry and people such as the present Prime Minister influence the way we conceive of the Don. Critics offering a less celebratory view do exist, but they must contend with the dominant institutions, texts and powerful people who have built a self-perpetuating 'guiding pattern' that ensures Bradman's heroism appears both 'natural' and 'normal'.[4] To challenge this pattern is to question the popular image of Bradman that successive generations of Australians have come to know. It is also to undercut the link that exists between the Don's story and a grand and victorious version of Australian history.

Challenges to the Bradman myth

Only two months after Bradman's passing in late February 2001, the criticisms made by former Test teammate Bill O'Reilly of Bradman resurfaced. O'Reilly's oral history recordings in the National Library, which caused the Don a great deal of anger when printed in *Wisden Cricket Monthly* in 1995 (see Chapter 2), were once again brought to public attention. I came across small stories in

The Courier-Mail and the *Sydney Morning Herald*, which included selections from the 'Tiger's' opinions on Bradman.[5] Readers were told that the Don stayed in a different hotel from teammates when first appointed as Australian captain and that he failed to come up with any 'brilliant' tactical ideas. Yet again, the accusation that he was not a 'team man' was aired.

These stories were in marked contrast to the eulogies and celebratory dedications that had recently appeared. The headlines of 27 February, after Bradman's death, included 'The Nation Loses its Hero' and 'A Loving Son and Nation Mourn Australia's Greatest Sports Hero'. The O'Reilly stories indicated that even a tidal wave of dedications could not completely silence people prepared to read against the grain of the Bradman myth. Response to the articles, however, was muted with no reaction evident in the letters pages, which is not surprising given that they were minor stories and these opinions on the Don were not new.

The first concerted challenge to Bradman's popular reputation after his death came at the start of the cricket season in November 2001. On consecutive days *The Australian*'s newspaper banner headlines announced, 'Bradman Snubbed His Family' and 'Bradman Fortune Born from a Scandal'. These stories, written by David Nason, told of the 'The Don We Never Knew' and featured on the front page of the Friday edition and as the cover story of the *Weekend Australian Magazine* on the Saturday.

The Friday story detailed his estrangement from his brother, Victor, and his failure to attend the funerals of members of his family – his mother Emily, father George, brother Victor and three sisters, Idy, Lily and May.[6] Bradman is also said to have neglected to visit his sister Lily in a Bowral nursing home when he returned to the town for the opening of the first stage of the Museum in 1989.

Nason's story tarnishes Bradman's reputation as a committed family man. This article might be interpreted as an unfair exposure of a family's private affairs, a stance that many Bradman admirers are likely to adopt. Of course it is nothing new for family members to become estranged. The significant revelation in the story is Bradman's failure to attend family funerals, especially those of his mother and his father for whom he is said to have made 'proper financial provision' from early on in his career.[7] Though living in Adelaide, Bradman was said to be in Sydney at the time of his mother's funeral and Nason writes that it was a cause of astonishment that he failed to appear at the service.[8] His non-appearance is a surprise as his mother had paid for the young Bradman's first new cricket bat and he had written weekly to her during the 1930s Ashes tour. Bradman's father had taken him to his first Test match in Sydney as a boy and had bowled to him in the backyard, memories that Sir Donald appears to have treasured. Nason's article generated an unfamiliar picture of the Don by presenting new biographical material, and more was added the following day.

The front page of the *Weekend Australian Magazine* on Saturday announced, 'The Don We Never Knew. How a national hero exploited a great financial scandal to launch his business career.'[9] Nason's article revisits the circumstances surrounding the 1945 collapse of the Adelaide stockbroking firm that employed Bradman, Hodgetts and Co. The closure of Hodgetts and Co., declared bankrupt with liabilities of £82,854 and 238 unsecured creditors, was the biggest financial scandal in South Australian history at the time; proprietor Henry Hodgetts was found guilty of fraud and false pretences and sent to jail for five years. The question within Adelaide business circles ever since has been whether Bradman, who was second in charge of the firm and Hodgetts' friend, had prior knowledge of the impending collapse.[10] The other topic discussed in the article concerned Bradman's unpopularity with many members of the Exchange and the Royal Adelaide Golf Club. As Tom Phillips, a former president of the Adelaide Stock Exchange, noted, 'No-one can doubt that he was a great cricketer, but all this man of honour stuff – where does that come from?'[11]

In regards to the company collapse, Nason's article questions whether due procedure was followed. Nason appears to imply that Bradman received favourable treatment from the receiver, George Weir Burns, and the committee of the Adelaide Stock Exchange, particularly when it was unclear whether Bradman had known of the impending collapse. Forty-eight hours after the closure of Hodgetts and Co., Don Bradman and Co. was operating from the offices of his former employer, with full access to Hodgetts' extensive client list.[12] Nason explains that this situation was unusual on three counts. First, it is unlikely that the receiver had had adequate time to establish whether Hodgetts and Co. could trade its way out of trouble. Second, the lease on Hodgetts' offices was transferred straight to Bradman without being put for tender. Third, the goodwill that was contained in Hodgetts' 4,000 plus client list was also passed directly to Bradman without being put to tender.[13] Furthermore, Bradman did not have to pay anything to achieve these exceptional outcomes. The impression created by Nason's article is that there is a possibility that Hodgetts' fall and Bradman's subsequent ascension occurred in dubious circumstances. Nason observes that this impression led to resentment towards Bradman among some members of the Adelaide Exchange that is said to still linger today.

Taken together, Nason's stories present a Don that jars against his scrupulously honest and morally upright image. The details also give rise to questions regarding the existing Bradman biographies. In presenting a full and balanced account of Bradman, why were these details not discussed by his biographers or at least alluded to? If they were not known, the breadth of the research contained in the Bradman biographies is brought into question, although

Rosenwater should perhaps be excused from this doubt given the excellent research that the majority of his biography contains.[14] If his biographers knew the contents of Nason's stories, were they ignored? Did the fear of possible libel action by Bradman prevent their publication? Hopefully, responses to these questions will feature in future writings on the Don.

Various reactions to Nason's stories were published and these help create a limited sense of 'public opinion'. The Bradman Foundation and the Bradman family issued a joint statement, published in *The Australian*, which defended Bradman but did not rebut the content of Nason's stories:

> The Bradman family and the Bradman Foundation do not intend publicly to respond to each and every allegation of wrongdoing or unfairness levelled at the late Sir Donald Bradman, whether in these articles or in any future publications ... They do intend, however, to act together to protect that good name and reputation of the late Sir Donald Bradman from unscrupulous abuse or exploitation.[15]

Richard Mulvaney noted that the family was not disputing the facts presented, but nor does 'that imply that they agree or believe in them', adding that the family had always 'acknowledged Bradman's "human failings"'.[16]

Two features stand out in the response of the Bradman Foundation and family. Firstly, the statement that they will not respond to 'each and every allegation of wrongdoing' levelled at Bradman, is surprising given that very few public allegations have been made against him in the past two decades (especially when compared to the praise and dedications showered upon him). Secondly, Mulvaney admits that Bradman had 'human failings'. It is worth speculating what the effect might have been if a 'human' rather than almost 'superhuman' Don had been more regularly presented to the public by stakeholders in the Bradman industry, such as biographers and the media. Arguably, had such a Bradman been more consistently portrayed, Nason's stories would not have warranted a response, or possibly would not have been written in the first place. As it stands, however, the substance of Nason's articles remains uncontested.

In line with their established pattern, the 'true believers' soon defended the Don's honour. Two commentators, Mike Gibson in the *Sunday Telegraph* and Frank Devine in *The Australian*, stood out in this respect, although in very different ways.[17] Gibson responded to Nason almost superficially. Gibson nostalgically rails against the industry surrounding celebrity and fame and refers to 'people who crawl out from under their rocks to discredit the reputations of those who are no longer able to defend themselves'.[18] Gibson admits surprise at Bradman's failure to attend family funerals, but expresses doubt as to whether the 'bile' emanating from Nason's 'tirade' has anything to offer.[19] The punch line to Gibson's outburst is his claim that he did not even read Nason's Saturday piece on Bradman's business dealings in Adelaide:

> I couldn't be bothered reading it.
> First his family. Then his finances. I couldn't stomach any more smears against someone who cannot answer because he is dead.[20]

The basis of Gibson's complaint is that a dead person cannot respond. He forgets that numerous people, such as himself, and high-profile organisations like the Bradman Foundation are able to defend the Don publicly. Perhaps Gibson simply wants to stop the critical examination of Bradman, the man with whom he had admitted a 'distant love affair' when the Don passed away.[21]

Frank Devine provided a thoughtful response to Nason. In referring to the article on Bradman's role in the Hodgetts and Co. imbroglio, he begins by separating himself from those who would sanctify the Don: 'We need to see him as a man in full, with flaws, foibles and even sins revealed and understood.' He is convinced that Nason performed 'useful work ... as the first post-mortem devil's advocate in the Bradman cause'.[22] Devine then provides his interpretation of Bradman's Adelaide business dealings, drawing upon over 40 hours of conversation he had with the Don. Devine observed that during these discussions Bradman was reluctant to 'concede much that did not show him in the best light ...'.[23] He explains that Bradman may have had a residual awareness of Hodgetts' impending collapse, but he thinks that Bradman did not allow himself to become suspicious of the firm's financial situation because of his insecurity about his skills away from cricket and fears he held about his long-term well-being. Devine also reveals that Bradman had friends who advised against him setting up his own stockbroking business. The article finishes by explaining that, when asked whether his return to cricket post-World War II was motivated by a desire to promote Don Bradman and Co., Bradman gave an inconclusive response.

In acknowledging the legitimacy of Nason's exposé and responding in a reasoned fashion, Devine added something to our understanding of Bradman. In defending the Don, Devine chose not to provide a point-by-point refutation of Nason's case, instead emphasising that Bradman's direct statements to him were 'unbendingly truthful'. This position sees Bradman stand as a dignified figure without Devine becoming embroiled in declaring him categorically innocent or guilty, or implying that he was infallible. The reader is told something not often disclosed about Bradman – that he was insecure and worried about his future away from the

game even in the later years of his cricket career. This image is
different from the popular 'Don the dominator' persona who took
all before him on the field and in life generally.

Readers' letters commenting on Nason's articles indicated that
public opinion on the Don had not been substantially altered.
Going by the five letters published, response was muted and not
always directed at Bradman personally. These responses highlight
that heroes and icons are evaluated as much for what they
represent culturally and historically as for their personal actions.
For example, one reader used Nason's articles to attack Prime
Minister John Howard over his claim that Bradman was the greatest
living Australian, which he believed was a ludicrous statement.
Another reader made a humorous criticism:

> The world is definitely a better place, now that we have been told that
> Joan of Arc was insane, Abraham Lincoln did not fight the Civil War
> to end slavery, Florence Nightingale was a lesbian, Baden Powell set
> the example that many scoutmasters followed, the ALP's losing the
> election was entirely Kim Beazley's fault and even Saint Don of the
> Wicket is tainted.
>
> Stand by for future disclosures about Weary Dunlop's voluntary
> pro-Japanese broadcasts, Mother Teresa's global heroin distribution
> network and Phillip Adams's secret membership of the Liberal
> Party.[24]

Other letters included two from Bradman devotees who felt
similarly to Mike Gibson and thought Nason 'a little jealous, spite-
ful and vindictive person', guilty of 'craven journalism'.[25] These
responses highlight that for some criticism of the Don only further
consolidates their admiration of him. Finally, one reader thought
that Nason's article 'thoroughly credible' and called for more of its

type.[26] This position appears to be a minority view on Bradman that is not often expressed in media forums.

The publication of Nason's articles and the varying responses to them indicate that they had limited impact in changing popular understandings of the Don. Respondents were grouped into familiar camps, either supporting or having to contend with the almost self-evident character of his heroism. Given that only one letter was published that openly supported the challenge to Bradman's pristine reputation, it would seem that the Don's long-established heroism will stand firm against most accusations. Media stakeholders in the Bradman myth also played a role, with Mike Gibson and Frank Devine arbiters of Nason's research and findings. Though using radically different approaches and styles, each sought to recuperate Bradman's reputation.

For all the discussion, Nason's stories scarcely dented Bradman's reputation, which has been under construction for over seventy years and appears more imposing then ever. Yet, the impetus to demythologise Bradman has not completely dissipated. Just as there will be innumerable stories and heroic representations of the Don on the anniversary of his death every year, so too will there be the occasional piece of analysis that digs for deeper meaning.

The elusive Australian spirit

This book has investigated two interconnected issues: the cultural and historical representation of an Australian icon, and ideas of the Australian national character. A figure such as Bradman does not simply reflect the national character; the ways in which icons are represented also actively construct this character. Bradman's security in the pantheon of Australian icons is thus the result of an ongoing cycle of reflection and constitution, and vice versa – stories Australians tell about themselves reveal much about dominant conceptions of Australianness, and the feted individuals who feature in these stories help to inform Australians who they are or perhaps who they imagine themselves to be.

Social, cultural, mythological, nationalist, economic, political and gendered processes have constructed the Don's representation and meanings. Various interrelated factors have been emphasised in this explanation of Bradman's heroism: his extraordinary cricket performances, the era in which he played, his longevity, his position as a hero from a 'golden age' of cricket, his emergence from the bush, his centrality to the events of the bodyline summer, the perception that he had little interest in financial matters, his seemingly apolitical character, and the selective highlighting of his masculinity.

Various cultural discourses and narratives that inform Australian iconography and mythologies have played a role in the Bradman myth. These include: ideas of nation building, the Australian legend, nationalist events such as the bodyline Tests, the commercial appeal of nationalist representations and products, political use of symbols of the nation and those who represent it, and popular images of what it is to be an 'Australian man.' The 'boy from Bowral' story, with its roots in the Australian bush myth, is probably the most obvious and potent of these narratives.

While never completely beyond challenge or revision, the dominant heroic interpretation of Bradman is 'anchored' very effectively.[27] Examples of popular meanings associated with the Don are his redemptive role as a 'nation-builder' during the dark years of the Depression and World War II and his increasing depiction by the media as a moral talisman representing cricket's 'traditional' values that are being 'destroyed' by corruption in the contemporary game. These meanings are accepted and support conservative ideals of Australian culture. The Australian legend,

the nation's experience of war, and honourable sporting achievement are thought by many to be positive motifs in an 'authentic'
Australian history. In other countries too, icons are integrated into
ideas of national, cultural and historical identity. Joe DiMaggio is
celebrated for filling the breach when America needed a hero
during World War II, Abraham Lincoln is read as holding out the
hope of racial justice and harmony, while Muhammad Ali cannot be
separated from the civil rights battle for African-Americans.[28] W.G.
Grace embodied the spirit of the age in Victorian England, while
soccer's Stanley Matthews offers faith in English democratic ideals
as he is 'proof' that an ordinary man can become a national hero.[29]
Nelson Mandela is the symbol of the long struggle to dismantle
apartheid in South Africa. The cultural meanings of icons resist
criticism because they are inextricably tied to ideals of the nation,
politics and culture. Analysing this relationship brings us closer to
an understanding of how meaning is created and expressed within
complex national communities.

Heroes tend to act either to transform or reproduce dominant
social values.[30] That the Don stands for stability and predicability
is evident on a number of fronts: his dominance in a sport that has
historically represented mono-cultural, white masculine privilege;
his upbringing in Bowral, a town with a history steeped in Protestantism and conservatism; his association with and appropriation
by politicians such as Menzies and Howard; and a personal
preference for socially conservative values. This is not the profile
associated with transformative or transgressive sporting figures
such as Muhammad Ali or Australia's Cathy Freeman. To the

satisfaction of some and the questioning of others, Don Bradman stands for an older, conservatively aligned nationalism.

This study suggests that little substantial change has occurred in the eight years since Graeme Turner stated in *Making It National* that the Australian nation is culturally dominated by 'spruced-up versions of ... old nationalisms'.[31] Bradman is understood through a bush–war–sport nexus that has long underpinned much of the nation's iconography and mythology. The national outpouring at news of his death and the coverage it received testify to the resonance of this vision. Such commemoration no doubt pleased those Australians who favour a return to 'traditional' values and who struggle to comprehend or resist the undercurrents of change within Australian society. Retreating to a golden age, however, cannot resolve the difficulties that accompany social and cultural transformation, and in any case, the age of order and harmony that Bradman represents is illusory: it is difficult to see the years of Bradman's dominance, which included the Depression and World War II, as either ordered or harmonious.

Perhaps the Don stands for an Australia that lies in an ever-elusive past and is part of an Anglo-centric (or Anglo-Protestant) dreaming.[32] A Bradman who is tied to romantic notions of a 'fair go' and the 'bush' in an Australia where 'everybody was about the same' may be a myth, but he nevertheless continues to be attractive to many. Martin Flanagan is half-right when he says that cricket is a game that clings tenaciously to its past and remains relatively untouched by recent changes in Australian society.[33] Cricket has been inattentive to the irrevocable social changes that have occurred in Australian society over the past two decades or more, yet it has been a leader when it comes to the ideology of economic competitiveness and marketing. For instance, the television-led one-day cricket revolution of the 1970s was a pioneering venture in the commodification of sport and culture that sits well alongside Australia's embrace of the free market, the rise of an individualist ethos and the gradual dismantling of the welfare state. The message underlying these changes is that winning is everything. This shift has drawn Australia into a new realm where appeals to the values of its national mythologies are mostly rhetorical: the 'whole-hearted pursuit of self-interest and ease and comfort is a step closer to American "individualism" and a step away from Australian "collectivism", "battlers" and the catch-phrase no Australian politician can resist, the "fair go"'.[34] The conditions produced by an untrammelled free market cannot guarantee the stable cultural and social order that is required if the notion of 'a fair go' is to have any meaning.[35] This disjuncture helps to fuel the nostalgia surrounding a figure such as the Don, who stands for an Australian past when fair play and honour are thought to have held sway. The irony is that the Don embraced the market and the individualist ethos and is loved by people such as the Prime Minister who have been at the forefront of making Australia a 'harder', more competitive society.

Longing and admiration for worn platitudes such as the notion of a 'fair go' may help to explain the continuing popularity of books on the Don, documentaries, articles, museums, and souvenirs. These items portray an Anglo-Celtic nation that is victorious and apolitical, and that enjoys honourable sporting competition among men who play for pleasure and not profit.

If the next generation of Australians begins to find continuous longing for and idealisation of the Bradman years tiresome and regressive, the homespun charm of the Bradman story will lose some of its lustre. Bradman followers will have to ensure that he continues to be thought of as more than just a cricketer, especially in light of the question as to why a 'bush' cricketer from the days of the White Australia Policy should serve as a symbol for a cosmopolitan Australian people? More level-headed and in-depth assessment of the Don and his cultural significance is needed in order to avoid him being reduced to a symbol for an older sepia-toned Australia.

A first step towards a more grounded estimation of the Don is to acknowledge that he is not necessarily a hero for *all* Australians or *the* hero of Australia. Occasionally, someone notes that 'he was only a cricketer',[36] and others have questioned whether the obsession with the Don has clouded our appreciation of other cricketers and features of Australian history.[37] In the end, he is but one hero in a rich and varied Australian history and culture, and needs to be placed alongside other great Australians – as Michael McGirr wrote when Bradman died, 'The uncomfortable truth is that no one individual can embody the elusive Australian spirit.'[38]

Appendix

TABLE 1 Bradman's batting records and achievements (selection)

Highest average of any Test cricketer: 99.94 runs per innings; scored 6,966 runs in 80 innings in 52 Test matches, with 29 centuries and 13 half-centuries; South African Graeme Pollock has the next highest average (60.97)
Second most Test match hundreds (29) and the most Test double hundreds (12)
Only batsman to have compiled 2 triple centuries in Tests
Equal highest score by an Australian in Test cricket: 334 runs in 1930, at that time a world record; former Australian captain, Mark Taylor, equalled this figure against Pakistan in 1998
Most Test runs in a day (309 runs versus England in 1930)
Fastest to 2,000 (22 innings), 3,000 (33 innings), 4,000 (48 innings), 5,000 (56 innings) and 6,000 (68 innings) Test runs
Co-holder of the highest partnership for the 2nd, 5th and 6th wicket in Test cricket
Scored a Test double century every 6.66 times he batted
Only player to have scored more than 4,000 runs against a single country (England)
Captained the 1948 Australian Ashes side – the 'Invincibles' – to an undefeated tour of England (in 2002 still the only side not to lose a match on tour)
A first-class batting average of 95.14 runs per innings; scored 28,067 runs in 338 innings in 234 matches
His 452 runs not out for New South Wales (NSW) against Queensland in 1930 remains the highest in Australia; at the time, this score was a first-class world record
Most first-class runs on a tour of England (2,960 runs in 1930)
One of only three batsmen to have scored 6 successive first-class centuries
Scored 1,000 runs in a first-class season 16 times (12 of them in Australia)
His 37 scores of 200 runs or more in first-class cricket are a world record
On average, scored a century once out of every three visits to the crease in first-class cricket
First former Test player to become chairman of the Australian Board of Control (1960–63, 1969–72)

TABLE 2 The Record of Bradman and the Australian Test Teams in which he played

YEAR	OPPONENT	SERIES RESULT		RUNS	50s	100s	AVERAGE
		Won	Lost				
1928–29	England	1	4	468	2	2	66.86
1930	England	2	1	974	–	4	139.14
1930–31	West Indies	4	1	447	–	2	74.50
1931–32	South Africa	5	0	806	–	4	201.50
1932–33	England	1	4	396	3	1	56.57
1934	England	2	1	758	1	2	94.75
1936–37*	England	3	2	810	1	3	90.00
1938*	England	1	1	434	1	3	108.50
1946–47*	England	3	0	680	3	2	97.14
1947–48*	India	4	0	715	1	4	178.75
1948*	England	4	0	508	1	2	72.57
TOTAL		W:8	L:2	6996	13	29	99.94
		D:1					

* Bradman was captain

TABLE 3 Bradman's awards and honours (selection)

A knighthood (1949); first Test cricketer so honoured

A Companion of the Order of Australia (1979)

In 1988, voted greatest male athlete of the past 200 years by the Australian Confederation of Sport

Selected by *International Who's Who* as one of only two Australians among the top 100 people who have done the most to shape the 20th century; the other (former) Australian was Rupert Murdoch. Bradman was also one of only three sportspeople selected, alongside boxer Muhammad Ali and soccer's Pele

Nominated among the top sportspeople of the 20th century by the World Confederation of Sport

Named male athlete of the century by the Sport Australia Hall of Fame

Voted sixth, and the highest ranked Australian, in *Reuter's Sports Personality of the 20th Century* list

Ranked eighth out of the 20 greatest world sporting champions of the 20th century by *The Australian* newspaper's *This Living Century* series; highest ranked Australian athlete

Ranked the number 1 Australian athlete of the 20th century by *Sports Illustrated* magazine

Voted the greatest cricketer of the 20th century by *Wisden Cricket Almanack*, unanimous decision by 100 judges

Nominated captain of the Australian Cricket Team of the Century

Captain of the team nominated the greatest of the century – the 1948 Invincibles

TABLE 4 New publications with 'Bradman' or 'The Don' in their title, or authored by Sir Donald Bradman, 1930–2001 (does not include reprints)

YEAR	AUTHOR/EDITOR	TITLE
1930	Sir Donald Bradman	Don Bradman's Book
1932	R.M. Davis	Don Bradman's Pictorial Test Record: South Africa – Australia Cricket
1933	R.M. Davis	Don Bradman's Pictorial Test Record: England – Australia Cricket
1934		In Quest of the Ashes: The Don Bradman Souvenir Booklet and Scoring Records
1935	Sir Donald Bradman, W.A. Oldfield, A. Mailey and A.G. Moyes	The News Cricket Hints
1936	G.N. Natu	Don Bradman
1939	Sir Donald Bradman	My Cricketing Life
1944	E.L. Roberts	Bradman 1927–1941
1945	Sir Donald Bradman	How to Play Cricket
1946	J.L. Ellis	Test Match: Records of All Games Australia v England 1877–1938: From Grace to Bradman
1948	A.G. Moyes	Bradman
1948	'Outfield'	The Bradman Book
1949	J.H. Fingleton	Brightly Fades the Don
1950	Sir Donald Bradman	Farewell to Cricket
1950	A. Flanagan	On Tour with Don Bradman
1951	P. Lindsay	Don Bradman
1953	C. Bax and Others	The Cricketing Lives of W.G. Grace, C.B. Fry, Maurice Tate and Don Bradman
1958	Sir Donald Bradman	The Art of Cricket
1959	B.J. Wakley	Bradman the Great
1960	A. Davis	Sir Donald Bradman
1964	R. Whitington	Bradman, Benaud and Goddard's Cinderellas
1974	W. Andrews	The Hand that Bowled Bradman: Memories of a Professional Cricketer

continued

YEAR	AUTHOR/EDITOR	TITLE
1974	W. Andrews	*Bradman to Chappell: A History of Australian–England Test Matches from 1946*
1978	E.W. Docker	*Bradman and the Bodyline Series*
1978	I. Rosenwater	*Sir Donald Bradman: A Biography*
1981	Introduction by Sir Donald Bradman	*Bradman's First Tour*
1981	T. Dexter	*From Bradman to Boycott: The Master Batsmen*
1983	M. Page	*Bradman: The Illustrated Biography*
1983	B. O'Reilly, compiled by J. Egan	*The Bradman Era*
1983	A. Mallett	*Don Bradman*
1983	K. Piesse	*Donald Bradman*
1984	M. Page and D. Fregon	*The Don: A Photographic Essay of a Legendary Life*
1985	J. Boyd	*The Quickest, the Brightest and the Best: Bradman's Fabulous Century*
1986	J. Pollard	*Australian Cricket 1918–1948: The Bradman Years*
1986		*Bradman to Border: A History of Australia–England Test Matches from 1946*
1987	P. Derriman	*Our Don Bradman: Sixty Years of Writing About Don Bradman*
1987	Introduction by Sir Donald Bradman	*The Bradman Albums, vols 1 and 2*
1991	D. Chase and V. Krantz	*Don Bradman: A Cricketing Legend*
1993	P. Derriman	*Our Don Bradman: The Don at the SCG*
1993	A. Mallett	*Clarrie Grimmett: The Bradman of Spin*
1994	G. Atkinson	*Bradman, the Man: A Short Biography*
1994	D. Christison	*Bradman: The Records*
1994	B. Morris	*Bradman: What They Said About Him*

continued

YEAR	AUTHOR/EDITOR	TITLE
1994	P. Allen and J. Kemsley	*Images of Bradman*
1995	R. Perry	*The Don: A Biography*
1996	C. Williams	*Bradman: An Australian Hero*
1997	M. Small	*Don Bradman: Cricketing Hero*
1998	G. Wright	*Wisden on Bradman*
1998	M. Coward	*Sir Donald Bradman A.C.*
1998	P. Allen	*The Invincibles: The Legend of Bradman's 1948 Australians*
1999	L.N. Mathur	*Don Bradman: Cricket Wizard*
2000	D. Hort	*Don Bradman*
2000	A. Mallett	*Bradman's Band*
2001	P. Allen	*Farewell to Bradman*
2001	R. Perry	*Bradman's Best*

Total: 55 publications

TABLE 5 Examples of prices achieved at auction for Bradman dedicated memorabilia

YEAR	AUCTION	ITEM	PRICE(A$)
1998	Christie's	Life-sized bronze sculpture of Bradman by Mitch Mitchell	74,750
1996	Phillips, London	Bat used by Bradman in scoring 212 runs against England in Adelaide in 1936–37	48,000
1997	Unknown	Bat used by Bradman during the 1930 Ashes tour of England	45,540
1998	Christie's	Bat used by Bradman	28,750
1999	Christie's	Bat used by Bradman for South Australia in 1935–36	28,000
1999	Christie's	Pair of Bradman batting gloves used on 1932 North American tour	24,000
1998	Unknown	Framed, signed photo of Bradman, Shane Warne and Sachin Tendulkar taken on Bradman's 90th birthday	22,000
2001	Christie's	Two Bradman letters	18,800
2000	NSW Hoteliers fundraising auction	Autographed Bradman bat	5,500
2000	International Auction House	Handmade 1960s Gunn and Moore bat signed by Bradman	5,000
1999	St Vincent's College, Sydney, fundraising auction	Autographed and framed Bradman bat	4,800
2000	Simply Cricket	Bradman signed limited edition framed bat, 'Sir Donald Bradman A.C.' (no. 1253 of 1500)	3,500
2000	St. Vincent's College, Sydney, fundraising auction	Autographed and framed Bradman bat	3,250
2001	Simply Cricket	Bradman 'Classic Collection' signed limited edition bat (no. 68 of 150)	3,150
2001	Simply Cricket	Bradman signed limited edition framed bat, 'Sir Donald Bradman A.C.' (no. 1258 of 1500)	2,300
2001	Simply Cricket	'Sir Donald Bradman. The Legend.' Limited edition signed framed photo (no.14 of 25)	2,100
2000	International Auction Gallery	Bradman Albums deluxe edition, signed by Bradman (production run limited to 500)	2,000

TABLE 6 Player associated items available on world wide web auction sites:
SOLD.com.au, eBay Australia, Stuff Auctions and GoFish (2000 except as indicated)

PLAYER	SIR DONALD BRADMAN	SHANE WARNE	ALLAN BORDER	STEVE WAUGH
7 April	168	11	15	8
8 May	178	16	15	8
7 June	172	10	10	12
5 July	168	12	9	11
7 Aug.	155	14	10	10
13 Sept.	102	14	8	7
9 Oct.	134	21	6	11
9 Nov.	157	29	11	17
9 Dec.	124	14	10	9
Bradman's death 25 February 2001				
15 March 2001	335	14	9	6
Total	1693	155	103	99
Average per month	169.3	15.5	10.3	9.9

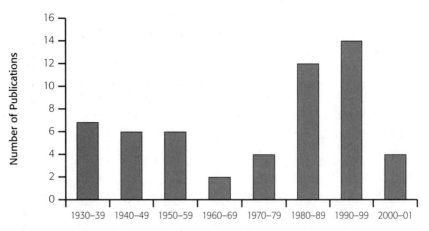

FIGURE 1 New publications with Bradman or The Don in the title, or authored by
Sir Donald Bradman, by decade 1930–2001 (does not include reprints)

Notes

1 Our one national hero?

1 J. Carroll, 'The Blessed Country: Australian Dreaming 1901–2001', *The Alfred Deakin Lectures 2001* (ABC Radio National, 12 May 2001).

2 D. Horne, *The Lucky Country: Australia in the Sixties*, 2nd edn (Sydney: Angus and Robertson, 1968), p. 40.

3 *Ibid.*

4 G. Turner, F. Bonner and D. Marshall, *Fame Games: The Production of Celebrity in Australia* (Cambridge: Cambridge University Press, 2000), p. 3.

5 *The Australian* (27 Feb. 2001), p. 3.

6 *Sydney Morning Herald* (27 Feb. 2001), p. 12.

7 *Sydney Morning Herald*, Tribute Edition (27 Feb. 2001), p. 6; R. Perry, *The Don: A Biography* (Sydney: Pan Macmillan, 1998), p. 600.

8 *Lateline*, ABC Television (26 Feb. 2001).

9 *The Bulletin* (6 March 2001), p. 10; *Bradman: A Tribute*, Inside Edge magazine (2001), p. 4.

10 B. Schwartz, 'The Social Context of Commemoration: A Study in Collective Memory', *Social Forces*, 61:2 (1982), p. 377.

11 G. Haigh, 'Bradman at Ninety', *Wisden Cricket Monthly* (Sept. 1998), p. 36.

12 D.L. Andrews and S.J. Jackson, 'Introduction: Sport Celebrities, Public Culture, and Private Experience', in D.L. Andrews and S.J. Jackson, eds, *Sports Stars: The Cultural Politics of Sporting Celebrity* (London: Routledge, 2001), p. 6.

13 *Sydney Morning Herald* (10 March 2000), p. 40.

14 C. Harte, *A History of Australian Cricket* (London: Andre Deutsch, 1993), p. 1.

15 N. Cardus, 'Six Giants of the Century – Sir Donald Bradman', reproduced from 1963 *Wisden Cricketers' Almanack*, in G. Wright, ed., *Wisden on Bradman* (South Yarra, Victoria: Hardie Grant Books, 1998), p. 32.

16 The other (former) Australian was Rupert Murdoch. Bradman was also one of only three sportspeople selected, alongside boxer Muhammad Ali and soccer's Pele.

17 A. Batchelder, 'Sir Donald Bradman A.C.' [Book review], *The Yorker*, 20 (Dec. 1998), p. 8.

18 Paraphrased from E.J. Gorn, 'Introduction', in E.J. Gorn, ed., *Muhammad Ali: The People's Champ* (Urbana: University of Illinois Press, 1995), p. xiii.

19 An approach drawn from M. Schudson, *Watergate in American Memory: How We Remember, Forget, and Reconstruct the Past* (New York: Basic Books, 1992).

20 Required next is a comprehensive study that bridges the gap between the end of Bradman's playing career and the contemporary context. Due to the particular aims and scope of this book it has not been possible to do justice to these years in which there is still much to uncover. A major challenge then for historians and biographers in the near future is to provide a detailed study of Bradman's business, cricket administration and personal activities between the 1950s and 1970s.

21 *Bradman: A Tribute*, Inside Edge magazine (2001), p. 55.

2 Looking for heroes

1 Mario Cuomo, Governor of New York, quotation from *Baseball: A Film by Ken Burns*, Episode 5 (Florentine Films, 1994).

2 W.F. Mandle, 'Cricket and Australian Nationalism in the Nineteenth Century', in T.D. Jaques and G.R. Pavia, eds, *Sport in Australia: Selected Readings in Physical Activity* (Sydney: McGraw-Hill, 1976), pp. 46–72.

3 R. Cashman, 'Australia', in B. Stoddart and K.A.P. Sandiford, eds, *The Imperial Game: Cricket, Culture and Society* (Manchester: Manchester University Press, 1998), p. 34.

4 Mandle, 'Cricket and Australian Nationalism', p. 61.

5 R. Sissons and B. Stoddart, *Cricket and Empire: The 1932–33 Bodyline Tour of Australia* (Sydney: Allen & Unwin, 1984), p. 37.

6 Mandle, 'Cricket and Australian Nationalism', p. 65.

7 G. Turner, *National Fictions: Literature, Film and the Construction of Australian Narrative* (St Leonards, NSW: Allen and Unwin, 1993); R. White, *Inventing Australia: Images and Identity 1688–1980* (Sydney: Angus and Robertson, 1981).

8 Mandle, 'Cricket and Australian Nationalism', p. 65.

9 Sissons and Stoddart, *Cricket and Empire*, p. 41.

10 W.F. Mandle, *Going it Alone: Australia's National Identity in the Twentieth Century* (Ringwood, Vic.: Allen Lane, 1977), p. 25. See also G. Haigh, *The Big Ship: Warwick Armstrong and the Making of Modern Cricket* (Melbourne: Text Publishing, 2001).

11 G. Turner, *Making It National: Nationalism and Australian Popular Culture* (St Leonards, NSW: Allen & Unwin, 1994), pp. 69, 123. Quotation from Z. Bauman, 'On Writing: On Writing Sociology', *Theory, Culture and Society*, 17:1 (2000), p. 81.

12 *Sydney Morning Herald* (1 Nov. 2000), p. 13. Myth making has obscured Simpson's origins as a working-class English immigrant and political radical of the Left who saved few, if any, lives. P. Cochrane, *Simpson and the Donkey: The Making of a Legend* (Melbourne: Melbourne University Press, 1992), p. 6.

13 D. Horne, *The Lucky Country: Australia in the Sixties*, 2nd edn (Sydney: Angus and Robertson, 1968).

14 P. Kelly, *The End of Certainty* (St Leonards, NSW: Allen & Unwin, 1992), p. 11.

15 For reference to Bradman's love of England and its people, see his autobiography. D.G. Bradman, *Farewell to Cricket*, originally published 1950 (Sydney: ETT Imprint, 1994), pp. 33, 79, 142, 144, 221, 232.

16 G. Wright, 'Introduction', in G. Wright, ed., *Wisden on Bradman* (South Yarra, Vic.: Hardie Grant Books, 1998), p. xiii. See also *Sydney Morning Herald* (14 Oct. 1989), p. 26.

17 A.G. Moyes, 'The Big Four', reproduced from 1954–55 in J. Maxwell, compiler, *The ABC Cricket Book: The First 60 Years* (Sydney: ABC Books, 1994), p. 93.

18 'The Importance of Timing and Measurement in 20th Century Sport', *The Sports Factor*, Radio National Transcripts (4 June 1999).

19 D.G. Bradman, *The Art of Cricket*, originally published 1958 (Sydney: ETT Imprint, 1998), pp. 75–76.

20 *Sun-Herald* (18 Oct. 1998), pp. 72–73; *Sydney Morning Herald* (20 Nov. 1998), p. 36.

21 *Boundary: The Journal of the Friends and Supporters of the Bradman Museum*, 11:2 (Autumn 2000), p. 1; C. Davis, *The Best of the Best: A New Look at the Great Cricketers and Their Changing Times* (Sydney: ABC Books, 2000); C. Davis, 'Cricket's Superman', *Wisden Cricketers' Almanack Australia 2001–02* (South Yarra: Hardie-Grant, 2001), pp. 10–17.

22 A. Guttmann, *From Ritual to Record: The Nature of Modern Sports* (New York: Columbia University Press, 1978), pp. 51–52.

23 C.L.R. James, *Beyond a Boundary*, originally published 1963 (Melbourne: Stanley Paul, 1986); J.H. Fingleton, *The Immortal Victor Trumper* (Sydney: Collins, 1978).

24 H.S. Altham, 'Tribute to Bradman', reprinted in *The Bradman Albums*, vol. 2, 1935–1949 (Sydney: Lansdowne, 1995), p. 790.

25 D. Harvey, *The Condition of Postmodernity: An Enquiry into the Origins of Cultural Change* (Cambridge, UK: Blackwell, 1989), p. 35.

26 Horne, *The Lucky Country*, p. 207.

27 R. Conway, 'Revolutionary Prowess', in M. Coward, co-ordinator, *Sir Donald Bradman A.C.* Ironbark Legends Series (Sydney: Pan Macmillan, 1998), p. 28.

28 F. Andrewes, "They Play in Your Home': Cricket, Media and Modernity in Pre-war Australia', *The International Journal of the History of Sport*, 17:2–3 (2000), p. 103.

29 I. Harriss, 'Cricket and Rational Economic Man', *Sporting Traditions*, 3:1 (1986), pp. 56–57; I. Harriss, 'Cricket and Capitalism: Batting and Capital

Accumulation in England, 1920–1960', *Melbourne Historical Journal*, 19 (1988), pp. 12–13.

30 N. Cardus, *Autobiography* (London: Collins, 1947), p. 152; J. Ellul, *The Technological Society* (New York: Alfred A. Knopf, 1964), p. 384.

31 I. Harriss, 'Cricket and Bourgeois Ideology', in G. Lawrence and D. Rowe, eds, *Power Play: The Commercialisation of Australian Sport* (Sydney: Hale and Iremonger, 1986), p. 185.

32 R. Holt, 'Cricket and Englishness: The Batsman as Hero', *The International Journal of the History of Sport*, 13:1 (1996), pp. 48–70.

33 *The Weekend Australian* (17–18 June 2000), p. 27.

34 P. Smith, 'Culture and Charisma: Outline of a Theory', *Acta Sociologica*, 43:2 (2000), pp. 101–111.

35 G. Haigh, 'O'Reilly's Gospel', *Wisden Cricket Monthly* (Feb. 1995), pp. 39–40; D.G. Bradman, 'The Don Hits Back', *Wisden Cricket Monthly* (July 1995), p. 4.

36 *Sydney Morning Herald* (21 Dec. 1998), p. 21.

37 *Sydney Morning Herald* (25 Jan. 2000), p. 10.

38 B. Hutchins and J. Mikosza, 'Australian Rugby League and Violence 1970 to 1995: A Case Study in the Maintenance of Masculine Hegemony', *Journal of Sociology*, 34:3 (1998), pp. 257–58.

39 A. McGilvray with N. Tasker, *The Game Goes On ...* (Sydney: ABC, 1987), p. 99.

40 D. Haskell and B. Bennett, 'Introduction', in B. Bennett and D. Haskell, eds, *Myths, Heroes and Anti-Heroes: Essays on Literature and Culture in the Asia-Pacific Region* (Perth: Centre for Studies in Australian Literature, University of Western Australia, 1992), p. vii.

41 During the 1956 series, Bradman's writing on the Australian team created the unprecedented situation where one of the men who had selected the side was commenting on their progress in the media. I. Rosenwater, *Sir Donald Bradman: A Biography* (London: BT Batsford, 1978), pp. 376–78.

42 *Sydney Morning Herald*, Tribute Edition Liftout (24 Aug. 1998), p. 1.

43 *The Cricketer International* (April 2001), p. 9.

44 *The Australian* (14 April 2000), p. 15.

45 'Transcript of the Prime Minister The Hon John Howard MP Sir Donald Bradman Oration, Melbourne', 17 August 2000, *Prime Minister of Australia News Room* http://www. pm. gov. au/news/speeches/2000/speech406. htm (13 Feb. 2001).

46 W. Franks, 'Notes by the Editor', *Wisden Cricketers' Almanack Australia 2001–02*, p. 4. To mankad a batsman involves the bowler breaking the stumps just before delivery if the batsman has left his ground, thereby running him out. Cricket etiquette generally dictates that a bowler first warns the batsman before doing this.

47 Bradman, *Farewell to Cricket*, p. 250.

48 *Sydney Morning Herald* (27 May 2000), p. 42; Franks, 'Notes by the Editor', pp. 2–3; *The Eye* (20 April–3 May 2000), pp. 46–47.

49 James, *Beyond a Boundary*, pp. 47–48.

50 *Daily Telegraph* (28 Feb. 2001), p. 30.

51 C. Harte, *A History of Australian Cricket* (London: Andre Deutsch, 1993), p. 383.

3   The boy from Bowral

1 *The Australian* (14 Oct. 1989).

2 *Sydney Morning Herald* (14 Oct. 1989), p. 26.

3 J. Pollard, *Australian Cricket 1918–1948: The Bradman Years* (Sydney: Book Company International, 1995), p. 244; R. Perry, *The Don: A Biography* (Sydney: Pan Macmillan, 1998), p. 598.

4 R. Cavalier, 'Exploring Frontiers', in M. Coward, co-ordinator, *Sir Donald Bradman A.C.* Ironbark Legends Series (Sydney: Pan Macmillan, 1998), pp. 4–23.

5 Perry, *The Don*, p. 18.

6 See H. Masterman-Smith and D. Cottle, ' "Bradstow Revisited": A Comparative Study of Class Politics in Bowral, 1974 and 1997', *Rural Society*, 11:1 (2001), p. 39–56; R.A. Wild, *Bradstow: A Study of Status, Class and Power in a Small Australian Town* (Sydney: Angus and Robertson, 1974).

7 Masterman-Smith and Cottle, 'Bradstow Revisited', pp. 46–47.

8 The 'Bradman Oration' is an initiative of the Australian Cricket Board.

9 W.F. Mandle, 'Sports History', in W.F. Mandle and G. Osborne, eds, *New History: Studying Australia Today* (Sydney: Allen and Unwin, 1982), p. 88.

10 R. Ward, *The Australian Legend*, originally published 1958 (Melbourne: Oxford University Press, 1989).

11 G. Turner, *Making It National: Nationalism and Australian Popular Culture* (St Leonards, NSW: Allen and Unwin, 1994), pp. 8–10.

12 R. Nile, 'Introduction', in R. Nile, ed., *The Australian Legend and Its Discontents* (St Lucia: University of Queensland Press, 2000), pp. 2–4; Turner, *Making It National*, p. 79.

13 H. Goodall, ' "Fixing" the Past: Modernity, Tradition and Memory in Rural Australia', *UTS Review*, 6:1 (2000), p. 23.

14 M. Clark, 'Heroes', in S.R. Graubard, ed., *Australia: The Daedalus Symposium* (North Ryde, NSW: Angus and Robertson, 1985), p. 80.

15 *Daily Telegraph* (28 Feb. 2001), p. 30.

16 P. Derriman, 'Sir Donald Bradman', *Wisden Cricketers' Almanack Australia 2001–02* (South Yarra, Vic.: Hardie-Grant Books, 2001), p. 19.

17　S. Waugh, 'Privileges in the Shadow', in Coward, co-ordinator, *Sir Donald Bradman A.C.*, p. 112; A. Mallett, *Bradman's Band* (St Lucia: University of Queensland Press, 2000), p. 201.

18　*Sydney Morning Herald* (27 Feb. 2001), p. 12.

19　*Boundary: Journal of the Friends of the Bradman Museum*, 6:4 (Spring 1995), p. 5.

20　*Ibid.*

21　P. Share, 'Beyond "Countrymindedness": Representation in the Post-Rural Era', in P. Share, ed., *Communication and Culture in Rural Areas* (Wagga Wagga: Centre for Rural Social Research, 1997), p. 10.

22　John Howard quotation from *This Fabulous Century*, Channel Seven (25 Sept. 1999).

23　Turner, *Making It National*, p. 51.

24　*Weekend Australian* (24–25 March), p. 26.

25　J. Bale, *Landscapes of Modern Sport* (London: Leicester University Press, 1994), pp. 120–121, 153–65.

26　*Bradman Museum Homepage*. http://bradman.org.au/home.html (9 June 2000).

27　B. Schwartz, 'Postmodernity and Historical Reputation: Abraham Lincoln in Late-Twentieth Century American Memory', *Social Forces*, 77:1 (1998), p. 91.

28　Share, 'Beyond "Countrymindedness"', p. 6.

29　Joan Thompson quotation from T. Blair, 'The Accessible Hero', *Time* magazine, reprinted in *Boundary*, 7:4 (Spring 1996), p. 5.

30　*Ibid.*

31　*Boundary*, 9:2 (Autumn 1998).

32　L. Kaino, 'Woop Woop(s) and Woolly Film-making: Rural Representations of Culture in Contemporary Australian Film Feature', *Rural Society*, 10:3 (2000), p. 320.

33　See Masterman-Smith and Cottle, 'Bradstow Revisited', pp. 47–48.

34　G. Bolton, *The Oxford History of Australia: The Middle Way 1942–1988* (Melbourne: Oxford University Press, 1993), p. 66; Perry, *The Don*, p. 566. See also A. Davis, *Sir Donald Bradman* (London: Cassell, 1960), p. 116.

35　D.G. Bradman, 'Introduction', in *The Bradman Albums*, vol. 1, 1925–1934 (Sydney: Lansdowne, 1995), p. 9.

36　*Ibid.*, p. 91.

37　Share, 'Beyond "Countrymindedness"', p. 13.

38　Cavalier, 'Exploring Frontiers', p. 22.

39　W.J. O'Reilly, *Cricket Conquest* (London: Werner Laurie, 1949), p. 200.

40　Davis, *Sir Donald Bradman*, p. 5.

41　For mention of Bradman's choice to play alone as a boy see Cavalier, 'Exploring Frontiers', p. 9; I. Rosenwater, *Sir Donald Bradman: A Biography* (London: BT Batsford, 1978), p. 24.

42 A.G. Moyes, *Bradman* (Sydney: Angus and Robertson, 1948), p. xvi.
43 D.G. Bradman, *The Art of Cricket*, originally published 1958 (Sydney: ETT Imprint, 1998), p. 95.
44 T. Thompson, 'Where Sir Donald Bradman Learnt His Cricket', *Sir Don Bradman (1908–2001)* http:// 167.216.192.98/cricket/donbradman/ 20010301don13.shtml (4 Jan. 2002); *Sydney Morning Herald*, The Bradman Legacy (3 March 2001), p. 2.
45 Thompson, 'Where Sir Donald Bradman Learnt His Cricket'.
46 *Ibid.*
47 *Ibid.*
48 Bradman, *The Art of Cricket*, p. 26.
49 *Ibid.*, p. 77.
50 Ward, *The Australian Legend*, p. 209.
51 R. Sissons and B. Stoddart, *Cricket and Empire: The 1932-33 Bodyline Tour of Australia* (Sydney: Allen and Unwin, 1984), p. 113 ; *Wisden Cricket Monthly* (April 2001), p. 1; K. Miller, *Cricket Crossfire* (London: Oldbourne Press, 1956), p. 20.
52 A.B. Paterson, 'Bradman', reproduced in P. Mullins and P. Derriman, eds, *Bat and Pad: Writings on Australian Cricket 1804–1984* (Melbourne: Oxford University Press, 1984), pp. 62–64.
53 'A Batsman of Promise', press article published in 1926, reproduced in P. Derriman, ed., *Our Don Bradman: Sixty Years of Writings About Don Bradman* (Melbourne: Macmillan, 1987), p. 11.
54 E. Thompson, *Fair Enough: Egalitarianism in Australia* (Sydney: University of New South Wales, 1994), pp. 152–53.

4   Bodyline and myth

1 *Sydney Morning Herald*, The Guide (16–22 July 1984), p. 1.
2 *The Age*, Green Guide (12 July 1984), p. 8.
3 *Bodyline* (Kennedy-Miller, 1984); P. Wheeler, *Bodyline: The Novel* (London: Faber and Faber, 1983).
4 It is arguable that comparing a television mini-series with a fictional novel is not comparing like with like. While conceding the point, I aim to review the major popular fictionalised and dramatised versions of the bodyline summer. Issues of media form and genre are an unavoidable part of this chapter and are addressed generally, but they remain in the background.
5 J. McKay, B. Hutchins and J. Mikosza, '"Shame and Scandal in the Family": Media Narratives of the IOC/SOCOG Scandal Matrix', *Olympika: The International Journal of Olympic Studies*, IX (2000), pp. 26–27.
6 See McKay *et al.*, 'Shame and Scandal in the Family'; A. Tomlinson and G. Whannel, eds, *Five Ring Circus: Money, Power and Politics at the Olympics* (London: Pluto, 1984).

7   D.R. Jardine, *In Quest of the Ashes*, originally published 1933 (Adelaide: Rigby, 1984).
8   R. Buchanan and J. James, 'Lest We Forget', *Arena*, 38 (Dec. 1998 – Jan. 1999), p. 27.
9   P. Derriman, *Bodyline* (Sydney: William Collins, 1984), p. 5.
10 For example, see *Ibid.*; E.W. Docker, *Bradman and the Bodyline* (North Ryde, NSW: Angus and Robertson, 1987); J.H. Fingleton, *Cricket Crisis* (Melbourne: Cassell and Co., 1946); H. Larwood with K. Perkins, *The Larwood Story* (Ringwood, Vic.: Penguin, 1982); L. Le Quesne, *The Bodyline Controversy* (Sydney: George Allen and Unwin, 1985); G. Mant, *A Cuckoo in the Bodyline Nest* (Kenthurst: Kangaroo Press, 1992); R. Sissons and B. Stoddart, *Cricket and Empire: The 1932–33 Bodyline Tour of Australia* (Sydney: Allen and Unwin, 1984); B. Stoddart, 'Cricket's Imperial Crisis', in R. Cashman and M. McKernan, eds, *Sport in History: The Making of Modern Sporting History* (St Lucia: University of Queensland Press, 1979), pp. 124–47.
11 P. Warner, *Cricket Between the Wars* (London: Chatto and Windus, 1943), p. 128.
12 Sissons and Stoddart, *Cricket and Empire*, pp. 141–42.
13 R. Robinson, *Between Wickets* (Sydney: Collins, 1949), pp. 83–91.
14 *Sydney Morning Herald* (14 Oct. 1989), p. 26.
15 *Sydney Morning Herald* (28 Jan. 2000).
16 G. Turner, *National Fictions: Literature, Film and the Construction of Australian Narrative* (St Leonards, NSW: Allen and Unwin, 1993), p. 114.
17 *Ibid.*, p. 119.
18 *Courier Mail* (17 July 1984), p. 9.
19 Marinos quotation from *The Age*, Green Guide (12 July 1984), p. 1.
20 *Ibid.*; *The Age* (17 July 1984), p. 2; *Sun-Herald* (15 July 1984), p. 53; *Courier Mail* (16 July 1984), p. 18; *Sydney Morning Herald*, The Guide (16–22 July 1984), pp. 1, 3; *The Age*, Green Guide (26 July 1984), p. 5; *Weekend Australian Magazine* (14–15 July 1984), p. 15. The negative review that criticised the language used and the depiction of class relations was in the *Sun-Herald* (22 July 1984), p. 54.
21 *Courier Mail* (16 July 1984), p. 18; *The Age* (17 July 1984), p. 2.
22 *Courier Mail* (16 July 1984), p. 18; *Weekend Australian Magazine* (14–15 July 1984), p. 15.
23 *Weekend Australian Magazine* (14–15 July 1984), p. 15.
24 *The Age*, Green Guide (26 July 1984), p. 5.
25 *Sydney Morning Herald*, The Guide (16–22 July 1984), pp. 1, 3.
26 *Sun-Herald* (15 July 1984), p. 53.
27 *Sun-Herald* (22 July 1984), p. 3.
28 *Sunday Mail* (22 July 1984), p. 55.

29 Buchan and James, 'Lest We Forget', pp. 25–30.
30 G. Lukács, *The Historical Novel* (London: Merlin Press, 1977), p. 19.
31 L.O. Sauerberg, *Fact into Fiction: Documentary Realism in the Contemporary Novel* (New York: St Martin's Press, 1991), pp. 56–57. See also T. Wolfe, *The New Journalism*, originally published 1973 (London: Picador, 1990); J. Birmingham, *Leviathan: The Unauthorised Biography of Sydney* (Sydney: Vintage, 2000).
32 J. Fiske, *Television Culture* (London: Routledge, 1987), pp. 306–308.
33 Sauerberg, *Fact into Fiction*, p. 62.
34 *Sydney Morning Herald*, Spectrum section (26–27 Jan. 2002), p. 7.
35 M.F. Oja, 'Fictional History and Historical Fiction: Solzhenitsyn and Kis as Exemplars', *History and Theory*, 27:2 (1988), p. 115.
36 *Punch* (5 Oct. 1983), pp. 62–64.
37 *Courier Mail* (24 Dec. 1983), p. 29; *Weekend Australian Magazine* (26–27 Nov. 1983), pp. 1–2; T. Slade, 'Bodyline – The Novel', [Book Review] *Sporting Traditions*, 1:1 (1984), pp. 119–120; *The Age Weekender* (22 Oct. 1983), p. 2; *The Weekend Australian* (10–11 Dec. 1983), p. 13; *Times Literary Supplement* (16 Sept. 1983), p. 1002.
38 *Punch* (5 Oct. 1983), pp. 62–64.
39 Wheeler, *Bodyline*, p. 168; *Time* magazine (23 Nov. 1998), p. 65.
40 *The Age Weekender* (22 Oct. 1983), p. 2; *Courier Mail* (24 Dec. 1983), p. 29.
41 *The Age Weekender* (22 Oct. 1983), p. 2.
42 *Ibid.*; *The Weekend Australian* (10–11 Dec. 1983), p. 13.
43 *Courier Mail* (24 Dec. 1983), p. 29. Neville Cardus indicates that Jardine did not possess some of the 'sinister qualities' attributed to him. See N. Cardus, *Fourth Innings With Cardus* (London: Souvenir Press, 1981), p. 103.
44 *Weekend Australian Magazine* (26–27 Nov. 1983), p. 2.
45 *Sydney Morning Herald* (31 May 2001), p. 13.
46 *The Age*, Green Guide (26 July 1984), p. 5.
47 Buchanan and James, 'Lest We Forget', p. 28.
48 R. Wagner-Pacifici and B. Schwartz, 'The Vietnam Veterans Memorial: Commemorating a Difficult Past', *American Journal of Sociology*, 97:2 (1991), p. 399.
49 James Mayo quotation from *Ibid.*, p. 380.
50 *Sunday Mail* (22 July 1984), p. 55.

5 An insatiable demand

1 *Bradman 87 Not Out* (South Yarra, Vic.: Visual Entertainment Group, under licence to Channel Nine, 1996).
2 *Australian Cricket Ashes Tour Guide 1998–99*, p. 36; R. Martin, 'Interviewing Sir Don Bradman', *The Sydney Papers*, 9:4 (1997), pp. 7–8.

3 R. Conway, 'Revolutionary Prowess', in M. Coward, co-ordinator, *Sir Donald Bradman A.C.* Ironbark Legends Series (Sydney: Pan Macmillan, 1998), p. 32. See also *Bradman 87 Not Out.*

4 *Bradman 87 Not Out.* See also *The Bulletin* (6 March 2001), p. 38; C. Williams, *Bradman: An Australian Hero* (London: Abacus, 1997), p. 47.

5 C. Harte, *SACA: The History of the South Australian Cricket Association* (Adelaide: Sports Marketing, 1990), pp. 270–72, 286, 288.

6 Thank you to Gideon Haigh for making this point to me.

7 *Sunday Age* (4 March 2001), p. 12.

8 Bradman quoted in I. Rosenwater, *Sir Donald Bradman: A Biography* (London: BT Batsford, 1978), p. 152.

9 R. Cashman, *'Ave a Go, Yer Mug!' Australian Cricket Crowds from Larrikin to Ocker* (Sydney: Collins, 1984), p. 92.

10 G. Haigh, 'Bradman at Ninety', *Wisden Cricket Monthly* (Sept. 1998), p. 39.

11 Rosenwater, *Sir Donald Bradman*, p. 130.

12 C. Cary, *Cricket Controversy: Test Matches in Australia 1946–1947* (London: T Werner Laurie Ltd., 1948), pp. 149–51; J.H. Fingleton, *Batting from Memory* (Sydney: William Collins Sons and Co., 1981), p. 105.

13 A.G. Moyes, *Bradman* (Sydney: Angus and Robertson, 1948), pp. 26, 52, 190, 204; M. Page, *Bradman: The Illustrated Biography* (Melbourne: Macmillan, 1983), p. 120; J.H. Fingleton, *Cricket Crisis* (Melbourne: Cassell and Co., 1946), pp. 120, 122.

14 *Sydney Morning Herald*, Spectrum section (12 Feb. 2000), p. 7.

15 R. Cashman, *Paradise of Sport: The Rise of Organised Sport in Australia* (Melbourne: Oxford University Press, 1995), pp. 188–90; W.F. Mandle, 'Games People Played: Cricket and Football in England and Victoria in the Late Nineteenth Century', *Historical Studies*, 15:60 (1973), pp. 511–35.

16 D.G. Bradman, 'Cricket at the Cross Roads', reproduced from 1939 *Wisden Cricketers' Almanack*, in G. Wright, ed., *Wisden on Bradman* (South Yarra, Vic.: Hardie Grant Books, 1998), p. 10.

17 Paraphrased from S. Frith, *Music for Pleasure: Essays in the Sociology of Pop* (New York: Routledge, 1988), p. 95.

18 Companies included Argo Investments (Australia's second largest listed equity investment group), Bounty Investments, Centurion, Clarkson, Endeavour, F.H. Faulding and Co., Kelvinator Australia, Leo Investments, Rigby (Books), South Australian Rubber Mills, Tecalemit Australia, Uniroyal Holdings, Wakefield Investments, and Mutual Acceptance.

19 J. Bannon, 'Of Adelaide and the Close of Play', in M. Coward, co-ordinator, *Sir Donald Bradman A.C.* Ironbark Legends Series (Sydney: Pan Macmillan, 1998), p. 105.

20 D.G. Bradman, *Farewell to Cricket*, originally published 1950 (Sydney: ETT Imprint, 1994), p. 86.

21 *The Bulletin* (6 March 2001), p. 36.

22 *Calypso Cricket*, ABC Television (22, 29 Nov. 2000).

23 D.G. Bradman, 'Introduction', originally published in 1987, *The Bradman Albums, Volume 1 1925–1934* (Sydney: Lansdowne, 1995), p. 9.

24 G. Haigh, *The Cricket War: The Inside Story of Kerry Packer's World Series Cricket* (Melbourne: Text Publishing, 1993), pp. 13–28; Haigh, 'Bradman at Ninety', p. 39.

25 New books: J. Boyd, *The Quickest, The Brightest and The Best: Bradman's Fabulous Century* (Blackheath, NSW: Blackheath Village and School Century Organisers, 1985); P. Derriman, *Bodyline* (Sydney: William Collins, 1984); M. Page and D. Fregon, *The Don: A Photographic Essay of a Legendary Life* (South Melbourne: Sun Books, 1984); R. Sissons and B. Stoddart, *Cricket and Empire: The 1932–33 Bodyline Tour of Australia* (Sydney: Allen & Unwin, 1984). Republished books: D.G. Bradman, *The Art of Cricket* (Sydney: ETT Imprint, 1998 and also in 1958, 1969, 1984, 1990); D.R. Jardine, *In Quest of the Ashes* (Adelaide: Rigby, 1933 and also in 1984); H. Larwood with K. Perkins, *The Larwood Story* (Ringwood, Vic.: Penguin, 1982 and also in 1984); L. Le Quesne, *The Bodyline Controversy* (Sydney: George Allen and Unwin, 1983 and also in 1985).

26 *Australian Cricket Ashes Tour Guide 1998–99*, pp. 37–38.

27 Ray Martin quotation from *Sir Donald George Bradman Memorial Service*, Channel Nine (25 March 2001).

28 F. Jameson, *Postmodernism: Or the Cultural Logic of Late Capitalism* (Durham: Duke University Press, 1990), pp. x, 45–54.

29 *Ibid.*

30 P.D. Marshall, *Celebrity and Power: Fame in Contemporary Culture* (Minneapolis: University of Minnesota Press, 1997), p. 69.

31 *Sydney Morning Herald* (25 April 2000), p. 13.

32 *Sir Donald Bradman 1908–2001 Commemorative Coin Program.*

33 R. Shields, 'The Individual, Consumption Cultures and the Fate of Community', in R. Shields, ed., *Lifestyle Shopping: The Subject of Consumption* (London: Routledge, 1992), p. 99.

34 W. Vamplew, 'Facts and Artefacts: Sports Historians and Sports Museums', *Journal of Sport History*, 25:2 (1998), p. 270.

35 T. Blair, 'The Accessible Hero', *Time* magazine, reprinted in *Boundary: Journal of the Friends of the Bradman Museum*, 7:4 (Spring 1996), p. 5.

36 *Bradman Museum Draft Business Plan 1998*, p. 7.

37 *Ibid.*, p.8.

38 Chairman's Message, *The Bradman Museum Trust and The Bradman Foundation 1994/95 Annual Report.*

39   Chairman's Message, *The Bradman Museum Trust and The Bradman Foundation 1995/96 Annual Report*; Chairman's Message, *The Bradman Museum Trust and The Bradman Foundation 1996/97 Annual Report*; Chairman's Message, *The Bradman Museum Trust and The Bradman Foundation 1994/95 Annual Report*.

40   *Sydney Morning Herald* (24–25 February 2001), p. 1.

41   *Courier-Mail* (23 Feb. 1992), p. 4; *Simply Cricket Cricket Memorabilia Auction #2* (18 June 2000).

42   *The Australian* (2 Aug. 2000), p. 3.

43   *Sydney Morning Herald* (23 Aug. 2000), p. 6.

44   *The Australian* (3 Aug. 2000), p. 3; *Sydney Morning Herald* (14 March 2001), p. 7.

45   *The Australian* (3 Aug. 2000), p. 3.

46   'Transcript of the Prime Minister The Hon John Howard MP Doorstop Interview, Melbourne', Media Interview 12 October 2000, *Prime Minister of Australia News Room* http://www.pm.gov.au/news/interviews/2000/interview486.htm (13 Feb. 2001). See also 'Sir Don Bradman', Media Release 12 October 2000, *Prime Minister of Australia News Room* http://www.pm.gov.au/news/media_releases/2000/ media_releases488.htm (13 Feb. 2001).

47   *Sydney Morning Herald* (11 Nov. 2000), p. 1; *The Weekend Australian* (11–12 Nov. 2000), p. 1; *Sun-Herald* (12 Nov. 2000), p. 3.

48   *The Weekend Australian* (1–2 Sept. 2001), p. 5.

49   *The Bradman Museum Trust and The Bradman Foundation Annual 1994/95 Report; The Bradman Museum Trust and The Bradman Foundation 1995/1996 Annual Report.*

50   *The Bradman Foundation 1993/94 Annual Report; The Bradman Museum Trust and The Bradman Foundation Annual 2001/2001 Report.*

51   Sponsors have included Shell Australia, the Commonwealth Bank, Rothschild Australia, Diners Club, Westfield Holdings, Toyota Australia, individuals including Kerry Packer and Bob Mansfield, and other organisations such as the British High Commission, the Australian Cricket Board and the New South Wales Cricket Association. Sir Ron Brierley has also been an important figure in the funding of the Museum. See *Boundary*, Souvenir Edition (1996), p. 16; A. Mallett, *Bradman's Band* (St Lucia: University of Queensland Press, 2000).

52   *Boundary*, 12:1 (2001), p. 4.

53   *The Bradman Foundation 1993/94 Annual Report; The Bradman Museum Trust and The Bradman Foundation 1999/2000 Annual Report.*

54   *Boundary*, 10:4 (Spring 1999), p. 4.

55   *Boundary*, 12:4 (Spring 2001), p. 10.

56 Chairman's Message, *The Bradman Museum Trust and The Bradman Foundation 1997/98 Annual Report*.

57 *Financial Review* (27 Feb. 2001), p. 3.

58 Haigh, 'Bradman at Ninety', pp. 36–39.

59 See C. Healy, 'Histories and Collecting: Museums, Objects and Memories', in K. Darian-Smith and P. Hamilton, eds, *Memory and History in Twentieth-Century Australia* (Melbourne: Oxford University Press, 1994), p. 47.

60 T. Bennett and J. Woollacott, *Bond and Beyond: The Political Career of a Popular Hero* (Hampshire: Macmillan Education, 1987), p. 44.

61 *The Australian* (17 Nov. 1999), p. 5.

62 *The Weekend Australian* (31 March – 1 April 2001), p. 40.

63 *Daily Telegraph* (28 Feb. 2001), p. 7.

64 *Courier-Mail* (27 Feb. 2001), p. 5.

65 *The Weekend Australian*, Personal Finance Section (16–17 Aug. 1997), p. 5.

66 Michael Ludgrove quotation from, 'Cricket Memorabilia', *The Sports Factor*, Radio National Transcripts (15 Aug. 1997).

67 *Sydney Morning Herald*, Tribute Edition (27 Feb. 2001), p. 6.

68 *The Weekend Australian*, Personal Finance Section (16–17 Aug. 1997), p. 1.

69 S. Moyle, Phone interview (14 Feb. 2000).

70 T. Greig, *Channel Nine Sport*, Fax correspondence (1 May 2000).

71 The survey was taken over nine months in 2000, plus a month from 2001 in order to assess the short-term impact of Bradman's death.

72 *Sun-Herald* (4 Feb. 2001), p. 89.

73 *Ibid*.

74 *Boundary*, 12:3 (Spring 2001), pp. 6–7.

6 Political connections

1 *Up Close and Personal with Ray Martin*, Channel Nine (Aug. 1998), as replayed on *Media Watch*, ABC Television (21 Sept. 1998).

2 Howard nominates four people as his heroes. There are two Australians, Bradman and Menzies, and two Englishman, Winston Churchill and Louis Mountbatten. G. Henderson, *Menzies' Child: The Liberal Party of Australia* (Sydney: Harper Collins, 1998), p. 6.

3 S.P. Baty, *American Monroe: The Making of a Body Politic* (Los Angeles: University of California Press, 1995) pp. 8–9.

4 Henderson, *Menzies' Child*, p. 3.

5 G. Haigh, *The Summer Game: Australia in Test Cricket 1949–71* (Melbourne: Text Publishing, 1997), p. 5; R. Cashman, 'Australia', in B. Stoddart and K.A.P. Sandiford, eds, *The Imperial Game: Cricket,*

Culture and Society (Manchester: Manchester University Press, 1998), p. 42.

6   Haigh, *The Summer Game*, p. 259.

7   P. Derriman, 'Sir Donald Bradman', *Wisden Cricketers' Almanack Australia 2001–02* (South Yarra: Hardie-Grant, 2001), pp. 22–23; Haigh, *The Summer Game*; A. Mallett, *Bradman's Band* (St Lucia: University of Queensland Press, 2000), pp. 124–146.

8   *Lateline*, ABC Television (26 Feb. 2001).

9   Henderson, *Menzies' Child*, p. 4.

10 *Sydney Morning Herald Good Weekend Magazine* (15 June 1996), p. 21; P. Williams, *The Victory* (St Leonards, NSW: Allen and Unwin, 1997), p. 92; Henderson, *Menzies' Child*, p. 7.

11 R. Martin, 'Interviewing Sir Don Bradman', *The Sydney Papers*, 9:4 (1997), p. 8; *Wisden Cricket Monthly* (April 2001), p. 15.

12 I. Rosenwater, *Sir Donald Bradman: A Biography* (London: BT Batsford, 1978), p. 296.

13 D.G. Bradman, *Farewell to Cricket*, originally published 1950 (Sydney: ETT Imprint, 1994), pp. 33, 79, 142, 144, 221, 232.

14 G. Henderson, *A Howard Government? Inside the Coalition* (Sydney: Harper Collins, 1995), p. 19.

15 Henderson, *Menzies' Child*, p. 5.

16 *Ibid.*, p. 6.

17 J. Brett, *Robert Menzies' Forgotten People* (Sydney: Pan Macmillan, 1992), p. 26.

18 'Transcript of the Prime Minister The Hon John Howard MP Sir Donald Bradman Oration, Melbourne', 17 August 2000, Prime Minister of Australia News Room; http://www.pm.gov.au/news/speeches/2000/speech406.htm (13 Feb. 2001).

19 *Sydney Morning Herald* (4 Nov. 2000), p. 46.

20 Henderson, *Menzies' Child*, p. 188.

21 Brett, *Robert Menzies' Forgotten People*, p. 172.

22 Henderson, *A Howard Government?* pp. 23–24.

23 A.W. Martin, *Robert Menzies: A Life. Volume 1, 1894–1943* (Melbourne: Melbourne University Press, 1993), p. 224.

24 Menzies, *The Measure of the Years*, p. 287; Menzies quotation from J. Maxwell, ed., *The ABC Cricket Magazine, 1996–97* Season (Sydney: ABC, 1996), p. 170.

25 Cited in Cashman, 'Australia', p. 43; Menzies quotation from Martin, *Robert Menzies*, p. 222.

26 Haigh, *The Summer Game*, p. 69; C. Harte, *A History of Australian Cricket* (London: Andre Deutsch, 1993), p. 441; B. Stoddart, 'At the End of the Day's Play: Reflections on Cricket, Culture and Meaning', in B. Stoddart and

K.A.P. Sandiford, eds, *The Imperial Game: Cricket, Culture and Society* (Manchester: Manchester University Press, 1998), p. 153.

27 *The Cricketer International* (April 2001), p. 12.

28 Henderson, *Menzies' Child*, p. 13.

29 *The Age* (15 Nov. 1997), p. 6.

30 J. Howard, 'Foreword', in M. Taylor with I. Heads, *Mark Taylor: Time to Declare* (Sydney: Ironbark, 1999).

31 Henderson, *Menzies' Child*, p. 21. For articles on the London visit see *The Australian* (16 June 1997), p. 9; *The Australian* (20 June 1997), pp. 1, 6; *The Australian* (26 June 1997), pp. 1-2.

32 *Sydney Morning Herald* (25 July 2000), p. 15.

33 Bradman, *Farewell to Cricket*, pp. 157, 181, 217.

34 Rosenwater, *Sir Donald Bradman*, pp. 362-63.

35 *Sydney Morning Herald* (29 Nov. 1999), p. 19.

36 See C. Tatz, *Obstacle Race: Aborigines in Sport* (Sydney: University of New South Wales Press, 1995); B. Whimpress, *Passport to Nowhere: Aborigines in Australian Cricket 1850-1939* (Sydney: Walla Walla, 2000).

37 J. Williams, *Cricket and Race* (Oxford: Berg, 2001).

38 Haigh, *The Summer Game*, p. 43.

39 *Ibid.*, p. 315; Bradman, *Farewell to Cricket*, p. 303.

40 Tatz, *Obstacle Race*, p. 67.

41 *Sydney Morning Herald* (15 Nov. 1999), p. 31. See also Stoddart, 'At the End of the Day's Play', p. 153.

42 R. Cashman, 'Cricket', in W. Vamplew and B. Stoddart, eds, *Sport in Australia: A Social History* (Melbourne: Cambridge University Press, 1994), pp. 67-71. See also R. Cashman and A. Weaver, *Wicket Women: Cricket and Women in Australia* (Sydney: New South Wales Press, 1991).

43 J. Bessant and R. Watts, *Sociology Australia* (Crows Nest, NSW: Allen and Unwin, 2002), p. 230.

44 G. Turner, *Making It National: Nationalism and Australian Popular Culture* (St Leonards NSW: Allen and Unwin, 1994), p. 50.

45 *Littlemore; Sydney Morning Herald*, The Bradman Legacy (3 March 2001), p. 3; *The Age*, News Extra (3 March 2001), p. 5.

46 J. Stratton, *Race Daze: Australia in Identity Crisis* (Annandale, NSW: Pluto Press, 1998); R. White, *Inventing Australia: Images and Identity 1688-1980* (Sydney: Angus and Robertson, 1981).

47 Henderson, *A Howard Government?* p. 29; *Time* magazine (28 Sept. 1998), p. 67.

48 *The Australian* (17 Nov. 1999), p. 17; *Sydney Morning Herald* (29 Nov. 1999), p. 19.

49 *Sydney Morning Herald* (29 Nov. 1999), p. 19.

50 *Sydney Morning Herald* (9 Sept. 1971), p. 1.

51 *Sydney Morning Herald* (9 Sept. 1971), p. 6; 'Springboks 1971', *The Sports Factor*, Radio National Transcripts (28 Dec. 2001).

52 D. Booth, *The Race Game: Sport and Politics in South Africa* (London: Frank Cass, 1998); J. Nauright, *Sport, Cultures and Identities in South Africa* (London: Leicester University Press, 1997).

53 Nauright, *Sport, Cultures and Identities in South Africa*, p. 37.

54 Nauright, *Sport, Cultures and Identities in South Africa*, p. 137; Booth, *The Race Game*, p. 90.

55 C. Merrett and J. Nauright, 'South Africa', in B. Stoddart and K.A.P. Sandiford, eds, *The Imperial Game: Cricket, Culture and Society* (Manchester: Manchester University Press, 1998), p. 73.

56 Booth, *The Race Game*, p. 117.

57 M. Page, *Bradman: The Illustrated Biography* (Melbourne: Macmillan, 1983), p. 356.

58 House of Representatives, *Hansard* (21 Aug. 1986).

59 *Sydney Morning Herald* (16 Nov. 1999), p. 7.

60 House of Representatives, *Hansard* (23 Aug. 1984).

7 Never quite typical

1 G. Haigh, 'Bradman at Ninety', *Wisden Cricket Monthly* (Sept. 1998), pp. 36, 38.

2 R. Martin, 'Interviewing Sir Don Bradman', *The Sydney Papers*, 9:4 (1997), p. 9.

3 See R.W. Connell, *Gender and Power* (Cambridge: Polity Press, 1987).

4 C.L.R. James, *Beyond a Boundary*, originally published 1963 (Melbourne: Stanley Paul, 1986), p. 175.

5 See J. Stratton, *Race Daze: Australia in Identity Crisis* (Annandale, NSW: Pluto Press, 1998), pp. 128–29.

6 R. Ward, *The Australian Legend*, originally published 1958 (Melbourne: Oxford University Press, 1989), pp. 1–2.

7 R.W. Connell, 'An Iron Man', in *The Men and the Boys* (St Leonards, NSW: Allen and Unwin, 2000), pp. 69–85.

8 G. Turner, *National Fictions: Literature, Film and the Construction of Australian Narrative* (St Leonards, NSW: Allen and Unwin, 1993), p. 123.

9 Kippax quotation from B. Morris, *Bradman: What They Said About Him* (Sydney: ABC Books, 1994), p. 210.

10 D.G. Bradman, *Farewell to Cricket*, originally published 1950 (Sydney: ETT Imprint, 1994), p. 302.

11 Richardson quotation from I. Rosenwater, *Sir Donald Bradman: A Biography* (London: B T Batsford, 1978), p. 136.

12 L. Le Quesne, *The Bodyline Controversy* (Sydney: George Allen & Unwin, 1985), p. 203; Rosenwater, *Sir Donald Bradman*, p. 197; R.S. Whitington, *Bradman, Benaud and Goddard's Cinderellas* (Adelaide: Rigby, 1964), p. 47.

13 A. Buzo, 'Cricket and the Media, 2000–01', *Wisden Cricketers' Almanack Australia 2001–02* (South Yarra: Hardie-Grant, 2001), p. 850.

14 C. Williams, *Bradman: An Australian Hero* (London: Abacus, 1997), p. 51; J.H. Fingleton, *Brightly Fades the Don* (Sydney: Collins, 1949), p. 217.

15 P. Derriman, 'Sir Donald Bradman', *Wisden Cricketers' Almanack Australia 2001–02* (South Yarra: Hardie-Grant, 2001), p. 20.

16 Kay Saunders, discussion with author (1 Dec. 2000).

17 O'Reilly quotation from *Sydney Morning Herald* (21–22 April 2001), p. 72. See also *Courier-Mail* (20 April 2001), p. 3.

18 Bradman, *Farewell to Cricket*, p. 257.

19 Cardus quotation from P. Allen, *The Invincibles: The Legend of Bradman's 1948 Australians* (Sydney: ABC Books, 1998), p. 69.

20 R.C. Robertson-Glasgow, 'Sir Donald Bradman', reproduced from 1949 *Wisden Cricketers' Almanack*, in G. Wright, ed., *Wisden on Bradman* (South Yarra, Vic.: Hardie Grant Books, 1998), pp. 15–30.

21 G. Davison, *The Use and Abuse of Australian History* (St Leonards, NSW: Allen & Unwin, 2000), p. 33.

22 A. Mallett, *Bradman's Band* (St Lucia: University of Queensland Press, 2000), pp. 44, 51.

23 R. Perry, *The Don: A Biography* (Sydney: Pan Macmillan, 1998), p. 151.

24 R. Robinson, *On Top Down Under: Australia's Cricketing Captains* (Stanmore, NSW: Cassell, 1976), p. 190.

25 *Sydney Morning Herald* (27 Feb. 2001), p. 8.

26 G. Haigh, *The Summer Game: Australia in Test Cricket 1949–71* (Melbourne: Text Publishing, 1997), p. 16.

27 *Ibid.*

28 Thank you to Geoff Lawrence for making this point to me.

29 Unidentified player quotation from Rosenwater, *Sir Donald Bradman*, p. 136.

30 *Boundary: Journal of the Friends of the Bradman Museum*, 6:4 (Spring 1995), p. 5.

31 *Bradman 87 Not Out* (South Yarra, Vic.: Visual Entertainment Group, under licence to Channel Nine, 1996).

32 Perry, *The Don*, p. 11; P. Derriman, *Bodyline* (Sydney: William Collins, 1984), p. 16; H. Larwood with K. Perkins, *The Larwood Story* (Ringwood, Vic.: Penguin, 1982), p. 106.

33 The *Daily Mail* newspaper quoted in M. Page, *Bradman The Illustrated Biography* (Melbourne: Macmillan, 1983), p. 215.

34 R. Cashman, *'Ave a Go, Yer Mug!' Australian Cricket Crowds from Larrikin to Ocker* (Sydney: Collins, 1984), pp. 69–73, 90–94.

35 *Ibid.*

36 Haigh, *The Summer Game*, p. 2.

37 Thank you to Toby Miller for making this point to me.

38 L. Murrie, 'The Australian Legend: Writing Australian Masculinity/Writing 'Australian' Masculine', *Journal of Australian Studies*, 56 (1998), p. 73.

39 Ward, *The Australian Legend*, pp. 96–98; E. Thompson, *Fair Enough, Egalitarianism in Australia* (Sydney: University of New South Wales, 1994), pp. 132–154.

40 G. Haigh, *The Cricket War: The Inside Story of Kerry Packer's World Series Cricket* (Melbourne: Text Publishing, 1993), pp. 13–28; Haigh, 'Bradman at Ninety', p.39.

41 M. Page, *Bradman: The Illustrated Biography* (Melbourne: Macmillan, 1983), p. 163.

42 R. Robinson, *Between Wickets* (Sydney: Collins, 1949), p. 87.

43 J.H. Fingleton, *Cricket Crisis* (Melbourne: Cassell and Co., 1946), p. 78.

44 Larwood with Perkins, *The Larwood Story*, pp. 248–49.

45 Fingleton, *Cricket Crisis*, pp. 64–66; J. McHarg, *Bill O'Reilly: A Cricketing Life* (Newtown, NSW: Millennium, 1990), pp. 76, 158.

46 J.C. Squire, 'A Whining Digger', reproduced in P. Mullins and P. Derriman, eds, *Bat and Pad: Writings on Australian Cricket 1804–1984* (Melbourne: Oxford University Press, 1984), p. 57.

47 Fingleton, *Cricket Crisis*, p. 65; Perry, *The Don*, p. 275.

48 Larwood with Perkins, *The Larwood Story*, pp. 214–15; Rosenwater, *Sir Donald Bradman*, pp. 199–200.

49 Perry, *The Don*, p. 276.

50 Bradman, *Farewell to Cricket*, p. 61.

51 Ward, *The Australian Legend*, p. 229; R. White, *Inventing Australia: Images and Identity 1688–1980* (Sydney: Angus and Robertson, 1981), pp. 128–130.

52 Rosenwater, *Sir Donald Bradman*, p. 18.

53 *Ibid.*, p. 293.

54 Williams, *Bradman*, pp. 188–89.

55 Haigh, *The Summer Game*, p. 4; Allen, *The Invincibles*, p. 69.

56 Murrie, 'The Australian Legend: Writing Australian Masculinity/Writing 'Australian' Masculine', p. 73.

57 Ward, *The Australian Legend*, pp. 95–97.

58 R. Waterhouse, 'Australian Legends: Representations of the Bush 1813–1913', *Australian Historical Studies*, 31:115 (2000), p. 207.

59 Perry, *The Don*, p. 20.

60 *Sydney Morning Herald* (11–12 Nov. 2000), p. 1.

61 Bradman, *Farewell to Cricket*, pp. 43, 119. See also Williams, *Bradman*, pp. 119–120, 206–207.

62 *The Weekend Australian* (17–18 June 2000), p. 27.
63 Allen, *The Invincibles*, p. 25.
64 Williams, *Bradman: An Australian Hero*.
65 Davison, *The Use and Abuse of Australian History*, p. 33.

8 Challenging the myth

1   *The Australian* (11 Dec. 2001), p. 1; *The Australian* (12 Dec. 2001), p. 5;
    The Australian (13 Dec. 2001), p. 3.
2   *Ibid.*
3   J. Carroll, 'The Blessed Country: Australian Dreaming 1901–2001', *The
    Alfred Deakin Lectures 2001* (ABC Radio National, 12 May 2001).
4   B. Schwartz, 'Social Change and Collective Memory: The Democratization of
    George Washington', *American Sociological Quarterly*, 56 (1991), p. 222.
5   *Courier-Mail* (20 April 2001), p. 3; *Sydney Morning Herald* (21–22 April
    2001), p. 72.
6   *The Australian* (16 Nov. 2001), p. 1, 3.
7   I. Rosenwater, *Sir Donald Bradman: A Biography* (London: BT Batsford,
    1978), p. 116.
8   *The Australian* (16 Nov. 2001), p. 3.
9   *Weekend Australian Magazine* (17–18 Nov. 2001).
10 *Ibid.*
11 *Ibid.*, p. 25.
12 *Ibid.*, p. 23.
13 *Ibid.*, pp. 22–25.
14 Rosenwater, *Sir Donald Bradman: A Biography*.
15 *The Australian* (23 Nov. 2001), p. 5.
16 *Ibid.*
17 *Sunday Telegraph* (18 Nov. 2001), p. 74; *The Australian* (22 Nov. 2001), p. 11.
18 *Sunday Telegraph* (18 Nov. 2001), p. 74.
19 *Ibid.*
20 *Ibid.*
21 *Daily Telegraph* (28 Feb. 2001), p. 81.
22 *The Australian* (22 Nov. 2001), p. 11.
23 *Ibid.*
24 Letter, *The Australian* (19 Nov. 2001), p. 12.
25 Letters, *Weekend Australian Magazine* (1–2 Dec. 2001).
26 *Ibid.*
27 S. Hall, 'Signification, Representation, Ideology: Althusser and the Post-
    Structuralist Debates,' *Critical Studies in Mass Communication*, 2:2 (1985),
    pp. 91–114.

28 M. Altimore, 'Gentleman Athlete: Joe DiMaggio and the Celebration and Submergence of Ethnicity', *International Review for the Sociology of Sport*, 34:4 (1999), pp. 359–67; B. Schwartz, 'Collective Memory and History: How Abraham Lincoln Became a Symbol of Racial Equality', *The Sociological Quarterly*, 38:3 (1997), pp. 469–96; E.J. Gorn, ed., *Muhammad Ali: The People's Champ* (Urbana: University of Illinois Press, 1995).

29 W.F. Mandle, 'W.G. Grace as a Victorian Hero', *Historical Studies*, 19:76 (1981), pp. 353–68; T. Mason, 'Stanley Matthews', in R. Holt, ed., *Sport and the Working Class in Modern Britain* (Manchester: Manchester University Press, 1990), pp. 159–78.

30 A.G. Ingham, J.W. Loy and R.D. Swetman, *Sport, Heroes and Society: Issues of Transformation and Reproduction*, Working Papers in the Sociological Study of Sport and Leisure, 2:4 (Ontario: Queen's University, 1979).

31 G. Turner, *Making It National: Nationalism and Australian Popular Culture* (St Leonards, NSW: Allen & Unwin, 1994), pp. 158–59.

32 See G. Rundle, 'The Opportunist', *Quarterly Essay*, No. 3 (2001).

33 *Sydney Morning Herald* (29 Dec. 2001), p. 15.

34 D. Watson, 'Rabbit Syndrome: Australia and America', *Quarterly Essay*, No. 4 (2001), p. 42.

35 *Ibid.*

36 Letter, *Daily Telegraph* (13 Nov. 2001), p. 22; Letter, *Sydney Morning Herald* (24 Jan. 2001), p. 15; Letters, *The Australian* (18–19 Nov. 2000), p. 20; *The Australian* (15 Nov. 2000), p. 13; *The Australian* (28 Feb. 2001), p. 4.

37 B. Whimpress, 'God, Saint, or the Hand that Signed the Paper?' *Baggy Green: Journal of Australian Cricket*, 3:2 (2001), pp. 19–28.

38 *The Age*, News Extra (3 March 2001), p. 5.

Bibliography

Books, book chapters and journal articles

Allen, P., *The Invincibles: The Legend of Bradman's 1948 Australians* (Sydney: ABC Books, 1998).

Altham, H.S., 'Tribute to Bradman', reprinted in *The Bradman Albums*, vol. 2, 1935–1949 (Sydney: Lansdowne, 1995).

Altimore, M., 'Gentleman Athlete: Joe DiMaggio and the Celebration and Submergence of Ethnicity', *International Review for the Sociology of Sport*, 34:4 (1999), pp. 359–367.

Andrewes, F., '"They Play in Your Home": Cricket, Media and Modernity in Pre-war Australia', *The International Journal of the History of Sport*, 17:2–3 (2000), pp. 93–110.

Andrews, B., 'Ginger Meggs: His Story', in S. Dermody, J. Docker and D. Modjeska, eds, *Nellie Melba, Ginger Meggs and Friends: Essays in Australian Cultural History*, pp. 211–233.

Andrews, D., 'Excavating Michael Jordan: Notes on a Critical Pedagogy of Sporting Representation', in G. Rail, ed., *Sport and Postmodern Times* (Albany: State University of New York Press, 1998), pp. 185–219.

Andrews, D.L. and Jackson, S.J., eds, *Sports Stars: The Cultural Politics of Sporting Celebrity* (London: Routledge, 2001).

Andrews, D.L. and Jackson, S.J., 'Introduction: Sport Celebrities, Public Culture, and Private Experience', in Andrews and Jackson, eds, *Sports Stars: The Cultural Politics of Sporting Celebrity*, pp. 1–19.

Atkinson, G., *Bradman The Man: A Short Biography* (Knoxfield, Vic.: Five Mile Press, 1994).

Bale, J., *Landscapes of Modern Sport* (London: Leicester University Press, 1994).

Bannon, J., 'Of Adelaide and the Close of Play', in M. Coward, *Sir Donald Bradman A.C.*, pp. 92–106.

Barnett, D. with Goward, P., *John Howard: Prime Minister* (Ringwood, Vic.: Penguin, 1997).

Barthes, R., 'The Discourse of History', *Comparative Criticism: A Yearbook*, 3 (1981), pp. 3–20.

Barthes, R., *Mythologies* (London: Paladin, 1973).

Batchelder, A., 'Sir Donald Bradman A.C.' [Book review], *The Yorker*, 20 (Dec. 1998), pp. 6–9.

'A Batsman of Promise', press article published in 1926, reproduced in P. Derriman, *Our Don Bradman: Sixty Years of Writings About Don Bradman* (Melbourne: Macmillan, 1987), p. 11.

Baty, S.P., *American Monroe: The Making of a Body Politic* (Los Angeles: University of California Press, 1995).

Bauman, Z., 'On Writing: On Writing Sociology', *Theory, Culture and Society*, 17:1 (2000), pp. 79–90.

Bennett, B. and Haskell, D., eds, *Myths, Heroes and Anti-Heroes: Essays on Literature and Culture in the Asia-Pacific Region* (Perth: Centre for Studies in Australian Literature, University of Western Australia, 1992).

Bennett, T. and Woollacott, J., *Bond and Beyond: The Political Career of a Popular Hero* (Hampshire: Macmillan Education, 1987).

Bentley, E., *A Century of Hero-Worship* (Boston: Beacon, 1957).

Bertrand, I., 'Censorship and National Image: Melba and Evensong', in S. Dermody, J. Docker and D. Modjeska, eds, *Nellie Melba, Ginger Meggs and Friends: Essays in Australian Cultural History*, pp. 76–88.

Bessant, J. and Watts, R., *Sociology Australia* (Crows Nest, NSW: Allen & Unwin, 2002).

Birmingham, J., *Leviathan: The Unauthorised Biography of Sydney* (Sydney: Vintage, 2000).

Blainey, G., *A Land Half Won* (Sydney: Sun Books, 1992).

Blair, T., 'The Accessible Hero', *Time*, reprinted in *Boundary: The Journal of the Friends of the Bradman Museum*, 7:4 (Spring 1996), p. 5.

Bolton, G., *The Oxford History of Australia: The Middle Way 1942–1988* (Melbourne: Oxford University Press, 1993).

Bonyhady, T., *Burke and Wills: From Melbourne to Myth* (Balmain, NSW: David Ell Press, 1991).

Boorstin, D., *The Image: A Guide to Pseudo-Events in America*, originally published 1961 (New York: Vintage Books, 1992).

Booth, D., *The Race Game: Sport and Politics in South Africa* (London: Frank Cass, 1998).

Boyd, J., *The Quickest, The Brightest and The Best: Bradman's Fabulous Century* (Blackheath, NSW: Blackheath Village and School Century Organisers, 1985).

Bradman, D.G., *The Art of Cricket*, originally published 1958 (Sydney: ETT Imprint, 1998).

Bradman, D.G., *Don Bradman's Book* (London: Hutchinson, 1930).

Bradman, D.G., *Farewell to Cricket*, originally published 1950 (Sydney: ETT Imprint, 1994).

Bradman, D.G., *How to Play Cricket* (Melbourne: Georgian House, 1945).

Bradman, D.G., *My Cricketing Life* (London: Stanley Paul and Co., 1938).

Bradman, D.G., 'Cricket at the Cross Roads', reproduced from 1939 *Wisden Cricketers' Almanack*, in G. Wright, ed., *Wisden on Bradman*, pp. 9–14.

Bradman, D.G., 'Cricket, Past, Present and Future', reproduced from 1978–79, in J. Maxwell, compiler, *The ABC Cricket Book: The First 60 Years*, pp. 166–170.

Bradman, D.G., 'Introduction', *The Bradman Albums*, vol. 1.

Bradman, D.G., 'The Don Hits Back', *Wisden Cricket Monthly* (July 1995), p. 4.

Bradman Albums, vol. 1, 1925–1934 (Sydney: Lansdowne, 1995).

Bradman Albums, vol. 2, 1935–1949 (Sydney: Lansdowne, 1995).

Bradman Museum Draft Business Plan (1998).

Bradman Museum Homepage. http://bradman.org.au/home.html.

Bradman: A Tribute, Inside Edge magazine (2001).

Braudy, L., *The Frenzy of Renown: Fame and Its History* (New York: Oxford University Press, 1986).

Brett, J., *Robert Menzies' Forgotten People* (Sydney: Macmillan, 1992).

Buchanan, R. and James, J., 'Lest We Forget', *Arena*, 38 (Dec. 1998 – Jan. 1999), pp. 25–30.

Buzo, A., 'Cricket and the Media, 2000–01', *Wisden Cricketers' Almanack Australia 2001–02*, pp. 848–851.

Cardus, N., *Cricket All the Year* (London: Collins, 1952).

Cardus, N., *Fourth Innings With Cardus* (London: Souvenir Press, 1981).

Cardus, N., 'Six Giants of the Century – Sir Donald Bradman', reproduced from 1963 *Wisden Cricketers' Almanack*, in G. Wright, ed., *Wisden on Bradman*, pp. 31–35.

Carlyle, T., *On Heroes, Hero-Worship, and the Heroic in History* (Berkeley: University of California Press, 1993).

Carter, D., 'Future Pasts', in D. Headon, J. Hooton and D. Horne, eds, *The Abundant Culture: Meaning and Significance in Everyday Australia* (St Leonards, NSW: Allen & Unwin, 1995), pp. 3–15.

Cary, C., *Cricket Controversy: Test Matches in Australia 1946–1947* (London: T. Werner Laurie Ltd, 1948).

Cashman, R., *'Ave a Go, Yer Mug!' Australian Cricket Crowds from Larrikin to Ocker* (Sydney: Collins, 1984).

Cashman, R., *The 'Demon' Spofforth* (Kensington, NSW: University of New South Wales Press, 1990).

Cashman, R., *Paradise of Sport: The Rise of Organised Sport in Australia* (Melbourne: Oxford University of Press, 1995).

Cashman, R., 'Australia', in B. Stoddart and K.A.P. Sandiford, eds, *The Imperial Game: Cricket, Culture and Society*, pp. 34–54.

Cashman, R., 'Cricket', in W. Vamplew and B. Stoddart, eds, *Sport in Australia: A Social History* (Cambridge: Cambridge University Press, 1994), pp. 58–76.

Cashman, R. and Weaver, A., *Wicket Women: Cricket and Women in Australia* (Sydney: New South Wales Press, 1991).

Cashman, R. and Weaver, A., *Wicket Women: Cricket and Women in Australia* (Sydney: New South Wales Press, 1991).

Cavalier, R., 'Exploring Frontiers', in M. Coward, *Sir Donald Bradman A.C.*, pp. 4–23.

Chairman's Message, *The Bradman Museum Foundation 1993–94 Annual Report.*
Chairman's Message, *The Bradman Museum Trust and The Bradman Foundation 1994/95 Annual Report* through to and including the *2000/2001 Annual Report.*
Chase, M. and Shaw, C., 'The Dimensions of Nostalgia', in C. Shaw and M. Chase, eds, *The Imagined Past: History and Nostalgia*, pp. 1–17.
Clark, M., *In Search of Henry Lawson* (Melbourne: Macmillan, 1978).
Clark, M., *Manning Clark's History of Australia*, abridged by M. Cathcart (Melbourne: Melbourne University Press, 1993).
Clark, M., 'Good Day to You, Ned Kelly', in *Ned Kelly: Man and Myth* (North Melbourne: Cassell, 1968), pp. 12–39.
Clark, M., 'Heroes', in S.R. Graubard, ed., *Australia: The Daedalus Symposium* (North Ryde, NSW: Angus and Robertson, 1985), pp. 57–84.
Cochrane, P., *Simpson and the Donkey: The Making of a Legend* (Melbourne: Melbourne University Press, 1992).
Connell, R.W., *Gender and Power* (Cambridge: Polity Press, 1987).
Connell, R.W., *Masculinities* (St Leonards, NSW: Allen & Unwin, 1995).
Connell, R.W., *The Men and the Boys* (St Leonards, NSW: Allen & Unwin, 2000).
Conway, R., 'Revolutionary Prowess', in M. Coward, *Sir Donald Bradman A.C.*, pp. 24–32.
Coward M., co-ordinator, *Sir Donald Bradman A.C.*, Ironbark Legends Series (Sydney: Pan Macmillan, 1998).
Cunningham, S., *Featuring Australia: The Cinema of Charles Chauvel* (North Sydney: Allen & Unwin, 1991).
Curthoys, A., 'Mythologies', in R. Nile, ed., *The Australian Legend and Its Discontents*, pp. 11–41.
Curthoys, A. and Docker, J., 'Is History Fiction?', *UTS Review*, 2:1 (1996), pp. 12–37.
Dale, L., 'Mainstreaming Australia', in R. Nile, ed., *The Australian Legend and Its Discontents*, pp. 311–325.
Davies, C., 'Sportsmen and Diggers', *Arena*, 97 (1991), pp. 30–36.
Davis, A., *Sir Donald Bradman* (London: Cassell, 1960).
Davis, C., *The Best of the Best: A New Look at the Great Cricketers and Their Changing Times* (Sydney: ABC Books, 2000).
Davis, C., 'Cricket's Superman', *Wisden Cricketers' Almanack Australia 2001–02*, pp. 10–17.
Davis, F., *Yearning for Yesterday* (New York: The Free Press, 1979).
Davison, G., *The Use and Abuse of Australian History* (St Leonards, NSW: Allen & Unwin, 2000).
Day, D., *Menzies and Churchill at War* (East Roseville, NSW: Simon and Schuster, 2001).

Dayan, D. and Katz, E., *Media Events* (Cambridge, MA: Harvard University Press, 1992).

DeLillo, D., *Libra* (New York: Viking, 1988).

Dening, G., *Mr Bligh's Bad Language: Passion, Power and Theatre on the Bounty* (Cambridge: Cambridge University Press, 1992).

Denzin, N.K., 'On Semiotics and Symbolic Interactionism', *Symbolic Interaction*, 10 (1987), pp. 1–19.

Dermody, S., Docker, J. and Modjeska, D., eds, *Nellie Melba, Ginger Meggs and Friends: Essays in Australian Cultural History* (Malmsbury, Vic.: Kibble Books, 1982).

Derriman, P., *Bodyline* (Sydney: William Collins, 1984).

Derriman, P., ed., *Our Don Bradman: The Don at the SCG* (Pymble, NSW: Playbill, 1993).

Derriman, P., 'Sir Donald Bradman', *Wisden Cricketers' Almanack Australia 2001–02*, pp. 18–24.

Docker, E.W., *Bradman and the Bodyline* (North Ryde, NSW: Angus and Robertson, 1987).

Ellul, J., *The Technological Society* (New York: Alfred A. Knopf, 1964).

Encel, S., 'Politicians', in R. Nile, ed., *Australian Civilisation*, pp. 141–161.

Fingleton, J.H., *Batting from Memory* (Sydney: William Collins, 1981).

Fingleton, J.H., *Brightly Fades the Don* (Sydney: Collins, 1949).

Fingleton, J.H., *Cricket Crisis* (Melbourne: Cassell and Co., 1946).

Fingleton, J.H., *The Immortal Victor Trumper* (Sydney: Collins, 1978).

Fingleton, J.H., 'Bodyline Remembered', reproduced in P. Mullins and P. Derriman, eds, *Bat and Pad: Writings on Australian Cricket 1804–1984*, pp. 48–51.

Fiske, J., *Television Culture* (London: Routledge, 1987).

Flanagan, A., *On Tour with Don Bradman* (Sydney: Halstead Press, 1950).

Foucault, M., 'Governmentality', in G. Burchell, C. Gordon and P. Miller, eds, *The Foucault Effect: Studies in Governmentality* (Chicago: University of Chicago Press, 1991), pp. 87–104.

Franks, W., 'Notes by the Editor', *Wisden Cricketers' Almanack Australia 2001–02*, pp. 1–9.

Frith, S., *Music for Pleasure: Essays in the Sociology of Pop* (New York: Routledge, 1988).

Giddens, A., *Modernity and Self-Identity: Self and Society in the Late Modern Age* (Stanford, California: Stanford University Press, 1991).

Goodall, H., ''Fixing' the Past: Modernity, Tradition and Memory in Rural Australia', *UTS Review*, 6:1 (2000), pp. 20–40.

Gorn, E.J., ed., *Muhammad Ali: The People's Champ* (Urbana: University of Illinois Press, 1995).

Gorn, E.J., 'Introduction', in Gorn, ed., *Muhammad Ali: The People's Champ* (Urbana: University of Illinois Press, 1995), pp. xi–xvii.

Greig, T., *Channel Nine Sport*, Fax correspondence (1 May 2000).

Gruneau, R., *Class, Sports and Social Development* (Champaign: Human Kinetics, 1999).

Guttmann, A., *From Ritual to Record: The Nature of Modern Sports* (New York: Columbia University Press, 1978).

Hage, G. (1998) *White Nation: Fantasies of White Supremacy in a Multicultural Society* (Annandale, NSW: Pluto, 1998).

Haigh, G., *The Big Ship: Warwick Armstrong and the Making of Modern Cricket* (Melbourne: Text Publishing, 2001).

Haigh, G., *The Cricket War: The Inside Story of Kerry Packer's World Series Cricket* (Melbourne: Text Publishing, 1993).

Haigh, G., *The Summer Game: Australia in Test Cricket 1949–71* (Melbourne: Text Publishing, 1997).

Haigh, G., 'Bradman at Ninety', *Wisden Cricket Monthly* (Sept. 1998), pp. 36–39.

Haigh, G., 'O'Reilly's Gospel', *Wisden Cricket Monthly* (Feb. 1995), pp. 39–40.

Halbwachs, M., *On Collective Memory* (Chicago: University of Chicago Press, 1992).

Hall, S., 'Signification, Representation, Ideology: Althusser and the Post-Structuralist Debates', *Critical Studies in Mass Communication*, 2:2 (1985), pp. 91–114.

Hancock, I., 'The Liberal Party and the Neglect of History', *The Sydney Papers*, 12:3 (2000), pp. 122–131.

Harriss, I., 'Cricket and Bourgeois Ideology', in G. Lawrence and D. Rowe, eds, *Power Play: The Commercialisation of Australian Sport* (Sydney: Hale and Iremonger, 1986), pp. 179–195.

Harriss, I., 'Cricket and Capitalism: Batting and Capital Accumulation in England, 1920–1960', *Melbourne Historical Journal*, 19 (1988), pp. 7–18.

Harriss, I., 'Cricket and Rational Economic Man', *Sporting Traditions*, 3:1 (1986), pp. 51–68.

Harte, C., *A History of Australian Cricket* (London: Andre Deutsch, 1993).

Harte, C., *SACA: The History of the South Australian Cricket Association* (Adelaide: Sports Marketing, 1990).

Harvey, D., *The Condition of Postmodernity: An Enquiry into the Origins of Cultural Change* (Cambridge: Blackwell, 1989).

Haskell, D. and Bennett, B., 'Introduction', in B. Bennett and D. Haskell, eds, *Myths, Heroes and Anti-Heroes: Essays on Literature and Culture in the Asia-Pacific Region*, pp. i–vii.

Healy, C., 'Histories and Collecting: Museums, Objects and Memories', in K. Darian-Smith and P. Hamilton, eds, *Memory and History in Twentieth-Century Australia* (Melbourne: Oxford University Press, 1994), pp. 33–51.

Henderson, G., *A Howard Government? Inside the Coalition* (Sydney: Harper Collins, 1995).

Henderson, G., *Menzies' Child: The Liberal Party of Australia* (Sydney: Harper Collins, 1998).

Hickie, T.V., *They Ran With the Ball: How Rugby Football Began in Australia* (Melbourne: Longman Cheshire, 1993).

Hoberman, J.M., *Mortal Engines: The Science of Performance and the Dehumanization of Modern Sport* (New York: The Free Press, 1992).

Holt, R., *Sport and the British: A Modern History* (Oxford: Clarendon Press, 1989).

Holt, R., 'Cricket and Englishness: The Batsman as Hero', *The International Journal of the History of Sport*, 13:1 (1996), pp. 48–70.

Holt, R., 'King Across the Border: Denis Law and Scottish Football', in G. Jarvie and G. Walker, eds, *Scottish Sport in the Making of the Nation: Ninety Minute Patriots?* (Leicester: Leicester University Press, 1994), pp. 58–74.

Hook, S., *The Hero in History: A Study in Limitation and Possibility* (Boston: Beacon Press, 1955).

Horne, D., *The Lucky Country: Australia in the Sixties*, 2nd edn (Sydney: Angus and Robertson, 1968).

Hossay, P., 'Methodological Madness: Why Accounting for Nationalism – and Many Other Political Phenomena – is Difficult for Social Scientists', *Critical Sociology*, 27:2 (2001), pp. 163–191.

House of Representatives, *Hansard*.

Howard, J., 'Foreword', in M. Taylor with I. Heads, *Mark Taylor: Time to Declare* (Sydney: Ironbark, 1999).

Hutchins, B. and Mikosza, J., 'Australian Rugby League and Violence 1970 to 1995: A Case Study in the Maintenance of Masculine Hegemony', *Journal of Sociology*, 34:3 (1998), pp. 246–263.

Ingham, A.G., Loy, J.W. and Swetman, R.D., *Sport, Heroes and Society: Issues of Transformation and Reproduction*, Working Papers in the Sociological Study of Sport and Leisure, 2:4 (Ontario: Queen's University, 1979).

Jackson, S.J., 'Gretzky, Crisis, and Canadian Identity in 1988: Rearticulating the Americanization of Culture Debate', *Sociology of Sport Journal*, 11 (1994), pp. 428–446.

Jackson, S.J. and Ponic, P., 'Pride and Prejudice: Reflecting on Sports Heroes, National Identity, and Crisis in Canada', *Culture, Sport, Society*, 4:2 (2001), pp. 43–62.

James, C.L.R., *Beyond a Boundary*, originally published 1963 (Melbourne: Stanley Paul, 1986).

Jameson, F., *Postmodernism: Or the Cultural Logic of Late Capitalism* (Durham: Duke University Press, 1990).

Jardine, D.R., *In Quest of the Ashes*, originally published 1933 (Adelaide: Rigby, 1984).

Kaino, L., 'Woop Woop(s) and Woolly Film-making: Rural Representations of Culture in Contemporary Australian Film Feature', *Rural Society*, 10:3 (2000), pp. 319–327.

Kellner, D., *Media Culture: Cultural Studies, Identity and Politics Between the Modern and Postmodern* (London: Routledge, 1995).

Kelly, P., *The End of Certainty: Power, Politics and Business in Australia* (St Leonards, NSW: Allen & Unwin, 1994).

Keneally, T., *Schindler's Ark* (Sydney: Hodder and Stoughton, 1982).

Kingston, M., *Off the Rails: The Pauline Hanson Trip* (St Leonards, NSW: Allen & Unwin, 1999).

Larwood, H. with Perkins, K., *The Larwood Story* (Ringwood, Vic.: Penguin, 1982).

Le Quesne, L., *The Bodyline Controversy* (Sydney: George Allen & Unwin, 1985).

Lindsay, P., *Don Bradman* (London: Phoenix House, 1951).

Lowenthal, D., *The Heritage Crusade and the Spoils of History* (Cambridge: Cambridge University Press, 1998).

Lowenthal, D., *The Past is a Foreign Country* (Cambridge: Cambridge University Press, 1985).

Lowenthal, D., 'Nostalgia Tells It Like It Wasn't', in C. Shaw and M. Chase, eds, *The Imagined Past: History and Nostalgia*, pp. 18–32.

Lowenthal, D., 'Uses of the Past in Australia', in B. Hocking, ed., *Australia Towards 2000* (London: Macmillan, 1990), pp. 46–54.

Lukács, G., *The Historical Novel* (London: Merlin Press, 1977).

MacAloon, J.J., 'Double Visions: Olympic Games and American Culture', *The Kenyon Review*, 4:1 (1982), pp. 98–112.

McGilvray, A. with Tasker, N., *The Game Goes On …* (Sydney: ABC, 1987).

McHarg, J., *Bill O'Reilly: A Cricketing Life* (Newtown, NSW: Millennium, 1990).

McKay, J., '"Just Do It": Corporate Sports Slogans and the Political Economy of "Enlightened Racism"', *Discourse: Studies in the Cultural Politics of Education*, 16:2 (1995), pp. 191–201.

McKay, J., Hutchins, B. and Mikosza, J., '"Shame and Scandal in the Family": Media Narratives of the IOC/SOCOG Scandal Matrix', *Olympika: The International Journal of Olympic Studies*, IX (2000), pp. 25–48.

McKay, J., Messner, M.A. and Sabo, D., eds, *Masculinities, Gender Relations, and Sport* (London: Sage, 2000).

Mallett, A., *Bradman's Band* (St Lucia: University of Queensland Press, 2000).

Mallett, A., *Clarrie Grimmett: The Bradman of Spin* (St Lucia: University of Queensland Press, 1993).

Mallett, A., *Don Bradman* (Richmond, Vic.: Hutchinson, 1983).

Mandle, W.F., *Going it Alone: Australia's National Identity in the Twentieth Century* (Ringwood, Vic.: Allen Lane, 1977).

Mandle, W.F., 'Cricket and Australian Nationalism in the Nineteenth Century', in T.D. Jaques and G.R. Pavia, eds, *Sport in Australia: Selected Readings in Physical Activity* (Sydney: McGraw-Hill, 1976), pp. 46–72.

Mandle, W.F., 'Games People Played: Cricket and Football in England and Victoria in the Late Nineteenth Century', *Historical Studies*, 15:60 (1973), pp. 511–535.

Mandle, W.F., 'Sports History', in W.F. Mandle and G. Osborne, eds, *New History: Studying Australia Today* (Sydney: Allen & Unwin, 1982), pp. 82–93.

Mandle, W.F., 'W.G. Grace as a Victorian Hero', *Historical Studies*, 19:76 (1981), pp. 353–368.

Mant, G., *A Cuckoo in the Bodyline Nest* (Kenthurst: Kangaroo Press, 1992).

Marcus, G., *Dead Elvis: A Chronicle of a Cultural Obsession* (London: Viking, 1992).

Marshall, P.D., *Celebrity and Power: Fame in Contemporary Culture* (Minneapolis: University of Minnesota Press, 1997).

Martin, A.W., *Robert Menzies: A Life. Vol. 1, 1894–1943* (Melbourne: Melbourne University Press, 1993).

Martin, R., 'Interviewing Sir Don Bradman', *The Sydney Papers*, 9:4 (1997), pp. 1–11.

Mason, T., 'Stanley Matthews', in R. Holt, ed., *Sport and the Working Class in Modern Britain* (Manchester: Manchester University Press, 1990), pp. 159–178.

Masterman-Smith, H. and Cottle, D., '"Bradstow Revisited": A Comparative Study of Class Politics in Bowral, 1974 and 1997', *Rural Society*, 11:1 (2001), pp. 39–56.

Maxwell, J., compiler, *The ABC Cricket Book: The First 60 Years* (Sydney: ABC Books, 1994).

Menzies, R.G., *Afternoon Light: Some Memories of Men and Events* (Sydney: Cassell, 1967).

Menzies, R.G., *The Measure of the Years* (London: Cassell, 1970).

Merrett, C. and Nauright, J., 'South Africa', in B. Stoddart and K.A.P. Sandiford, eds, *The Imperial Game: Cricket, Culture and Society*, pp. 55–78.

Mikosza, J., 'Gender, Nationalism and the Media', *M/C Reviews*, Feature no. 10 (18 Oct 2000); http://www.media-culture.org.au/reviews/features/olympic/mikosza.html.

Miller, K., *Cricket Crossfire* (London: Oldbourne Press, 1956).

Miller, K. and Whitington, R.S., *Cricket Caravan* (London: Lativer House, 1950).

Miller, T., *Technologies of Truth: Cultural Citizenship and the Popular Media* (Minneapolis: University of Minnesota Press, 1998).

Miller, T., 'Radio', in S. Cunningham and G. Turner, eds, *The Media in Australia: Industries, Texts, Audiences* (St Leonards, NSW: Allen & Unwin, 1993), pp. 41–58.

Mills, C.W., *The Sociological Imagination* (New York: Oxford University Press, 1959).

Morris, B., *Bradman: What They Said About Him* (Sydney: ABC Books, 1994).

Moyes, A.G., *Bradman* (Sydney: Angus and Robertson, 1948).

Moyes, A.G., 'The Big Four', reproduced from 1954–55 in J. Maxwell, compiler, *The ABC Cricket Book: The First 60 Years*, pp. 92–93.

Moyle, S., Phone interview (14 Feb. 2000).

Mullins, P. and Derriman, P., eds, *Bat and Pad: Writings on Australian Cricket 1804–1984* (Melbourne: Oxford University Press, 1984).

Murrie, L., 'The Australian Legend: Writing Australian Masculinity/Writing "Australian" Masculine', *Journal of Australian Studies*, 56 (1998), pp. 68–77.

Nauright, J., *Sport, Cultures and Identities in South Africa* (London: Leicester University Press, 1997).

Nile, R., ed., *Australian Civilisation* (Melbourne: Oxford University Press, 1994).

Nile, R., ed., *The Australian Legend and Its Discontents* (St Lucia: University of Queensland Press, 2000).

Nile, R., 'Introduction', in Nile, ed., *The Australian Legend and Its Discontents*, pp. 1–7.

O'Reilly, W.J., *Cricket Conquest* (London: Werner Laurie, 1949).

O'Reilly, B., compiled by Egan, J., *The Bradman Era* (Sydney: ABC and William Collins, 1983).

Oja, M.F., 'Fictional History and Historical Fiction: Solzhenitsyn and Kis as Exemplars', *History and Theory*, 27:2 (1988), pp. 111–124.

Oriard, M., *Reading Football: How the Popular Press Created an American Spectacle* (Chapel Hill: University of North Carolina, 1993).

Oriard, M., 'Muhammad Ali: The Hero in the Age of Mass Media', in E.J. Gorn, ed., *Muhammad Ali: The People's Champ*, pp. 5–23.

Page, M., *Bradman: The Illustrated Biography* (Melbourne: Macmillan, 1983).

Page, M. and Fregon, D., *The Don: A Photographic Essay of a Legendary Life* (South Melbourne: Sun Books, 1984).

Paterson, A.B., 'Bradman', reproduced in P. Mullins and P. Derriman, eds, *Bat and Pad: Writings on Australian Cricket 1804–1984*, pp. 62–64.

Perry, R., *Bradman's Best* (Milson's Point, NSW: Random House, 2001).

Perry, R., *The Don: A Biography* (Sydney: Pan Macmillan, 1998).

Phillips, M.G. and Moore, K., 'The Champion Boxer Les Darcy: A Victim of Class Conflict and Sectarian Bitterness in Australia During World War One', *The International Journal of the History of Sport*, 11:1 (1994), pp. 102–114.

Pollard, J., *Australian Cricket 1918–1948: The Bradman Years* (Sydney: Book Company International, 1995).

Raiji, V., 'The Unseen God', in M. Coward, *Sir Donald Bradman A.C.*, pp. 56–68.

Roberts, E.L., *Bradman 1927–1941* (Birmingham: E.F. Hudson, 1944).

Robertson-Glasgow, R.C., 'Sir Donald Bradman', reproduced from 1949 *Wisden Cricketers' Almanack*, in G. Wright, ed., *Wisden on Bradman*, pp. 15–30.

Robinson, R., *Between Wickets* (Sydney: Collins, 1949).

Robinson, R., *From the Boundary* (Sydney: Collins, 1950).

Robinson, R., *On Top Down Under: Australia's Cricketing Captains* (Stanmore, NSW: Cassell, 1976).

Rosenwater, I., *Sir Donald Bradman: A Biography* (London: BT Batsford, 1978).

Rosenwater, I., 'Sir Donald Bradman – Selector', reproduced from 1972 *Wisden Cricketers' Almanack*, in G. Wright, ed., *Wisden on Bradman*, pp. 37–44.

Rowe, D., *Popular Cultures: Rock Music, Sport and the Politics of Pleasure* (London: Sage, 1995).

Rowe, D., 'Apollo Undone: The Sports Scandal', in J. Lull and S. Hinerman, eds, *Media Scandals: Morality and Desire in the Popular Culture Marketplace* (Oxford: Polity Press, 1997), pp. 203–221.

Rundle, G., 'The Opportunist', *Quarterly Essay*, no. 3 (2001).

Ryan, G., '"Extravagance of Thought and Feeling": New Zealand Reactions to the 1932/33 Bodyline Controversy', *Sporting Traditions*, 13:2 (1997), pp. 41–58.

Sauerberg, L.O., *Fact into Fiction: Documentary Realism in the Contemporary Novel* (New York: St Martin's Press, 1991).

Saunders, K., discussion with author (1 Dec. 2000).

Schudson, M., *Watergate in American Memory: How We Remember, Forget, and Reconstruct the Past* (New York: Basic Books, 1992).

Schudson, M., 'The Present in the Past versus the Past in the Present', *Communication*, 11 (1989), pp. 105–113.

Schwartz, B., 'Collective Memory and History: How Abraham Lincoln Became a Symbol of Racial Equality', *The Sociological Quarterly*, 38:3 (1997), pp. 469–496.

Schwartz, B., 'Introduction: The Expanding Past', *Qualitative Sociology*, 19:3 (1996), pp. 275–282.

Schwartz, B., 'Postmodernity and Historical Reputation: Abraham Lincoln in Late Twentieth-Century American Memory', *Social Forces*, 77:1 (1998), pp. 63–103.

Schwartz, B., 'Social Change and Collective Memory: The Democratization of George Washington', *American Sociological Quarterly*, 56 (1991), pp. 221–236.

Schwartz, B., 'The Social Context of Commemoration: A Study in Collective Memory', *Social Forces*, 61:2 (1982), pp. 374–397.

Seal, G., *Ned Kelly in Popular Tradition* (Melbourne: Hyland House, 1980).

Selth, D., *The Prime Minister's XI: The Story of the Prime Minister's XI Matches Menzies to Hawke* (Canberra: D.V. Selth, 1990).

Share, P., 'Beyond "Countrymindedness": Representation in the Post-Rural Era',
   in P. Share, ed., *Communication and Culture in Rural Areas* (Wagga Wagga,
   NSW: Centre for Rural Social Research, 1997), pp. 1–23.

Shaw, C. and Chase, M., eds, *The Imagined Past: History and Nostalgia*
   (Manchester: Manchester University Press, 1989).

Shields, R., 'The Individual, Consumption Cultures and the Fate of Community',
   in R. Shields, ed., *Lifestyle Shopping: The Subject of Consumption* (London:
   Routledge, 1992), pp. 99–113.

'Sir Don Bradman', Media Release 12 October 2000, Prime Minister of
   Australia News Room; http://www.pm.gov.au/news/media_releases/2000/
   media_releases488.htm (13 Feb. 2001).

Sissons, R., *The Don Meets the Babe: The 1932 Australian Cricket Tour of
   North America* (Cambridge: J.W. McKenzie, 1995).

Sissons, R. and Stoddart, B., *Cricket and Empire: The 1932–33 Bodyline Tour
   of Australia* (Sydney: Allen & Unwin, 1984).

Slade, T., 'Bodyline – The Novel' [Book review], *Sporting Traditions*, 1:1 (1984),
   pp. 119–120.

Smith, P., 'Culture and Charisma: Outline of a Theory', *Acta Sociologica*, 43:2
   (2000), pp. 101–111.

Spillman, L. (1997) *Nation and Commemoration: Creating National Identities
   in the United States and Australia* (Cambridge: Cambridge University Press,
   1997).

Squire, J.C., 'A Whining Digger', reproduced in P. Mullins and P. Derriman, eds,
   Bat and Pad: Writings on Australian Cricket 1804–1984, p. 57.

Stauth, G. and Turner, B.S., 'Nostalgia, Postmodernism and the Critique of Mass
   Culture', *Theory, Culture and Society*, 5:2-3 (1988), pp. 509–526.

Stewart, K., 'Nostalgia – A Polemic', *Cultural Anthropology*, 3:3 (1988),
   pp. 227–241.

Stoddart, B., 'At the End of the Day's Play: Reflections on Cricket, Culture and
   Meaning', in B. Stoddart and K.A.P. Sandiford, eds, *The Imperial Game:
   Cricket, Culture and Society*, pp. 150–166.

Stoddart, B., 'Cricket's Imperial Crisis', in R. Cashman and M. McKernan, eds,
   Sport in History: The Making of Modern Sporting History (St Lucia:
   University of Queensland Press, 1979), pp. 124–147.

Stoddart, B. and Sandiford, K.A.P., eds, *The Imperial Game: Cricket, Culture
   and Society* (Manchester: Manchester University Press, 1998).

Stratton, J., *Race Daze: Australia in Identity Crisis* (Annandale, NSW: Pluto
   Press, 1998).

Tannock, S., 'Nostalgia Critique', *Cultural Studies*, 9:3 (1995),
   pp. 453–464.

Tatz, C., *Obstacle Race: Aborigines in Sport* (Sydney: University of New South
   Wales Press, 1995).

Thompson, E., *Fair Enough: Egalitarianism in Australia* (Sydney: University of New South Wales, 1994).

Thompson, T., 'Where Sir Donald Bradman Learnt His Cricket', *Sir Don Bradman (1908–2001)*; http://167.216.192.98/cricket/donbradman/20010301don13.shtml (4 Jan. 2002).

Tomlinson, A. and Whannel, G., eds, *Five Ring Circus: Money, Power and Politics at the Olympics* (London: Pluto, 1984).

'Transcript of the Prime Minister The Hon John Howard MP Doorstop Interview, Melbourne', Media interview, 12 October 2000, Prime Minister of Australia News Room; http://www.pm.gov.au/news/interviews/2000/interview486.htm (13 Feb. 2001).

'Transcript of the Prime Minister The Hon John Howard MP Sir Donald Bradman Oration, Melbourne', 17 August 2000, Prime Minister of Australia News Room; http://www.pm.gov.au/news/speeches/2000/speech406.htm (13 Feb. 2001).

Trujillo, N., *The Meaning of Nolan Ryan* (College Station: Texas A and M University Press, 1994).

Turner, B.S., 'A Note on Nostalgia', *Theory, Culture and Society*, 4 (1987), pp. 147–156.

Turner, G., *Making It National: Nationalism and Australian Popular Culture* (St Leonards, NSW: Allen & Unwin, 1994).

Turner, G., *National Fictions: Literature, Film and the Construction of Australian Narrative* (St Leonards, NSW: Allen & Unwin, 1993).

Turner, G., Bonner, F. and Marshall, D., *Fame Games: The Production of Celebrity in Australia* (Cambridge: Cambridge University Press, 2000).

Vamplew, W., 'Facts and Artefacts: Sports Historians and Sports Museums', *Journal of Sport History*, 25:2 (1998), pp. 568–282.

Wagner-Pacifici, R. and Schwartz, B., 'The Vietnam Veterans Memorial: Commemorating a Difficult Past', *American Journal of Sociology*, 97:2 (1991), pp. 376–420.

Wakley, B.J., *Bradman the Great* (London: Nicholas Kaye, 1959).

Ward, R., *The Australian Legend*, originally published 1958 (Melbourne: Oxford University Press, 1989).

Warner, P., *Cricket Between the Wars* (London: Chatto and Windus, 1943).

Waterhouse, R., 'Australian Legends: Representations of the Bush 1813–1913', *Australian Historical Studies*, 31:115 (2000), pp. 201–221.

Watson, D., 'Rabbit Syndrome: Australia and America', *Quarterly Essay*, no. 4 (2001).

Waugh, S., 'Privileges in the Shadow', in M. Coward, *Sir Donald Bradman A.C.*, pp. 108–114.

Weber, M., *On Charisma and Institution Building* (Chicago: University of Chicago Press, 1968).

Wheeler, P., *Bodyline: The Novel* (London: Faber and Faber, 1983).

Whimpress, B., *Passport to Nowhere: Aborigines in Australian Cricket 1850–1939* (Sydney: Walla Walla, 2000).

Whimpress, B., 'God, Saint, or the Hand that Signed the Paper?' *Baggy Green: Journal of Australian Cricket*, 3:2 (2001), pp. 19–28.

Whimpress, B., 'Rhyme If Not Reason: Christies' Memorabilia Auction 1999', *Baggy Green: Journal of Australian Cricket*, 2:1 (1999), pp. 44–47.

White, R., *Inventing Australia: Images and Identity 1688–1980* (Sydney: Angus and Robertson, 1981).

White, R.S., 'Don Bradman: That Inscrutable Object of Adulation', in B. Bennett and D. Haskell, eds, *Myths, Heroes and Anti-Heroes: Essays on Literature and Culture in the Asia-Pacific Region*, pp. 193–200.

Whitington, R.S., *Bradman, Benaud and Goddard's Cinderellas* (Adelaide: Rigby, 1964).

Wild, R.A., *Bradstow: A Study of Status, Class and Power in a Small Australian Town* (Sydney: Angus and Robertson, 1974).

Williams, C., *Bradman: An Australian Hero* (London: Abacus, 1997).

Williams, J., *Cricket and Race* (Oxford: Berg, 2001).

Williams, P., *The Victory* (St Leonards, NSW: Allen & Unwin, 1997).

Wisden Cricketers' Almanack Australia 2001–02 (South Yarra: Hardie Grant, 2001).

Wolfe, T., *The New Journalism*, originally published 1973 (London: Picador, 1990).

Wright, G., ed., *Wisden on Bradman* (South Yarra, Vic.: Hardie Grant Books, 1998).

Wright, G., 'Introduction', in Wright, ed., *Wisden on Bradman*, pp. xi–xvi.

Yoselloff, A.A., 'From Ethnic Hero to National Icon: The Americanization of Joe DiMaggio', *International Journal of the History of Sport*, 16:3 (1999), pp. 1–20

Zelizer, B., *Covering the Body: The Kennedy Assassination, the Media, and the Shaping of Collective Memory* (Chicago: University of Chicago Press, 1992).

Newspapers and perodicals

ABC Cricket Magazine, 1996–97 Season
Age, The
Age Weekender, The
Australian, The
Australian Cricket Ashes Tour Guide 1998–99
Australian Country Experience
Australian Country Style
Australian Financial Review

Boundary: The Journal of the Friends of the Bradman Museum
Boundary: The Journal of the Friends and Supporters of the Bradman Museum
Bulletin magazine
Cricketer International
Courier-Mail
Daily Telegraph
Eye, The
Gold Coast Bulletin
Herald Sun
Inside Edge
Mercury, The
Punch
Queensland Times
Sydney Morning Herald
Sydney Morning Herald Good Weekend Magazine
Sun-Herald
Sunday Age
Sunday Mail
Sunday Telegraph
Time magazine
Times Literary Supplement
Weekend Australian
Weekend Australian Magazine
Wisden Cricket Monthly

Audio-visual sources

Baseball: A Film by Ken Burns (Florentine Films, 1994).
Bodyline (Kennedy-Miller, 1984).
Bradman (ABC Video, 1991).
Bradman 87 Not Out (South Yarra, Vic.: Visual Entertainment Group, under licence to Channel Nine, 1996).
Bradman: The Don Declares (ABC Radio, 1988).
Calypso Cricket, ABC Television (22, 29 Nov. 2000).
Carroll, J., 'The Blessed Country: Australian Dreaming 1901–2001', *The Alfred Deakin Lectures 2001* (ABC Radio National, 12 May 2001).
'Cricket Memorabilia', *The Sports Factor*, Radio National Transcripts (15 Aug. 1997).
A Current Affair, Channel Nine (26 Feb. 2001).
Donald Bradman: Sir Donald's Speech at the Opening of the Museum (Sydney: Australian Broadcasting Corporation, 1990).
'Fixing Cricket', *Four Corners*, ABC Television (24 July 2000).

How I Play Cricket by Don Bradman (Australia: A MOD Production, 1994).

Lateline, ABC Television (26 Feb. 2001).

Littlemore, ABC Television (5 March 2001).

Media Watch, ABC Television (21 Sept. 1998).

Sir Donald George Bradman Memorial Service, ABC Television (25 March 2001).

Sir Donald George Bradman Memorial Service, Channel Nine (25 March 2001).

'Springboks 1971', *The Sports Factor*, Radio National Transcripts (28 Dec. 2001).

The Bradman Era (ABC Video, 1991).

The Don, Channel Nine (26 Feb. 2001).

The Invincibles (ABC Video, 1998).

This Fabulous Century, Channel Seven (25 Sept. 1999).

Words from the Don: A Collection of Speeches by the Great Sir Donald Bradman (South Australian State Library, year unidentified).

World At Noon, ABC Television (26 Feb. 2001).

Index